ACKNOWLEDGEMENTS

We gratefully acknowledge the support of Neil Davidson for his comments throughout the planning and production of this publication; Hillna Fountaine (Keyboard) for her enthusiasm and transcribing skills; Sally Phillips for her assistance with some of the sub-editing; RAP for their typical flexibility, which enabled us to produce this book with such speed; Geoff Dench for 'provoking' the idea for the book; and all our contributors, who responded so positively, enthusiastically and quickly.

This book is dedicated to our fathers,
Albert Lloyd and George Wood.

What Next for Men?

Contents

INTRODUCTION

As co-editors of *Working With Men* — one of the few publications that offers itself as a forum for those developing work with men — we get to see most books that take men and masculinity as their major theme. Through this same role, we also hear about the ways that work with men is developing and make a point of keeping up with media coverage about men.

Consequently, we get some sense of where, and what, the current debates are surrounding men. The media tend to lead on the 'hot' debates — young men's failure within schools, 'joy riding' and other 'male' crimes, the irresponsibility of fathers etc., etc. Four years ago, the publication of Neil Lyndon's 'No More Sex War' provoked a massive media interest in relationships between men and women, and, three years ago, Robert Bly's 'Iron John' gave more than a few journalists the opportunity to go on weekend retreats to drum, sweat, chant and listen to myths and return to their desks to write often trite articles about their experience. Books that provoke media debate are fairly rare. Only those that have a popular attraction and carry with them conflict and strong emotions tend to generate media and public interest.

There are debate sites apart from the popularist media. In the first two months of 1996, *Working With Men* received 16 new books about men. These were mostly academic, spanning the social, cultural and psychological fields, concentrating on men generally and competing for the 'gender and masculinities' territory.

Disturbingly, these books, on the whole, do not address what we can do about the many and varied problems and difficulties they highlight. Some would argue, of course, that academia adds to our knowledge of the problem and this is their

1

contribution to the solution. But, from a scan of the 16 books received, you would get the impression that 'ideas' about men have run off on their own, rather than contributing to resolving our current questions about men.

'What Next for Men?' has come out of the belief that books (especially academic and research-based books), the media, public debate and developing policy and practice need to be kept as close to each other as possible. Currently, policy and practice on masculinity issues generally sadly trail behind theoretical and media debate; it's difficult to see whether this situation has taken us any further than simply to an increasingly common view that men are a problem.

The format for this book came out of Trefor Lloyd's reading Geoff Dench's 'The Frog, the Prince and the Problem with Men'. He found himself arguing with the book: while he disagreed with so many of the conclusions Dench made, he found the many questions the book raised extremely stimulating. Here was an academic who was prepared to take ideas into more traditional policy areas, asking, "If we draw this conclusion, what does this mean?". Too often, those involved and interested in theory stop at understanding the problem, the media exhibit the figures and trends and make a stab at understanding the problem, and those developing policy and practice are so focused on the task of working with men that they have difficulties addressing the wider issues and trends. What we needed was some lateral thinking that took the growing body of knowledge (research, statistics and trends), placed this within a theoretical perspective (or made this understandable), and then suggested what we might do about it.

So this is the concept and the aims of 'What Next for Men?' — to take the statistical and research trends, place these within the context of an understanding of men and suggest what can we do about the problems which men (and, indeed, British society as a whole) are currently confronting.

Contributors were provided with 'the evidence' which forms the first section of this book and asked to respond to the statistics and trends, outlining how they perceive 'the problem' and what they would do about it. They were invited to think of themselves as 'Minister for Men' — indeed, one contribution (Richard Fletcher's) has been written precisely from this perspective.

Initially, some 50 politicians, academics, policy makers, researchers, journalists, writers, commentators and those working with men were invited to contribute to the book. We selected these people on the basis of their known interest in the field, and their previous willingness to speak about the situation men find themselves in. We did not want this book to reflect narrow perspectives on men, but the broad range that exists in what is still a very limited topic of study and comment.

Half of those invited agreed to contribute. Of course, every book has at least one story to tell about its shaping and production, and — particularly with so many contributors — this one is no exception. Life has a habit of interfering with schedules and deadlines. Contributors changed jobs (one from a strong gender-related responsibility to the field of transport), had computers stolen (along with their hard disk contribution), and had to deal with family illness and deaths. Of course, the more general 'pressures' of other work also contributed to a chopping and changing of who participated and what arrived.

What you will find in 'What Next for Men?' is variety. We have not sought out similar perspectives, and we also have not looked for similar styles and approaches. Some contributors have written in a more academic style, while others have gone for a more open 'essay' form: other contributions take the form of interviews. Some contributors have focussed on specific aspects of 'the evidence' (such as Sandy Ruxton's piece on young criminals), while others have taken themes which cut across it (such as Jeff Hearn's analysis of 'the body').

All of the contributions, however, do not rest simply on theory or policy, but go on to suggest practical steps for addressing the needs of men in society in undergoing the changes which all of us are experiencing. The book aims to stimulate you, the reader, to think past 'the problem of men' and begin to consider what can actually be done about the problems and issues indicated by 'the evidence'.

This may require some readers to approach this book in a

slightly different way. Some people read to have their views confirmed. Books provide them with reassurance, and sometimes the confidence that their ideas and understandings have credence. Some may read books they know they do not agree with, either so they 'know the arguments', or so they can 'build a critique' of the ideas. A 'good book', we believe, is one that makes you think and that helps you make sense of what you know, or introduces you to issues and questions you had not previously thought about.

This book requires you to approach reading it with this frame of mind. Please argue with it, throw it at the wall, caress it — but above all use it to think about what's next for men.

Trefor Lloyd & Tristan Wood.
London 1996.

THE EVIDENCE

Each contributor was sent a copy of the statistics, research and trends covered in this section, some of which is referred to in the articles that follow. While we all (quite rightly) approach this type of material with some scepticism, this data is presented here for you to gain an understanding of the current context for men in Britain, and for you to refer back to when reading the 'Responses' section. Where information has been updated since contributors were first contacted, the most recent data is reproduced.

Employment Trends

In 1979, there were 13.1 million men and 9.4 million women in employment. By April 1993, this had changed to 10.7 million men and 10.1 million women. An estimated 90% of the jobs created in these 14 years have been seen as 'women's work' (low pay, part-time, requiring finger work) and a similar percentage of jobs lost were 'men's jobs' (wages high enough to keep a family, manual or skilled work). The majority of British workers will very soon be female. *Income Data Services (IDS) 1993 and Annual Abstract of Statistics, 1993, HMSO.*

Both men and women still regard certain occupations as being predominantly suitable for one sex. For instance, in 1987, 73% of men and 62% of women regarded a car mechanic as an exclusively male occupation. Although there was a shift in attitudes towards occupations such as bus driving and policing, where more than half thought that men and women were equally suitable, a substantial minority of men and women thought these jobs were still suitable for men only. *British Social Attitudes Survey, Social Community Planning Research, GB, 1987.*

92% of men and 52% of women who are working, work at least 35 hours a week, with men averaging 43.9 hours and women 30.3 hours per week. These averages place men at the top of the European Union (average 40.7 hours), and women second bottom (average 33.4 hours). *Labour Force Survey, Employment Department, GB, 1989 and Statistical Office of the European Communities, 1988.*

There are about 127,000 males aged 18-24 who have been unemployed for a year or more. Only 38,800 women fall in the same category.

The unemployment rate for 16-24 year-old black males in London is 62%, and young black men are three times more likely to be jobless than young white men. *Labour Force Survey, Employment Department, GB, 1992.*

Up to 40% of men without qualifications are out of work and the numbers are growing, according to a labour analysis of official figures. Even the most conservative Department of Employment figures show that 21% of unskilled men are jobless. In 1990, the figure was 13%.

10.78 million people have been unemployed at some point in the last five years — 39% of the workforce. Some 6.87 million men (44% of the male workforce) and 3.9 million women (33%) experienced unemployment during this period. *Harriet Harman, obtained from the Common's Library from unpublished Department of Employment data, 1995.*

The experience of unemployment has been shown to destroy men's personal and social identity (especially their 'breadwinner' identity), often resulting in a life crisis, with the inevitable increase in stress; leading to more families being poor; to effects on diet and other basic needs; and inevitably to illness. Long-standing illness is 40% higher amongst unemployed men, compared to men in work. Other studies have shown a deterioration in men's mental health when unemployed, with an improvement if they returned to work. *Tom Lewis. Unemployment and men's health. Nursing, vol 3 No 26, February 1988. M. Brenner. Mortality and the national economy. Lancet 1979, 2: pp568-9.*

Health

Life expectancy for those born between 1985 and 1990 is 78.1 years for women and 72.4 years for men. Virtually throughout this century, there has been at least 5 years difference between men's and women's expectancy, and this difference is also reflected in the EU (7.1 years). *OHE Compendium of Health Statistics, 1992, 8th Edition.*

Accidents, while only accounting for 1.9% of all deaths in 1991, reflect 42% of all deaths of 15-24 year-olds, and 17% of deaths of 25-44 year-old men.
Risk-taking behaviour, combined with lack of experience, alcohol and (to a lesser extent) drugs, are significant factors in accident causation for this age group. In addition to deaths, an estimated 10,000 children a year are left with long-term health problems from accidents: a large proportion of these are male. *Key Area Handbook on accidents (1991). HMSO.*

While suicide rates have been steadily decreasing since the mid-seventies for women, there has been a corresponding increase for men — especially young men. Men from social classes I and V are most likely to commit suicide, as are unemployed men (2-3 times); single, divorced and widowed men (3 times); men with AIDS; men in prison; or abusers of alcohol and drugs. *John Charlton et. al. Suicide deaths in England and Wales: trends in factors associated with suicide deaths. Population Trends, No 71, Spring 93. pp34-43.*

While, in England, 9% of girls (aged 9-15), compared to 7% of boys, were smokers in 1988, boys were the heavier smokers, averaging 35 cigarettes a week (compared to 28 for girls). *OPCS. Smoking among secondary school children in England in 1988, HMSO.*

In 1981, approximately 53% of males and 41% of females were found to be overweight (i.e. a Body Mass Index of 25 or above). *OPCS, The height and weights of adults in Great Britain, 1994.*

In 1988, 27% of men over the age of 16 years drank more than 21 units a week (the recommended level), with 14% drinking at least 36 units per week. These men were spread fairly evenly over all socio-economic groups. *General Household Survey. Figures for Great Britain.*

Research has shown that the male gender role leads men to ignore their health needs. Explanations for the higher mortality rates for men have included differences in risk-taking, "the outcome of differential risks acquired from role, stress, lifestyle, and preventative health practices. Psycho-social factors — how men and women perceive and evaluate symptoms, and their readiness and ability to take therapeutic action". *Robert Skelton. Man's role in society and its effect on health. Nursing 26, vol 3, No. 26, February 1988. D.L. Wingard. The sex differential in morbidity, mortality and lifestyle. Ann Rev Public Health 1984, 5, pp433-58.*

Fewer men go to visit their GP, and those men that do visit less often than women — men visited 67 million times in 1990, while women visited 143 million times in the same period (1:2.1). While the total number of visits by women will be inflated by family planning, pregnancy, childbirth and children, these differences are thought to highlight the way GP's are used by women (as a point of referral) and by men, who go more hesitantly. *General Household Survey, OPCS, 1991.*

Marriage (or living with a female partner) acts as a protection from ill-health. Other men, and particularly separated and divorced men, have higher mortality and morbidity rates. Widowed, divorced and separated men are also more likely to risk their health by smoking and drinking excessively. (There is no comparable data for homosexual couples, so whether it is being in a relationship, or being in a relationship with a woman, that protects men from ill-health is difficult to determine). *Gove W. Sex, Marital Status and Mortality, American Journal of Sociology, 1979, pp. 45-67. OPCS, 1986.*

Men often have a different perception of their health than others'; they may see themselves as fit, even though, to others, they look overweight and unfit. Men feel they need to be in control and self-sufficient, which often stops them from asking for external help. When over 20,000 young people were asked, "If you wanted to share health problems, to whom would you probably turn?", 12.8% of 12-year-old boys answered, "No one" (with only 6.9% of girls answering similarly), and, by 15 years-of-age, this response had risen to 13.8% (5.8% of girls). When asked, "When you have a problem, what do you do about it?", 18.8% of 12-year-old boys answered that they "do nothing". Briscoe suggests that, "from an early age, girls become orientated towards the tendency to seek medical care for a wide variety of complaints, whereas boys learn to disregard pain and avoid doctors; hence an association is formed between being feminine and being more concerned with health". *Blaxter, Mildred. Health and Lifestyles. Tavistock / Routledge, London, 1990, pp. 87-99. Good. GE, Dell. DM, Mintz. LB. Male Role and Gender Role Conflict: Relations to Help Seeking in Men. J. Counselling Psych 1989, 36(3), pp. 295-300. Baldings. John. Young People in 1992. Schools Health Education Unit, University of Exeter, 1993. Monica E. Briscoe. Sex Differences in Mental Health. Update, 1st November 1989. pp834-839.*

Crime

The number of young offenders (10-20 years) has fallen since 1983 (10-17 years by 37%, and 18-20 years by 8%), while there's been a corresponding fall of this age range in the population of 19%: 77% of young offenders (10-17 years) committing indicable offences in England and Wales were male (100,200) and 85.6% of those aged 18-20 were also male (77,500).

For males aged 10-13 found guilty or cautioned for indictable offences, 61% (13,600) had committed offences of theft or handling stolen goods; 18% (4,000) had committed burglary and 9% (2,100) had committed violence against the person. For males aged 14-17, the primary figures were 48% (37,400) in theft and handling stolen goods; 18% (13,900) in burglary; and 13% (10,200) in offences of violence against the person. For males aged 18-20, the figures were 38% (29,500) in theft or handling stolen goods; 14% (11,200) in burglary; 17% (13,300) in drug offences; and 11% (8,300) in offences of violence against the person. *NACRO Youth Crime Section: Factsheet about Young Offenders in 1993.*

97% of the prison population in 1989 were men (34,389M:1,175F). These percentages are reflected in those found guilty of offences (87.6%M), those cautioned (73.5%M), and those sentenced for indictable offences (87.7%M). *Home Office, England and Wales, 1992/93.*

A National Association of Probation Officers (NAPO) investigation, which analysed the circumstances of 3,279 people on probation, found that 56% misused drugs and alcohol and nearly three-quarters had committed their last offence to maintain their addiction. Parallel surveys found that 53% of 2,473 prisoners and 41% of those on community supervision were in the same circumstances. NAPO estimates that more than 95% of those surveyed were unemployed at the time of the crime, and as many as half of them had nowhere permanent to live. *NAPO, 1994.*

The number of male drug addicts notified to the Home Office has tripled from 2,979 in 1983 to 8,981 in 1993, with 21 to 30-year-olds increasing by 1,562 to 5,058. Males account for 77.7% of all addicts. 72% of males are under 30 years of age. *Home Office Statistical Bulletin, 10/94.*

Crimes committed by people aged between 10 and 20 cost the country more than £7bn a year. This age group accounted for half of all crimes in 1992 and the proportions attributed were £444m to criminal damage, £170m to motoring offences, £160m to damage during burglary, £582m to violence against people, £3.5m to the criminal justice system and £640m to private security. *Prevention Strategy for Young People in Trouble, Cooper & Lybrand, 1994.*

Sixty-seven per cent of victims of violent crime are male, of which at least 43% are victims of either pub or street brawls. This compares to 27% for female victims: 32% of females are victims of domestic violence. *Criminal Statistics England and Wales. Government Statistical Service, 1990.*

One in three men born in 1953 had been convicted of a serious offence by the age of 30. Most of their first convictions occurred at the age of 17; males first convicted in their early teens are more likely to continue offending than those convicted later. *Criminal Statistics England and Wales. Government Statistical Service, 1990.*

Sexual and Domestic Violence

Notifiable sexual offences in England and Wales have risen from 21,107 in 1980 to 29,0440 in 1990. Of these, rape has risen from 1,225 to 3,391, indecent assault on a female from 11,498 to 15,783, and unlawful sexual intercourse with a girl under 16 has dropped from 3,109 to 1,993 (although gross indecency with a child has increased from none to 1,050). Indecent assault on a male has risen from 2,288 to 3,43 and indecency between males has dropped from 1,421 to 1,121. *Criminal Statistics England and Wales, 1990. HMSO 1992.*

Education

In 1993, 45.8% of girls achieved 5 top grade GCSEs (grade A, B, or C), compared with only 36.8% of boys. 16% of girls gained three or more A-levels, compared to 14% of boys. Females make up 53% of the university population: 45.4% of women graduates are in work within six months of leaving university, as opposed to 42.3% of men. After a year, 12% of male graduates are unemployed, but only 8% of women. *Sunday Times, 19th June 1994.*

Up to 12% of boys aged 11 to 16 are unhappy and disillusioned at school — double the proportion of girls. Boys are also twice as likely to truant, do no homework and misbehave in lessons. *Keele University, 1994.*

Class is a major factor in the levels of qualifications attained. 75% of 25-69 year-olds described as 'unskilled manual' men had no qualifications, compared to 73% of women from the same group. The major changes seem to be occurring in the 'intermediate and junior non-manual' grouping. *General Household Survey, Great Britain, 1991 and 1992 combined.*

Boys outnumber girls 2:1 in Britain's schools for children with learning difficulties. In special units for behavioural problems, there are six boys for every girl. *Department of Education. 1993.*

African-Caribbean boys are four times more likely to be excluded from school than white boys. African-Caribbean children represent 8.1% of all children excluded, while comprising only 2% of the school population. *Department of Education figures and MORI poll of 79 local authorities, commissioned by Panorama in March 1993.*

Fatherhood

There has been a 50% drop in sperm count and a 50% drop in the numbers of sperm per ejaculation in the last 50 years. Research has now led to the belief that exposure to oestrogens during critical periods of male productive development has led to 'feminisation' of eels in France, alligators in Florida and fish in Britain. Further reductions in sperm counts will lead to an increase in infertility and genital abnormalities. *Richard M. Sharpe and Niels E Skakkeback. Are oestrogens involved in falling sperm counts and disorders of the male reproductive tract? The Lancet Vol 341, May 29 1993. p1392.*

More than 900 fathers abducted their children from Britain in 1993. *The Independent, 10th January 1994. 'Desperate to be a proper father'.*

38% of boys with criminal fathers acquired a criminal record, compared with 15% of comparable juveniles with non criminal fathers. Arrested fathers tended to have children showing similar rates and types of offences. The association between parental criminality and delinquency is strongest when the parent's criminal record is recidivist and extends into the time period during which the children are being reared. *Robins L.N, West P.A., and Herjanic B.L (1975). 'Arrests and delinquency in two generations. A study of black urban families and their children'. Journal of Child Psychology and Psychiatry, 16, pp125-140. West D.J. (1982) Delinquency. Its Roots, Careers and prospects. London, Heinemann Educational Books.*

The proportion of divorced and separated lone mothers has increased from 4% in 1971 to 10.6% in 1993. In the same period the number of families that comprise a married or cohabiting couple has dropped from nine to eight out of ten, and continues to fall. *General Household Survey, 1993 (OPCS Monitor SS92/1).*

Among families with children, only 13% of wives of unemployed men are themselves in employment, whereas 69% of wives of employed men are in employment. *General Household Survey, 1992. 1994, HMSO.*

There seems to be a trend towards fathers spending more time with their children. Fathers in dual income families do this more than their counterparts in single income families where the father is the income earner. *Lamb, M.E. (1988). The Changing Role of Fathers: The Father's Role — Applied Perspectives.*

A third of both men and women believe that it is a husband's job to earn the money, and a wife's job to look after the home and family. However, a greater proportion (45%) reject the traditional 'man as breadwinner / woman as homemaker', this is particularly the case with the 18-34 age group (65% of men and 68% of women). *British Social Attitudes Survey, 1992. HMSO.*

RESPONSES

From the Co-Minister for Gender Affairs

(Speech given on the Launch of the Father Care Project of Great Britain: London, 6th September 1999)

Richard Fletcher

After working in education for several years, Richard Fletcher was contracted to the Health Promotion Unit in Newcastle, Australia, as a research fellow to examine domestic violence prevention. As a result, he became interested in male health issues and pioneered the development of Men's Health and Boys' Health as areas of study, teaching male health studies to teachers, nurses, occupational therapists and medical students as a lecturer in Health Studies at the University of Newcastle's Discipline of Paediatrics. He also founded a group to conduct Stopping Rape workshops with teenage boys in schools. Now co-ordinator of the Men's Health Project, Family Action Centre, University of Newcastle, Richard's most recent publications are 'Boys in Schools: addressing the real issues — behaviour, values and relationships' (co-edited with Rollo Browne) and 'An Introduction to the new 'Men's Health''.

Mrs Prime Minster, distinguished guests, friends. As I was driving here today, I passed through a section of my constituency which, over the 20 years I have been a resident, has been known as a rough area, an area where you wouldn't leave your car unlocked, certainly an area where you wouldn't go alone, especially if you were female. I am pleased to say, of course, that my Government has begun to take action in boroughs precisely like this one to address many of the deep social problems which form the legacy, even 20 years later, of Thatcherism in our country.

Today, I am pleased to say, unemployment, oppression and repression of men and women is no longer the norm. Driving through the borough, there are signs of hope and progress. Things are happening. The opening of the 100th work-based daycare centre, the completion of the community health centre programme and the establishment of the first fully-integrated human transit system are just three recent accomplishments — accomplishments of which my Government can be justly proud, although, of course, we didn't make these things happen. What we did was to get off the backs of the people there so that they could make things happen. Get off their backs and get others off their backs too. To let the community take the lead, with our encouragement, in making a safe, clean and co-operative environment where children can learn, where communities and businesses can prosper together. All we claim credit for is assisting and encouraging.

However, what I want to tell you about is not the broad social parameters of change, but a tiny incident: a minute example of the specific changes that we are here about today. Because, driving through Elswick-on-Lloyd while stopped at a traffic light, I saw a small child, probably about three years old, trip on a piece of scaffolding set up across the footpath and hurt herself. Before the lights had had time to change, two men, one about 18 or 20 and the other an older man, had gone to the child, picked her up, dried her tears, dusted her off, soothed her and set her off running again. From my observation, neither of the men knew the girl. One came from a shop across the road, the other from the building site behind her. They asked her name, they acted respectfully concerned, as you would with a hurt child whom you didn't know, and — and this is the part that took my attention — neither of them looked the least bit self-conscious about what they were doing, neither of them looked around for a woman to fix it, or to check if other men might jibe at them for their tenderness, or maybe someone accuse them of nasty intentions.

What we as a community are starting to realise — and the programme we are here to launch today is evidence of the change in our thinking — is that, if we get off the backs of the men in our community, if we put in place the structures, the institutional arrangements which will allow men to interact well with children, then forcing men or punishing men to make us more caring, to make us more considerate of others, is totally unnecessary. We (that is, men) already have all the programming we need to be caring. We have the software inside us to allow us to be caring. What we need is the hardware in the community, the systems in place to allow and encourage that caring to come out. And that is precisely what this Project we are here to launch today is designed to do.

No project, no one system, of course, can, by itself, bring about the sort of change we are looking for in our community. Most of you will have seen the Minster for Justice's statement on physical punishment of children, and many of you know that we are in the process of adopting the Australian sick leave provisions for male carers as part of the gender reform of our industrial relations system. But we want to go beyond removing impediments to actually valuing male carers in our community, and that is what we are about today.

The Father Care Project is a comprehensive, multi-level package which has one simple aim and one simple premise. The aim is to have more frequent, more enjoyable, more socially productive interactions between fathers of all descriptions and the children in our communities. Dads, and here I mean, of course, not just biological fathers, but uncles, so called defacto fathers, older male friends — men, in short, from our community — are to be encouraged to spend more time, in more mutually productive ways, with a variety of children in their locality. This will take place in schools, in parks, in organised activities and in recreational and social settings.

In their participation, these men will fundamentally challenge the notion that children somehow belong to, are the responsibility of, and should be exclusively or predominantly cared for by, women. This Project, and the other measures my Government is undertaking in the same vein, are not in any way an attack or a criticism of the mothering and caring already done by women in our community. As my Co-Minister for Gender has made clear in her speeches to the House, this Project has the full and enthusiastic support of every major women's association in the country. The Project will benefit every member of the community. For too long, the expectation that women would take care of the children has been a central part of our thinking. In challenging this assumption, we also need to make perfectly clear that a parallel assumption has been just as powerful in limiting the lives of parents, children and community members in general. This assumption is that men are somehow genetically or wilfully incapable of providing consistently loving and competent care for children. It is this assumption that we wish to expunge from our policies, our work practices, our schools and childcare centres. This is a two-sided process. Men have been told, for ever and a day, not only that children are women's work, but that men are constituted differently, that we are naturally suited to competitive games and war and striving for material achievement, but that we do not have, and could not possible achieve, the skills and competencies to successfully interact with children.

Some of you will be thinking of your own children, and the enjoyable times you have had with them. You may be wondering if I am exaggerating the bleakness of this picture of what men have been told. Let me say firstly that we have been very mindful of the trap of thinking that all men are the same. As I hope will be clear from the description of the Project which follows, we have gone to considerable trouble to build an array of strategies to address the needs of different groups of men and children in our community. But, before detailing the way that this Project hopes to address the caring father issue, let me first point to the evidence that we do not already have sufficient male involvement with children at any age.

From the annual surveys published by HMSO, we know that, across Britain, the average time spent by adult males with their own children — and I stress this is their own children, not the broader focus of this Project — averages 11 minutes per week. That is an increase, of course, on the previous years, and the trend is definitely rising. But there are few who would say that this amount of time is sufficient. When we break this into occupation groups, some important differences arise. Contrary to the view that the rich enjoy better lifestyles, there is no correlation between income and time spent with children. Among the unemployed, and among professionals, for example, there is enormous variation. Some men manage to spend considerable time in child-based activity, others spend less than the average.

But the family setting, especially the much-invoked family unit (the fetish, you might say, of every Conservative since Disraeli), is not the only place where children encounter adults, and it should not be the only place where we look to improve the relationship between children and fathers and adult men in our communities. In preparing for this Project, my Department commissioned a variety of ground-breaking research into the issue of children's contact with men. One measure examined was just how much time was spent, not in the home with mother or father, but how much time the average child spent with adult males throughout their whole day. We conducted a gender audit, if you like, totting up the hours a child spends with men or women during the week. We did this in different locations where children, from pre-school age to teenagers, spend their time.

The findings are, in a sense, what you would expect. Everyone knows that there are more female primary school teachers and nurses than there are males. But it may be a shock to you (it certainly was to me) to see the extent to which males are removed from the world of children. Here are just some of the percentages, of the week the average child spends with a female, that is an adult female, compared to male contact. Childcare 94% female; Libraries 87% female; Accident and Emergency Departments 80%

female; Retail outlets 79% female; Infants Schools 92% female; Welfare agencies 78% female; Youth clubs 69% female; Primary Schools 87% female; and Comprehensive Secondary Schools 71% female.

This evidence points to the structural, the institutional forces which shape men and women's and children's perception of who should be with children. This is not the man deciding whether to bath the kids in the isolation of his own home. These figures demonstrate the public values we hold, the gender arrangements we as a society are actively promoting. And this is what we hope, and are determined, to change.

In order for people (men and women) to change, of course there has to be some incentive, some drive for a better situation, a better result. Here we also have commissioned new research, because what is becoming very clear in the development of this Project is that the understanding that we have of men in our community is very often a guess based on an assumption. We are just now coming to realise how little we really know about what men think. In relation to children, we asked men from round the nation, from all walks of life, to tell us what they think about their interaction with children. Not just their own children, but the children in their immediate area.

One of the most important findings of this research, and it is a finding I should say which applies to the vast majority of sub-groups sampled in this wide-ranging research project, is that machismo — the notion that men do the things they do out of some ideal of toughness — is a minor player (a very minor player) in this process. This will come as a shock, I realise, to many of the Press, or at least their editors, here today. Machismo for too long has been the shorthand — and we now see incorrect — explanation of every social ill related to male behaviour. The major stumbling block for men getting involved with children is not a desire to be or look as tough as possible. On the contrary, what men say, in a variety of ways, is that they feel awkward, incompetent or stupid in crucial areas of dealing with children. The factor identified in our research was a cluster of feelings and apprehensions best described as looking like an idiot or a fool.

Embarrassment, if you like, proved to be the major single reason for men not wanting to do things around children.

This is an important finding. Because you can do things about embarrassment. You can set up situations where the idiot factor is reduced. Training, explanation, gradation, familiarisation — there are a host of strategies which we know make a difference, which avoid people looking like an idiot. If, on the other hand, you think it's all about machismo, what have you got? About the best you can do is say, "Don't be tough".

Now let me describe for you the basic elements of the Father Care Project. Of those areas I listed before to you, retail to pre-school, the site where most mileage can be made, where most impact can be made and where there is a clear mandate from the community, is in the school and pre-school sectors. So the primary focus of the Project is in schools, pre-schools and in comprehensive secondary schools. We wish to have fathers productively interacting with children, but what does 'productively' mean? Productively, for this Project, means to the mutual satisfaction of both parties; it means the adult man listening to the child, not abdicating his knowledge and experience as a grown man , but not simply instructing the child either. So we are not talking about males taking over teachers' jobs, although, of course, in the long run, we would like to see a gender balance in the classroom, just as we strive for a gender balance in the principal's office. But, as anyone who has spent any time at all in a school knows, there are many, many situations where adults who are not teachers can meaningfully interact with students. Volunteers have many important roles in schools, and fathers traditionally have been conspicuous by their absence. But we will be encouraging fathers, in the broad sense of that term, to be highly visible, in numbers and enthusiasm, in the roles of helping with reading, of serving in the canteen, in being assistants to the sports teachers, in mentoring students with difficulties.

How will we encourage this? Caring, like most crucial aspects of fostering children, is not something which can be applied mechanically. We have come a long way since the early studies of institutionalised children demonstrated that simply feeding, clothing and watching over children is nowhere near proper caring. So that, when we propose caring fathers, we do not simply intend for fathers to be on the premises, or even in the same room, but to actively engage with children. Further, we see engagement as more than discipline, more than coaching the football (although coaches can, of course, be caring); we mean engagement which includes warmth and respect. The engagement can be playful or serious, it can be task-related or just hanging around, and it might include energetic physical play, sports, be outdoors or indoors, and involve large or small groups. This is where we can be prescriptive in saying that we want more than the traditional disciplinarian approach. But there is enormous scope for individual dads and schools to create enjoyable ways to do things together.

Do dads already know how to do this? Yes and no. We men already have the potential and the capacity — what most of us lack is the experience. Based on the research conclusion of the importance of the idiot factor, we have built into the Project a strong development component, for schools, pre-schools and secondary schools to work out with the fathers and men in their communities how best to engage dads.

Some schools have already made significant steps in this direction. Members of the Project Team have met and talked with dozens of groups across all regions who have already pioneered effective strategies with fathers. It gives me great pleasure, as part of the official launch of this Project, to show you the first 'Fathercare Works' booklet, which documents the various successful strategies used by these pre-schools and schools to build a climate of involvement with fathers. As you can see by the photo on the cover, this is not exclusively about middle-class tertiary-educated fathers, in fact one surprising feature was how many schools in so-called disadvantaged areas have really targeted the men in their area, and many have succeeded. Their stories, not glib, promotional propaganda, but readily accessible accounts, warts and all, of what happened, are in here and a copy of this booklet will go to every school body in the next few weeks. But any resource book, no matter how good, can only be implemented with real people to make things happen. We need not just stimulus and novel ideas, but real expertise.

To this end, I am also pleased to present today, the inaugural Fathercare Leaders Certificates for the 16 fathers from Islington Public School District, North London, who have completed the Fathercare Leaders course at their local college. This Certificate, which has been accorded national accreditation by the Manpower Services Board, recognises the skills that these men have developed in recruiting strategies for fathers, in developing school-based activities for men, in planning and implementing father involvement and in liaising with men's organisations. This is a genuine educational qualification, with an intellectual and practical component. These 16 men worked with three schools in the area to actually plan and implement the involvement of men in the day-to-day activities of the schools. There have been notable successes, as well as some important lessons. At St Michael's, for example, at the conclusion of the course, not only were men for the first time helping with reading and with sports supervision, but a fathers' project linking men seeking carpentry skills with suitable trainers was formed. In another school, the literacy needs of the fathers themselves were recognised and addressed. A crucial point raised by the men in this course was that fathers have some important differences in their roles with boys and girls. In many cases, the fathers' role is the same, of course, but, as school teachers well know, it is the boys in our schools who have the most difficulty with reading, with discipline, with the humanities subjects. With boys, fathers have a special role in providing leadership, companionship and mentoring in the transition to becoming men.

Another important point about this model programme is that the men worked not only within the schools. An essential aspect of community involvement is to engage not just individual men, but men's organisations. In the case of Islington, the Islamic Association became the staunchest supporter of the project, even to the point of adopting the idea as part of their own members charter. The Islington Juniors Football Club became another major sponsor, and this model suggested to us a way of involving significant numbers of men from right across the land.

A third aspect of this Project, which I am delighted to announce, is the Fathercare Cup. This Cup, and the cash prize of £25,000, will be presented annually by Littlewoods to the football team whose registered members can accrue the highest total of Fathercare hours (that is, activities falling within the guidelines) in their local schools. Here, let me just return briefly to the research base for this Project. As the Mori polls regularly find, men and women are most concerned with issues such as unemployment or the national debt. Children, and looking after children's needs, do not regularly appear in lists of issues considered most important. However, when our researchers interviewed men about their concerns, if the interview was allowed to run past a few minutes, concern for children was raised by fathers themselves in 77% of cases. This 77% is a considerable mandate for involving men in children's issues. If — and, I repeat, if — it is presented in the right way, the Fathercare Cup, our initial research suggests, might be one way to translate this genuine concern into action. Contact with football clubs from Glasgow to Brighton has revealed considerable interest and, in league with sports administrators and, of course, school communities, we expect a big turnout for the final round next year.

But what of fathers who cannot, for legitimate reasons of work hours, visit their schools for activities? Time, the most important invention of the Industrial Revolution, is accepted by many as the most concrete barrier to men's participation in the activities of schools. Here, we can take a leaf from the way military training is sponsored in our society. Since the 1940's, voluntary military service is given priority over work commitments for those involved. Employers are reimbursed for the time a man is off training to defend his country. Since probably the end of World War II, but certainly since the end of the Cold War, it has become perfectly clear that our real struggle is with the social issues here at home. For this reason, it makes perfect sense to reimburse employers for the hours lost when men leave work to attend Fathercare activities in their school. By our estimates, the cost of this scheme in the first 12 months will amount to £5-8 million. The expected increase in subsequent years will, my Government believes, be money well spent, since it will reflect the movement of men into the caring role which is crucial to our future. These estimates, I should point out, are based on the experience at two industrial sites, Jencks Engineering's plant at Hexham, where 120 men out of a workforce of 400 were involved, and the Woolworths' distribution centres at Heathrow, Glasgow, Liverpool and Belfast, where, out of a total male workforce of 17,000, just over 6,000 men took some part in school-based activities through the initiative. Two public sector organisations were also trialed, The Inland Revenue office in Leeds and the Second Grenadiers Regiment, based in Clyde. In both these organisations, over 30% of eligible men were involved. Initial reports from all areas suggest that schools and children were delighted with the men's involvement. Some of the experiences from these schools form part of the 'Fathercare Works' publication I referred to earlier.

These four elements are, of course, just a beginning. But they are, I believe, a significant start to one of the most important issues ever tackled by Her Majesty's Government. In closing, I would just like to leave you with a comment made in one of the discussion groups conducted at the Jencks Engineering plant. It came from a 32-year-old boiler attendant, the father of four, a man who hardly saw his own father during daylight hours and who eventually became deeply involved in every aspect of the project at the plant. In the discussion following the presentation of the project at the shop committee he said, "You know, that's right, we ought to be grabbing this opportunity to do things with our kids. After all, when was the last time you heard a man on his deathbed say he wished he'd spent more time at work?".

Bringing the Male Crisis
Into the Open

Peter Baker

Peter Baker is a writer and journalist specialising in gender and health issues. He is currently contributing health and fitness editor for Maxim magazine and has co-authored a self-help book for men, 'The MANual', to be published by Thorsons in autumn 1996. He has also been an honorary visiting research fellow in applied social studies at Bradford University.

The traditional certainties of men's lives appear to be crumbling as fast as their sperm counts and now look as dated as the tuxedo James Bond wore under his wet suit. No longer guaranteed superior status through work, or emotional security through marriage, many men are responding to the rapid changes in social, economic and gender roles with resignation, confusion, despair, or, in some cases, downright panic. A few seek a new way of being through the burgeoning 'men's movements' — typically involving a mix of new-age therapy and old-age rituals — while many more attempt to counter a sense of growing powerlessness through crime, violence, pornography, 'workaholism', or an obsession with achieving the perfect 'masculine' body. The explosion in the use of muscle-swelling anabolic steroids, as well as the inexorable rise of cosmetic surgery for men, are striking testaments to male anxiety.

Other men, meanwhile, seem to be retreating into a kind of permanent adolescence or laddishness, a condition celebrated by *Loaded* magazine and the television sitcom *Men Behaving Badly*. The only significant political response comes not from pro-feminist men rushing to embrace the changes in men's lives, but from the 'backlash'-inspired 'men's rights' lobby. Grandly co-opting for itself the title 'The UK Men's Movement', this grouping seeks to destroy feminism — a movement it frequently equates with Nazism — and restore men to their 'rightful' place at the head of the table. But perhaps the most worrying male reaction to change is reflected in The Samaritans' statistics. They now receive more calls from men than women, and four times as many men actually kill themselves. If these figures are a barometer of the modern male psyche, it is clear Nineties Man is beset by some pretty serious problems.

But there is now no turning back: traditional masculinity has had its day. After all, what place would Rambo have in the brave new multinational world of McDonald's and Microsoft? He would just damage the equipment and frighten the customers. The economy increasingly needs workers with more 'feminine' skills, such as being able to communicate and to handle complex and fast-changing work-loads. At home, moreover, men are now expected to be caring partners and sharing parents, not Bruce Willis clones who cannot even find the time to phone because they are too busy reducing America to rubble. There are signs that even Arnold Schwarzenegger — the 'real' man's 'real' man — has realised the game is up. Present at the birth of his daughter, Conan the Babysitter even cut the umbilical cord and now claims to enjoy little more than spending the early hours rocking her to sleep. But most men are not as adaptable as Arnie and they face the problem of how to come to terms successfully with what is, without much exaggeration, the real new world order.

Understandably, many will have little sympathy with men's

predicament. After all, with the exception of a few, isolated cultures, men have been on top since humans first roamed the primeval swamps in search of a juicy mammoth and a warm cave to eat it in. It is easy to believe, therefore, that men should take their turn to suffer insecurity and disadvantage. But this stance is unsatisfactory for two reasons. First, if it is wrong in principle for women to suffer because of their gender, it is also wrong for men. Secondly, and more concretely, it is counterproductive. If the threats to traditional masculinity are not properly understood or responded to, the result could be gender conflict on a considerable scale. The UK Men's Movement may, as yet, seem eccentric, even mildly comical, but the well-organised, high-profile USA men's rights lobby provides a more worrying insight into what could happen here. Moreover, the response of many men will not just be organisational or political. A sense of growing powerlessness could well result in a range of destructive behaviour, damaging to both men and women.

The solution is not to reassure men by attempting to halt change, let alone trying to recreate gender relationships now firmly belonging to the past, but rather to help them find ways of adapting to, and accepting, their emerging new role. This means enabling men not only to come to terms with what they have lost, but also to appreciate how much they stand to gain from adopting a different kind of masculinity. The process of adjustment could be eased by including men within the framework of political and social concern through public acknowledgement of their position, as well as beginning a serious debate about the role of men in the 21st century. Enhancing men's emotional skills could enable them both to accept change and to develop a more positive and empowered sense of themselves. Greater involvement in parenting, better relationships and significantly improved health are also among the top prizes on offer to men able to adapt to their new role. Ultimately, what is becoming available to men is not a choice between being a 'strong' Clint Eastwood or a 'wimpy' Woody Allen, but a more complete, rounded and human form of maleness, one in which men can pick and mix the best qualities of traditional femininity and traditional masculinity.

Inducements alone may not be enough, however. They need to be combined with regulation to ensure men are unable to reassert traditional gender inequality. This requires a new determination on the part of government to eradicate sex discrimination, unequal pay and sexual harassment. With women generally earning considerably less than men (in only 13% of couples does a woman earn £50 more than her partner) and much less likely to become senior managers, there is still a clear need for a renewed effort to eradicate prejudice through both legislation and education. This conclusion is reinforced, and given even greater urgency, by the appalling facts that one in four women has been raped and one in three has suffered domestic violence. The process of change in the roles and relationships of men and women could also be managed much more easily in a society in which there existed a genuine commitment by government to full employment and social welfare, rather than one in which uncertainty, insecurity, fear and individualism have become prevalent. Current economic and social circumstances do not make it easy for a citizen to relinquish any advantage he or she may have.

Suggesting men's issues should be more widely discussed is not an attempt to create a new class of 'victims' or to claim men are the new 'second-class citizens' — that would be absurd given their continued dominance in many areas of public and private life. But it would surely be easier for men to adapt to apparently inevitable changes if they were taking place in a context where there was at least a widely-expressed understanding of, and sympathy for, the problems of adjustment. Men may know their feelings of unhappiness, frustration, fear, anger or sadness stem from anxieties about their work, their relationships, or even their football team's position at the bottom of the Second Division, but they are less likely to relate their unease to their feelings about themselves as men, in particular their expectations of themselves, the expectations they believe others have of them and their inability to live up to them. The emergence of an understanding among men that being male is a key factor in determining how they feel about their experiences would enable them to appreciate better how their lives are affected by change, and to participate far more effectively in a debate about their position.

Yet when did a politician last encourage debate on the changing role and position of men? When did a policy statement, whether from a political party or a social policy organisation, discuss men's roles? Any examples are notable largely for their rarity. A major transformation in the lives of half of the population is happening without any significant recognition or debate. Politicians and policy-makers do not hesitate to pontificate about most social issues, but this one certainly seems to have escaped their attention.

If a politician had to select just one aspect of men's lives for public discussion, he or she could do no better than to choose employment. It is men's changing connection to work — and the sense of identity it confers — that lies behind many of the other key developments affecting their lives, particularly in parenting, health and personal relationships. Although it has become commonplace to acknowledge the general effect of the decline of traditional industries and the rise of mass unemployment on communities, little has been said about the impact on men specifically. Even for men in white-collar jobs, the rapidly approaching end of 'the job for life', even of the very idea of 'a career', together with women's increasing participation in the labour force, is effectively terminating any sense men might have of themselves as 'providers'. While it is easy to applaud the demise of male domination of the workplace — an outcome certainly long overdue — it is nevertheless still crucial to acknowledge the profound effect such a change has on men's sense of themselves. It cannot be right that so many men are simply left feeling confused, angry, dispossessed and powerless without that experience being publicly acknowledged and discussed.

But the situation requires more than a few speeches empathising with the difficulties facing men. The pace of change requires nothing less than a significant public debate about men and masculinity. The best way to achieve this would be for the Government — or perhaps (and more likely) a major charity or think-tank committed to the development of public policy — to initiate a high-profile, independent investigation into the challenges now facing men, as well as their future role. The remit would include work, the family, education, crime, health, sexuality and any other relevant area. Evidence could be taken in public, research commissioned and submissions invited from all interested parties. The slowly growing (although somewhat disparate) experience of work with men would also need to be brought together and analysed. A highly-publicised final report could significantly encourage politicians, policy-makers and 'ordinary' men and women to begin an informed debate about men's role beyond the millennium.

The inquiry would certainly need to consider the many claims now being made about discrimination against men. Because any overall comparison of the lives of men and women unquestioningly shows that women are significantly more disadvantaged, there has been an understandable reluctance to accept the existence of areas where men do suffer. But just because the majority of people affected by domestic violence are women, it does not follow that women cannot sometimes be perpetrators and men victims. Men can also be discriminated against at work and in the divorce courts, be sexually harassed and be sexually objectified in advertising and pornography. This area is so fraught with claim and counter-claim, however, that the commissioning of objective and independent research would seem to represent the best way forward. It is, of course, also vital that the inquiry does not lose sight of the many ways in which men still discriminate and act abusively against women. A central part of its role would be to suggest what further steps are needed to challenge unacceptable male behaviour and promote greater gender equality.

So, what steps could be taken to bring about progress in important areas like men and their emotions, male violence, fatherhood, men's health, sexuality and work with men generally?

Any experience of unwanted change is stressful, even traumatic. Bereavement, for instance, is an obviously painful experience, requiring a period of grieving and adjustment before acceptance. Men's changing role is no less stressful, even though it is not represented by a sudden event, but is taking place over a long period of time. The slow 'death' of traditional masculinity also requires an emotional response, although this is hard for many men, given their notorious 'emotional illiteracy'. Yet if men could feel and express their feelings — particularly grief and fear — it would make adjustment to a new role much easier. It would reduce the chances of men's anger leading to self-victimising and women-blaming. It would also improve their physical and mental health, their relationships with partners and children, and have a big impact on their propensity for violence.

The emotional male is no longer a complete unknown, of course. We have become used to sports stars weeping on the field of play and 'regular guys' can often be seen parading their feelings on talk-shows like *Oprah* and *Esther*. The increasing level of crises in men's lives (especially in relation to work and relationships) is also inevitably bringing them into greater contact with their emotions — even the stiffest of upper lips can quiver when faced with redundancy or divorce. Moreover, we all now live in a culture in which therapy-speak is evermore widespread and emotional expression increasingly validated. But most men still need to go much further before they can finally shake off the claim that they are actually little more emotional than a robot encased in bubble-wrap.

A campaign to educate the public, and men in particular, about the importance of understanding and expressing feelings would help. Based on the slogan 'Big Boys Do Cry', the campaign could be organised jointly by the Health Education Authority, the Royal College of Psychiatrists, The Samaritans, the British Association for Counselling and the UK Council for Psychotherapy. Such an initiative needs to be broader than publicity involving the experiences of celebrity role models, important though that could be. There has to be institutional change, with employers encouraged to provide counselling as part of their occupational health service, and primary health care providers urged to set up on-site, short-term counselling or therapy and to recommend it to more of their male patients. Given many men's reluctance to talk face-to-face, however, a national telephone helpline (and e-mail) counselling service could also be established with a wider remit than that currently provided by The Samaritans. Organisations of all kinds — including workplaces, trade unions and voluntary groups — could also ask their male staff, members or users to consider meeting together in order to share and learn from common experiences and as a means of providing mutual, self-help support.

Counsellors working with men need to be more aware of masculinity and how it can affect the counselling process. Counsellors and therapists often do not take into account just how hard it is for many men to articulate their feelings. "How do you feel today?" might seem a straightforward enough question to ask a client, but a man who has struggled to repress his inner self since childhood might well find it about as confusing as a knitting pattern. In fact, the first stage in counselling many men has to be tuition in identifying feelings and asking the kind of information-seeking questions they often find it easier to respond to. If the counsellor has the expectation that the approach used for female clients will work equally well with men, he or she is likely to accumulate a considerable number of disappointed male customers. It is vital these issues form a significant part of counselling training.

One specialist area of counselling work with men for which considerable evidence of effectiveness already exists is work with perpetrators of violence against women. There are a number of small-scale schemes operating around the country and, although their methods are different, many do seem to be achieving results. If this is confirmed by independent evaluation — already completed for some projects, currently underway at others — then a properly funded national network of agencies should be created. The lessons learned could also be incorporated into the work of other organisations working with violent men, especially the probation and prison services. Counselling these men should not be seen as an alternative to legal sanctions, however, and women's safety must always remain a paramount concern.

Improving emotional literacy is not an issue for adult men alone. The social pressures limiting a male's emotional life begin early. It is not for nothing that almost the first question people ask about a baby is whether it is a boy or a girl: we need to know so we can provide what seems the 'appropriate' gendered response. This suggests an important role for both parents and, later, teachers. While it would be unrealistic to expect parents to bring up their sons in a way that is completely gender-neutral — even those that try often seem to end up disappointed and disillusioned — it is not unreasonable to believe many parents could show greater gender-consciousness. The belief that boys should not cry or show their vulnerability could be challenged from ante-natal classes onwards, for example, and parents can become more aware of the many ways in which their own behaviour influences a child's perception of sex roles. At school, discussion of emotions and relationships could become part of the curriculum, not just confined to counselling for young people with special problems.

Although men might sometimes seem a bit like the computers they spend so much time playing with, there is at least one crucial difference — men's brains contain the software necessary for travel down the emotional super-highway; it merely requires activation. Greater emotionality would do more for men than enable them to deal better with change and to enrich their lives, important though that is. It would also help to improve communication between men and women, vital in any relationship. With family breakdowns a key contemporary issue, such a development could play a part in maintaining some relationships, as well as enabling separations to occur with less damaging emotional fall-out. More male openness about feelings could also increase the demand for relationship counselling. Existing services, including Relate, are already overstretched and there is a clear need for the development of adequate national provision able to respond quickly to couples' emotional crises. Outreach work to men could also be an important objective for an expanded service.

Fathers now routinely attend births; many cut the umbilical cord. It is no longer unusual to see a man pushing a buggy — even if it is just with one hand — or even changing the occasional nappy. Men are already more likely to have a greater role in childcare than their own fathers, especially if they are unemployed or in dual-income households. Men's changing role now offers them an opportunity to become more involved parents. Not only are there greater social — including partner — expectations that they 'should' get their hands dirty, but men's changing relationship with work could also leave many more likely to seek a sense of self-identity through parenting.

But there are still factors inhibiting men's greater involvement in childcare. One is the belief, still held by too many men, that childcare is essentially 'women's work' and, basically, a bit 'sissy'. There are also, of course, major institutional problems confronting any man wanting to be an active parent, not least long working hours, job insecurity and the non-existence of statutory paternity leave. While establishing maximum hours of work, together with a more gender-neutral system of parental leave, could definitely help, giving men more time to be with their children does not, in itself, guarantee that they will not choose to do something else instead. The result could simply be more anglers on riverbanks, a boom in membership of snooker halls and a surge in surfing on the Internet.

Greater encouragement of fathering could come through education. Some young offenders' institutions already give boys training in parenting skills and there is no obvious reason why these programmes should not be made more widely available. There cannot be many schools currently teaching their male students how to sterilise a bottle, puree soft fruits and burp a baby. Midwives and doctors could provide more information about the possible role of fathers, even if it is only in the form of leaflets. There is also a clear need for more positive role models of men as fathers. The media currently tends to depict them either as the angst-ridden dads of *Thirtysomething* or as incompetent 'dorks' populating television advertisements for washing liquids or fish fingers. Public lavatory providers could also take one small but important step by replacing 'mother-and-baby' rooms with 'parent-and-baby' facilities.

One area where there has already been some public recognition of men's particular problems is health. The

Government's Chief Medical Officer devoted a chapter to men in his 1992 annual report and the Health Minister addressed a major men's health conference in 1995. With two new men's health magazines recently launched, and a series of BBC television and radio programmes on men's health broadcast in early 1996, the subject is certainly creeping up the public agenda. But, while some younger men in particular seem susceptible to healthy lifestyle messages, many more males apparently remain content to push their bodies to the limit with booze and burgers, fags and fast cars. Men in general still share an apparent predilection for ill-health and premature death.

Much of men's reluctance to take their health seriously flows from a fear of appearing weak or vulnerable — after all, a 'real' man would be as likely to visit the doctor as wear a pinny and bake cakes. The broadening of men's emotional repertoire would certainly help here and more involved parenting could increase men's contact with health care services. A sustained health promotion campaign aimed at men and led by the Health Education Authority could also make a significant difference. So far, the HEA's work specifically with men has been limited, yet there is a clear need for television, cinema and newspaper advertisements, street posters and widely-available leaflets on key men's health issues. Every library and leisure centre, as well as every doctor's surgery, should (at the very least) contain accessible information on diseases of the testes and prostate.

A national, free network of 'well man' (or 'well person') clinics attached to GP surgeries, work and sports facilities should also be established. While there are legitimate doubts about whether preventive health screening makes a value-for-money difference, such clinics could provide the vital function of encouraging men to see a health care professional and of normalising the notion that it is acceptable for men to pay attention to their health. An opportunity would be created for men to discuss concerns and anxieties, as well as to receive information on diet, exercise and smoking. Telephone helplines on health also have a role, and consideration should therefore be given to publicising and expanding the Medical Advisory Service's provision for men.

It is impossible to discuss the changing role of men without considering gay men. That is not only because gay men remain a large group of men affected by discrimination, but also because homophobia is a key factor that inhibits all men from changing their traditional role. As long as gay men are oppressed, socially or legally, there remains a significant disincentive for any men to adopt any behaviour that could be interpreted as gay. That extends from showing emotions (apart from anger) to touching another man (except when drunk or on the football field) to showing an interest in cooking, cleaning or childcare. While attitudes are slowly changing, especially in some larger cities, further steps are urgently needed, not only for gay men themselves, but for all men. There is no rational reason to maintain a higher age of consent for gay men, or a bar on military service, and discrimination on the grounds of sexual orientation should be made illegal.

There is, as yet, limited public understanding of men and masculinity, but there is also surprisingly little understanding among those whose job it is to work with men in a context where gender is acutely relevant — this certainly includes police officers, probation and prison officers, social workers, health care professionals and teachers. Given the rapidly changing context of men's lives, and the fact that men constitute the most problematic group now dealt with by many agencies, it is more important than ever for all those working with men to have an understanding of their issues. But, when gender is addressed in professional training programmes, it is normally as an option and concerned solely with women, rather than incorporating a critical understanding of masculinity. This seems outdated and unworkable, perhaps most obviously in the case of violent men, for whom the traditional — and obviously largely useless — response is imprisonment combined with neglect. A greater understanding of the psychological roots of violent behaviour, intertwined as they are with masculinity, would create the opportunity for a more creative, and more effective, approach.

Taken together, this package of measures would not only acknowledge the changing position of men, but also create a basis for a positive and practical response. Crucially, it would bring men's experience, which is seldom recognised (even by many men themselves), into the public domain and enable the development of initiatives that would improve the quality of men's lives, as well as the lives of the women and children around them. While more resources will clearly be needed, it is vital that these are not taken from services for women, since they are also chronically underfunded. But it should be clear to any far-sighted analyst that, although the short-term costs might be considerable, the long-term savings could be greater. A male population which is, to quote a phrase perhaps more memorable than the politician who used it, 'at ease with itself' will be physically and emotionally healthier, less disposed to violence, more active in parenting and more accepting of change. These initiatives will help men understand that they are not so much being 'emasculated' as 'remasculated' — in other words, now that traditional masculinity has become as obsolete as many of the jobs that once underpinned it, a new, more flexible and human masculinity at last has the opportunity to emerge.

Try Supporting Feminism!
(Observations from the U.S.A.)

Michael S. Kimmel

Michael S. Kimmel is Professor of Sociology at State University of New York at Stony Brook. His books include 'Changing Men' (1987), 'Men Confront Pornography' (1990), 'Against the Tide: Profeminist Men in the United States, 1776-1990' (1992), 'Men's Lives' (3rd ed. 1995) and 'Manhood in America: A Cultural History' (1995). He edits 'masculinities', an interdisciplinary scholarly journal; a book series on men and masculinities at University of California Press; and the Sage Series, 'Men and Masculinities'. He is spokesperson for the National Organisation for Men Against Sexism (NOMAS) and lectures extensively on campuses in the U.S.A. and abroad.

There's been a revolution going on for the past 25 years or so — a seismic shift in the social world that has been so profound, so sweeping, so irrevocable that our lives will never be the same. Unfortunately, men may not have noticed.

I think back to the world of my father's generation. Now in his late 60's, my father could go to an all-male college, serve in an all-male military and spend his entire working life in a virtually all-male working environment. He entered the middle class with every expectation of upward mobility and enormous opportunities in the professions. His era witnessed the first hints of a sexual revolution that made the pursuit of pleasure a consumer option.

In my generation (I am in my mid-40's), his world began to crumble; today it has completely disappeared. The path of upward mobility is blocked; we are a downwardly-mobile culture. Most Americans are less successful now than their parents were at the same age. It now takes two incomes to provide the same standard of living that one income provided about a generation ago. Most middle-class young adults who were raised in the suburbs of major metropolitan areas have probably lived in the nicest houses they will ever live in, as they will never be able to afford to buy the houses in which they were brought up. Virtually all previously all-male colleges have become coeducational, the military has been opened up to women, and large numbers of women have entered the workforce.[1] There is virtually no occupation that a young man can choose in which he will not have a woman colleague, a woman co-worker, or a woman boss.

There's been a revolution, all right. And it's been among women. Their lives have changed dramatically in the past three decades, and it is this that provides the context for the dramatic transformation of men's lives.

Let me point to four different areas in which I believe the changes in women's lives have already changed the topography of men's lives, and then suggest some of the issues that these changes augur for men.

First, the feminist revolution has made gender visible. Women have demonstrated the centrality of gender in social life; in the past two decades, gender has joined race and class as the three primordial axes around which social life is organized, one of the primary building-blocks of identity. The visibility of gender has transformed the university, where virtually every curriculum has a women's studies program and every university press boasts a women's studies book list.

Second, women have transformed the workplace. Almost half the labour force is female and women are in the workplace to stay. I often demonstrate this point to my university classes by asking the women who intend to have careers to raise their hands. All do. Then I ask them to keep their hands raised if their mothers have had a career outside the home for more than 10 years. Half put their hands down. Then I ask them to keep their hands raised if their grandmothers had a career for 10 years. Virtually no hands remain raised. In three generations, they can visibly see the difference in women's working lives.

This has led to the third area of change — women's efforts to balance work and family life. Currently, women face the difficult and painful choice of putting career or family first, but they are not willing to make such a choice: they want both career and family. "Having it all" — that strange phrase for women in the 1980's — has become a symbol of the modern woman; she can have a glamorous, rewarding career and a great loving family. But isn't it men who have, until now, "had it all" all along? We have had the rewarding careers outside the home and the rich and emotionally-satisfying family lives, and women have been unable to have it all precisely because of this! So, if women are going to have it all, they are going to need men to share housework and childcare. Women have consequently begun to question the 'second shift,' the household shift that has traditionally been their task after the workplace shift is over.[2]

Finally, women have changed the sexual landscape. As the dust is settling from the sexual revolution, what emerges in unmistakably finer detail is that it's been women, not men, who are our era's real sexual pioneers. We men like to think that the sexual revolution, with its promises of more access to more partners with less emotional commitment, was tailor-made for male sexuality's fullest flowering. But, in fact, it's been women's sexuality that's changed in the past two decades, not men's. Women now feel empowered to claim sexual desire. Women can like sex, can want sex, can seek sex, can even — gasp! — get horny. Women feel entitled to pleasure. They have learned to say yes to their own desires, claiming, in the process, sexual agency.[3]

And men? What's been happening with men? To put it bluntly, not very much. Sure, some men have changed in some ways, but most men have not undergone a comparable revolution. Our revolution has stalled, and in the growing gender gap men lag increasingly behind women in feeling empowered to implement change in their lives. This is, I think, the reason that so many men seem so confused about the meaning of masculinity these days.

Our lives have changed dramatically, but what has not changed are the ideas we have about what it means to be a man. The structure of our lives has changed, but not their culture, the ideologies that give that structure meaning. This is what social scientists used to call 'culture lag,' where the technology and institutional framework of a society changes more rapidly than the culture's stock of meanings and interpretations of social structure.

The 1990's have found men constantly bumping up against the limitations of the traditional definition of what it means to be a man, but without much of a sense of direction about where they might go to look for alternatives. Alan Alda never replaced Rambo; neither is today seen as an adequate role model for today's men (despite my admiration for Alda). We chafe against the edges of traditional masculinity, but seem unable, or unwilling, to break out of the constraints we feel. Thus the defensiveness, the anger, the confusion that is everywhere in evidence.

These limits will become most visible around the four areas in which women have changed most dramatically: making gender visible, the workplace, the balance between work and home, and sexuality. It is these changes which suggest the issues that must be placed on the agenda for men.

The first task is making gender visible to men, for, though we now know that gender is a central axis around which social life revolves, most men do not know they are gendered beings. Courses on gender are still populated mostly by women, and those gender studies books on every university press list are still read virtually entirely by women.

I often tell a story about a conversation I observed in a feminist theory seminar that I participated in about a decade ago. A white woman was explaining to a black woman how their common experience of oppression under patriarchy bound them together as sisters. All women, she explained, faced a common enemy, and therefore they were in the same position.

The black woman demurred from quick agreement. "When you wake up in the morning and look in the mirror," she asked the white woman, "what do you see?" "I see a woman," responded the white woman hopefully. "That's the problem," the black woman replied, "I see a black woman. To me, race is visible, because it is how I am not privileged in society. Because you are privileged by race, race is invisible to you. It is a luxury, a privilege not to have to think about race every second of your life."

I groaned, embarrassed. And, as the only man in the room, all eyes turned to me. "When I wake up and look in the mirror," I confessed, "I see a human being. The generic person. As a middle-class white man, I have no class, no race and no gender. I'm universally generalizable. I am Everyman."

Lately, I've come to think that it was on that day in 1980 that I became a middle-class white man, that these categories actually became operative to me. The privilege of privilege is that the terms of privilege are rendered invisible. It is a luxury not to have to think about race, or class, or gender. That is what privilege looks like — like the air, like the level playing field, like nothing at all. Only those marginalized by some category understand how powerful that category is when deployed against them.

Becoming aware of ourselves as gendered, recognizing the power of gender as a shaping influence in our lives, is made more difficult by the fact that there is no adequate mechanism for men to experience a secure gender identity. Specifically, the problem we will face in the 1990's is developing some mechanism of initiation to a secure sense of masculinity, a rite of passage through which young men can successfully demonstrate their manhood. Masculinity is a public enactment, demonstrated and proved in the public domain before the evaluative eyes of other men. Yet there is no recognizable way in which adolescent men can pass through some ceremony to achieve a secure manhood. As a result, masculinity becomes a relentless test, never completely proved, with always the nagging suspicion that one false move will destroy everything one's done to prove it.

Men are haunted by the specter of the sissy. I have a standing bet with a friend that I can walk onto any playground where several five- or six-year-old boys are happily playing, and, by asking one question, I can provoke a fight. That question is simple: "Who's a sissy around here?" Once posed, the challenge is made. One of two things is likely to happen. One boy will accuse another of being a sissy, to which that boy will respond that he is not a sissy, that the first boy is. They may have to fight it out to see who's lying. Or, a whole group of boys will surround one boy and all shout, "He is! He is!". That boy will either burst into tears and run home crying, disgraced, or he will have to take on several boys at once, to prove that he's not a sissy. (And what will his father or older brothers tell him if he chooses to run home crying?). It will be some time before he regains any sense of self-respect.

Or think about how this works itself out in college. I often ask my students to imagine the most confident guy in the school, the guy who has absolutely no questions or concerns about proving his manhood, who is completely and utterly secure in his masculinity. Now, imagine that this guy walks into the school snack bar past a table where four other guys are sitting. One of them says, "Will you look at that fairy!". Another says, "Yeah, what a faggot!". The third says, "Yeah, the pussy!". The fourth says, "Ugh, what a wimp!".

Now what's Mr. Cool and Confident doing? How does he react? Suddenly we might be in a scene from *Taxi Driver*: "You talkin' to me? You talkin' to me?" He's been called out, his masculinity has been publicly challenged. What will he do? And remember, this is the most confident guy you know! Imagine what life must be like for the rest of us poor slobs!

One of the more graphic illustrations of this lifelong quest to prove one's manhood — actually, one of the most revealing moments in the history of American manhood — occurred at the Academy Awards presentation in 1992. As aging, tough-guy actor Jack Palance accepted the award for Best Supporting Actor for his role in the cowboy comedy *City Slickers*, he commented that people, especially film producers, thought that, because he was 71 years old, he was all washed up, no longer competent. "Can we take a risk on this guy?" he quoted them as saying, before he dropped to the floor to do a set of one-armed push-ups. It was pathetic to see such an accomplished actor still having to prove that he is virile enough to work and, as he also commented at the podium, that he can still "get it up." When does it end?

Or, does it? To admit weakness, frailty or fragility is to be seen as a wimp, a sissy, not a real man. This fear of being seen as a sissy haunts men all their lives, but it is never more palpable than during adolescence, that fragile moment of transition between childhood and adulthood, a moment when sexual awakening is coupled with the craving for a secure gender identity. Thus sexuality and gender identity become intimately entwined with one another, and this is the moment when systematically avoiding the feminine becomes crucially important. One's manhood is at stake.

Without clear, definable mechanisms for boys to feel secure in their manhood, we will invent our own, dangerous and destructively-distorted ways to prove it to others, and thereby, hopefully, to ourselves. These efforts are shaped (distorted, really) by those two forces that shape and distort everything else in our culture: sexism and homophobia — the power that men have over women, and the power that some men have over other men. Sexism and homophobia become the organizing principles of these distorted initiation processes; is it any coincidence that it is almost always adolescent males who are attacking gays in our cities, dousing drunks ('failed' men) with lighter fluid and setting them on fire as sport, or gang-raping drunk, unconscious women at parties?

As a culture, we must confront adolescent males' need for developing a secure, confident, inner sense of themselves as men, which, I believe, can only be accomplished by changing what it means to be a real man. Otherwise, we shall continue to face the dangerous consequences that come from our twisted efforts to prove ourselves. Unless we as a society deal with these young men's needs for a secure identity in constructive ways, lawyers, police, courts, and prisons will continue to have to deal with the terrifying consequences of this emptiness.

The second area to focus on is the changing workplace. Most men derive their identity as breadwinners, but the economic landscape has changed dramatically; more and more men feel as though they haven't made the grade — they feel damaged, injured, powerless, and in need of demonstrating their masculinity all over again.

Just when men's economic breadwinner status is threatened, women have come into the workplace in unprecedented numbers as easy targets for men's anger. This is the context in which we must consider the question of sexual harassment. Sexual harassment at work is a distorted effort to put women back in their place, to remind women that they are not equal to men in the workplace, that they are, still, "just women". In the 1990's, sexual harassment will become an increasingly visible problem.

Every major corporation, law firm, and university is scrambling to implement sexual harassment policies, to make sure that sexual harassment will be recognized and punished. But our challenge is greater than admonition and post-hoc counselling. Our challenge will be to prevent sexual harassment before it happens. And that means working with men.

Politically, we need strong measures that clearly spell out our society's growing intolerance for sexual harassment, measures that clearly and unequivocally explain formal and informal mechanisms for adjudication of these events. More than that, we need to intervene directly into workplace dynamics, to work to prevent sexual harassment by working with men at their worksites, to enable men to accept and welcome women colleagues and co-workers. We will also need to explore the ways in which our personal relationships with women will actually improve if we support women's efforts to end sexual harassment.

Thirdly, men will need to sort out the balance between work and family life, to recover our capacities for manly nurture, if we are to experience the richness of interior life that we have come to believe is our right, but for which we are ill-equipped and unskilled. What has traditionally made men reliable in a crisis is also what makes us unavailable emotionally to others.

Fatherhood, friendship, partnership, all require emotional resources that have traditionally been in short supply among men — resources such as patience, compassion, tenderness, attention to process. As Alan Alda once wrote, in his brilliant dissection of excessive masculinity ('testosterone poisoning' he called it), a "man isn't someone you'd want around in a crisis — like raising children or growing old together."[4]

We are increasingly finding that our relationships with other men, and with our children, are impoverished by precisely the things that we thought would make us real men. Sexism and homophobia distort our experiences with other men and with our children, making us uneasy around other men and fearful of feminization around children. But the emotional impoverishment of our own lives, coupled with the demands of women that we participate in childcare — as well as our own desires to do so — will make it imperative that we raise these issues.

What steps are we taking to become better fathers? At best, men say they "help out" around the house, that they "pitch in" with the housework, and that they spend 'quality time' with their children. But it is not 'quality time' that will provide the deep intimate relationships that we say we want, either with our partners or with our children. It's 'quantity time' — putting in those long, hard hours of thankless, unnoticed drudge work. It's 'quantity time' that creates the foundation of intimacy. Nurture is doing the unheralded tasks, like holding someone when they are sick, doing the laundry, the ironing, washing the dishes. Nurturing is putting in those hours, unseen, uncelebrated.

The experience of intimacy, of nurturing relationships — with our partners, with our children, with our friends — requires that we do the routine work to experience those peak moments. We men are smart enough to learn how to do this. But, in this world, it is women — as mothers, as wives, as friends — who are the intimacy experts, the ones who do that work. So we have to learn from women how to be nurturing and caring, how to do the 'quantity time' work. Such a strategy makes more sense than fighting with our spouses about custody after we've separated, when we haven't made any attention to taking care of children before the separation. And it certainly makes a lot more sense than running off to the woods, to chant, drum and bond with other men in an effort to achieve, or retrieve, some manly sense of nurture. Frankly, I'd rather see a whole lot more "Ironing Johns" and a lot fewer "Iron Johns" in my neighbourhood.

Workplace and family life are also joined in the public sphere. Several different kinds of policy reforms have been proposed to make the workplace more 'family-friendly', more hospitable to our efforts to balance work and family. These reforms generally revolve around three issues: on-site childcare, flexible working hours, and parental leave. But how do we usually think of these family-friendly workplace reforms? As women's issues, as it is women who campaign for and want them. But on-site childcare, flexi-time and parental leave are not women's issues, they're parents' issues, and to the extent that we, men, identify ourselves as parents, they are reforms that we will want. Because they will enable us to live the lives we say we want to live.[5]

Finally, we come to the bedroom. This is where men confirm their masculinity — in a relentless effort to get sex. We're always supposed to be "ready for it", to want it, to go for it. But now many of us come to bed with far more trepidation than before. Although one might think that men would have welcomed women's new sexual assertiveness, the evidence is somewhat more mixed. For example, 20 years ago, the most common sexual problem for which men sought sex therapy was premature ejaculation, which, if nothing else, indicated that the man was a bit over-eager. Today, he is far more likely to present with 'inhibited sexual desire', which translates into a growing indifference to sex. He just doesn't want to anymore — men are literally wilting in the face of female sexual assertiveness. But, if we men say we want to have sex with partners who are as hot, horny and passionate as we are, then it would seem that we would be wiser to re-examine our definitions of sexuality, and meet these new women on an equal playing field.

Also, just at the moment in which women are saying "yes" to their own sexual desires, there's an epidemic of date and acquaintance rape on our nation's campuses. In one recent study, 45% of all college women said that they had had some form of sexual contact against their will, and a full 25% had been pressed or forced to have sexual intercourse against their will. When a UCLA psychologist asked freshmen men over the past 10 years if they would commit rape were they certain they could get away with it, almost one-half said they would.

It's as if men were afflicted with a strange hearing disorder, a socialized deafness, the inability to hear when women say "no". Surely, here is an arena where we need strong measures to make clear our intolerance for date and acquaintance rape, laws that protect women, social attitudes that believe women who do come forward. Here, again, men's support of feminism will enable us to live the lives we say we want to live. If we make it clear that we, as men, will not tolerate a world in which women do not feel safe, and if we make it clear to our individual partners that we understand that no means "No", then — and only then — can women begin to articulate the "yes" that is also their right.

Safety is a precondition for women's sexual agency; it is also a necessity in this age of AIDS. Surprisingly AIDS was omitted from the evidence given at the start of this book — yet, how is it possible to speak about what's next for men without discussing AIDS?

After all, AIDS is men's No 1 health problem in both Britain and the U.S. In the States, over 90% of all AIDS patients are men, and AIDS is now the leading cause of death for men aged 33-45. Except for those diseases like hemophilia or uterine or prostate cancer, in which only men or only women are susceptible, no other disease has ever attacked one gender so disproportionately. AIDS could affect both men and women equally (in Africa, it seems to come closer to gender parity), but, in the United States and Britain, AIDS patients are overwhelmingly men. (Of course, one must recognize that women are as likely to get AIDS from engaging in the same high risk behaviours as men. But that's precisely my point. Women don't engage in those behaviours at rates anything like men.)[6]

With AIDS, then, male behaviour — activities that ignore potential health risks for more immediate pleasures — puts both women and other men at risk. For example, sharing needles is both a defiant flaunting of health risks and an expression of community among male IV drug users, while the capacity for high-risk sexual behaviours, for instance, unprotected anal intercourse with a large number of partners — the ability to take it, despite any potential pain — is also a confirmation of masculinity.

The most effective way to prevent AIDS is to use sterile needles for intravenous drug injections and to practice 'safer sex.' Safer sex programs encourage men to have fewer partners, to avoid certain particularly dangerous practices, and to use condoms when having any sex that involves the exchange of bodily fluids. But, to men, 'safe sex' is an oxymoron, one of those juxtapositions of terms that produce a nonsensical outcome. Sex is about danger, risk, excitement; safety is about comfort, softness and security. Safer sex programs encourage men to stop having sex like men.

What heterosexual men could learn from the gay community's response to AIDS is how to eroticize the responsibility for safety — something that women have been trying to teach men for decades. And straight men could also learn a thing or two about caring for one another through illness, supporting one another in grief, and maintaining a resilience in the face of a devastating disease and the callous indifference of the larger society.

But, to do that, we will need to transform the definition of what it means to be a man. The victims of men's adherence to these crazy norms of masculinity — AIDS patients, rape victims, victims of sexual harassment — did not become victims intentionally; they did not "ask for it." They do not deserve blame. Until we change the meaning of manhood, sexual risk-taking and conquest will remain part of the rhetoric of masculinity. The male date rapists, sexual harassers and AIDS patients are not "perverts" or "deviants" who have strayed from the norms of masculinity. They are, if anything, over-conformists to destructive norms of male sexual behaviour.

So, what's next for men? Just now, we seem to be pursuing several avenues at once. Some proponents of 'men's rights' seek to reverse feminist gains of the past three decades, whining that today men are the new victims of sex discrimination. The growing racism, sexism and heterosexism of America's "angry white males" indicates a defensive circling of the wagons, a vain effort to preserve what's left of male privilege. Some men seek solace in the company of other men, retreating to the woods to heal their wounds, to experience manly nurture. These have always been American men's ways of proving masculinity in an uncertain world.[7]

I propose a different path, both politically and personally. Rather than resisting the transformation of our lives that has already begun, or escaping to the woods, we should embrace these changes, both because they offer us the possibilities of social and economic equality, and because they also offer us the possibilities of richer, fuller, and happier lives with our friends, lovers, partners, and children. As men, we should support feminism — both at work and at home. At work, it means working to end sexual harassment, supporting family-friendly workplace policies, becoming publicly compassionate about AIDS patients, and advocating draconian measures to end the scourge of date and acquaintance rape, violence and abuse that terrorize women in our societies. At home, it means sharing housework and childcare, as much because our partners demand it as because we want to spend that time with our children, and because housework is a conventional way of nurturing and loving. It means bringing the idea of safety to the centre of our sexual vocabulary, and treating our partners with integrity and respect.

The feminist transformation of society is a revolution-in-progress. For nearly two centuries, we men have met insecurity by frantically shoring up our privilege, or by running away. These strategies have never brought us the security and the peace we have sought. Perhaps now, as men, we can stand with women and embrace the rest of this revolution — embrace it because of our sense of justice and fairness, embrace it for our children, our wives, our partners, and ourselves.

ENDNOTES

1. In the U.S., Wabash and Hampden-Sydney remain as small private single-sex colleagues, while VMI and The Citadel are publicity supported all-male military schools whose admissions policies are currently under judicial review as examples of sex discrimination.

2. See, for example, Arlie Hochschild, The Second Shift (New York: Viking, 1989).

3. There is a mountain of sex research that might illustrate such a point. Let me suggest only two examples. Thirty years ago, only one-half of women under 25 had masturbated to orgasm; today, the figure is closer to 90%. About half of the women surveyed in 1994 had masturbated during the preceding year. Twenty-five years ago, sociologist Lillian Rubin found that three-quarters of the women she interviewed had faked orgasm; last year, she asked again and found that less than two in 10 had faked it. In the most recent sex survey, a maximum of 15% of women might have faked an orgasm during the previous year.

4. Alan Alda, "What Every Woman Should Know About Men" in 'Ms 4(4)', October, 1975.

5. For more about men's efforts to balance work and family see my "What Do Men Want?" in 'The Harvard Business Review', November-December 1993.

6. In Britain, women are now contracting AIDS at a faster rate than men. Cases of AIDS in females rose by 10% between 1990 and 1995, while cases in males fell by 14% during the same period. Nevertheless, the vast majority of HIV-positive women have acquired the infection through unprotected sex with a man (Eds.).

7. I tell this story in great detail in 'Manhood in America: A Cultural History' (New York: The Free Press, 1995).

Just Around the River Bend?[1]

George Mair

George Mair has worked for a number of years in the Home Office Research and Planning Unit, latterly as Principal Research Officer in charge of work on community penalties. Since September 1995, he has been Professor of Criminal Justice at Liverpool John Moores University. He is the author of many Home Office research studies, 'Part Time Punishment' (1991) and joint editor (with Tim Newburn) of 'Working With Men' (1996).

In Disney's latest commercial success, we see the heroine, Pocahontas, paddling down a river in her canoe wondering what the future holds for her — will it be smooth water and a quiet and dull life, or will it be rapids and an exciting whitewater ride? She makes it quite clear that she would opt for the latter (mainly because she associates the former with marriage to a worthy but dull and serious warrior). But what lies just around the river bend for men? Is it more of the same; some slight changes, but nothing dramatic; or profound, radical change? The starting point of this book is that men are in a mess and something needs to be done — the question, of course, is what?

Men have become used to being top dogs; they take for granted their superiority in all walks of life (except, of course, where this is biologically impossible, and any achievements here tend to be dismissed or treated condescendingly), but — as the evidence which is collected at the beginning of this book shows — such superiority has not been achieved without some cost, and there are some disturbing suggestions about changes. Men do not live as long as women; they are much more likely to ignore symptoms of ill-health than are women; they take more risks of all kinds than women; and they internalise such matters, rather than talking about them to others. Men work longer hours than women — and there is increasing evidence that, as a result of recession, and fearful of losing their jobs, men are working even harder, doubtless with detrimental effects on their health, relationships and social lives. Because of their hitherto unchallenged place in the job market and the way men have defined themselves primarily in terms of their work, the effects of unemployment on men can be catastrophic. Increasingly, unemployment and the growth of fixed-term contracts and unstable employment patterns have begun to hit middle-class men (while, if you are young, male, black and without qualifications, then you might as well resign yourself to life on the dole).

Everyone knows that men are overwhelmingly over-represented in crime: in 1994, 275,000 men were found guilty of indictable offences in England and Wales, whereas the comparable figure for women was 40,000. Of these, 50,200 men were sentenced to immediate custodial sentences, compared to 2,700 women; 30,400 men received community service orders, compared to 2,500 women; and 27,900 men received probation orders, compared to 6,900 women. So the criminal justice system is dealing for the most part with men — a fact which is only beginning to be recognised as an issue in itself[2].

Education does not seem to offer a way out. Girls are more likely to do better at school than boys and thus are more likely to go on to university. Boys seem to be more disenchanted with the educational process and this can have obvious repercussions for employment.

All of this paints a rather unhealthy and fairly disturbing picture of men. So, what is to be done?

Lenin famously asked this same question more than 90 years ago — at least he had an answer to it. With regard to men, as we move towards the 21st century, there are no easy answers. Indeed, it might be simplest to treat the question as a rhetorical one and move on to something else — a cop-out, which, in this case, must be resisted.

The evidence mentioned earlier offers only the symptoms of a problem. The real issue lies in the disjunction, which is becoming more and more obvious, between the myth of being a man and the reality. The myth is founded upon man's traditional omnipotence which became entrenched with the Industrial Revolution in the middle of the last century. Like so much of Britain's casual assumption of superiority over the rest of the world, men became bogged down in this belief and trusted that it would last forever. Britain is still coming to terms with the loss of Empire and its increasingly marginal role in world affairs; and men are only beginning to suspect that something may have gone wrong in terms of their position with respect to women. If nothing else, the rapidly-growing literature on the subject of men and masculinities is a clear sign of unease (although it may also be seen as an effort by men to colonise the growing field of gender studies).

Ironically, all of this interest in men has — of course — been sparked by feminism. It is in many ways a sign of the success of the feminist agenda that more and more men are discussing what it means to be a man and the difficulties associated with this. But, despite this interest, the number of such men remains small relative to the general male population; it is very much a middle-class phenomenon; and discussions remain essentially at the theoretical level. As one example, take Joseph Boone's essay 'Of me(n) and feminism'[3]. Despite the post-modern use of parenthesis in the title, this is an interesting paper discussing the relationships between men and feminism in academic literary criticism, but when the author moves on to offer some suggestions about how male academics might respond to feminist criticism, the words 'irrelevant' and 'impractical' spring to mind. Boone suggests that men should be encouraged to identify with feminism; they should "make their own oppressive structures (ideological, social, psychological) present for critique, rather than hiding them under a veil of abstract musing"; they should be willing to acknowledge differences in male sexuality; and they should form 'communal networks of relationships' in order to share their ideas as feminists have done. All well and good, but how many men do such prescriptions affect, and how should such suggestions be acted upon in practice: it is rather too easily assumed that such men are already predisposed to feminism — at least as a form of literary criticism.

The impact of such well-meaning suggestions as those posited by Boone are likely to be marginal at best. The vast majority of men will be untouched by them and remain trapped in the disjunction between the myth and the reality of being a man. Being so trapped is bad enough, but, if things carry on as usual, men will naturally try to live up to the myth as they always have done; they will be socialised — for the most part — into becoming traditional, heterosexual males with all of the attendant problems noted at the beginning of this book. This 'more-of-the-same' scenario is depressing enough, but all of the signs are that men may be fighting back (the 'New Laddism' and *Loaded* magazine being just two examples) and this could constitute a serious backlash against feminism in particular, and against women in general. Indeed, even the interest in masculinity, which in many ways uses feminism as a model, could lead to any gains women have made being threatened. As Bob Connell has recently written[4]: "The political risk run by an individualized project of reforming masculinity is that it will ultimately help modernize patriarchy rather than abolish it" — not an outcome to be looked forward to with relish. So, breaking out of the cage will be no easy task for men, especially if it is not to be achieved at the expense of women.

Whatever might be done will not be done quickly. It is difficult to change attitudes and practices, as years of equal opportunities training have demonstrated. It may well be that men are in no mood to change their way of life, or their attitudes towards women. Any perceived threat to male dominance is (not surprisingly) likely to be greeted with unease and provoke defensiveness, rather than a willingness to accept change. Even more of a problem is the fact that power structures are still dominated by men; why should they collude in giving up their much-cherished power bases? Where would this leave them? Power and authority are seen as crucial components of being a man, so lacking these would raise all sorts of questions about manhood in the short term. What's next for men will not, therefore, involve any sudden, radical changes; slow, incremental steps are far more likely — they are more feasible in every sense, although they may not please feminists who desire faster and more profound changes.

Whatever may be next for men will certainly involve women. It would simplify matters immensely if I could suggest enlisting the help of women as a means of moving things forward for men, but it is not as easy as that. In the first place, women are seen by many men as a threat; or they are dismissed as raving feminists who want all men to be castrated; or, third, they are assumed to be meek, subordinate creatures who know their place and are comfortable with it. How could help be accepted from any of these groups — what could they possibly offer to men? And how many women would want to join with men in helping to refashion them? They would certainly be suspicious, and rightly so. Such a project could lead to a weakening of their position, and a further strengthening of men. But, overall, it must be to the advantage of both men and women to have more 'healthy' men, just as, overall, the rise of feminism has been of benefit to both sexes. It will be hard work and will require considerable amounts of goodwill and trust, but alliances must be forged between men and women as much as possible.

As an academic, I would be failing in my duty if I were not to make the ritual claim for further research. As I have noted, the literature on masculinity is increasing rapidly, but much of this is theoretical and/or based on very small samples of specific groups of men. What is needed is more field research into men; much greater numbers of men need to be involved, comparisons between different types of men are required, longitudinal studies of boys growing up to become men are lacking. Why do men act as they do? How important are the various institutions or groups which socialise them into becoming men (family, friends, school, etc.)? Where do young men take their role models from, and how do they grow out of them (if they do)? Are there various options available to men in practice — how are these chosen, and how far adhered to? Far more work is required to examine the masculine power-base in industry and organisations: how deeply is this founded, and what mechanisms uphold it? Are there successful contra-examples, and how do they work? Studies of the numbers and distribution of men and women in jobs might help to explain gender imbalances, which, in turn, might lead to suggestions about how to rectify these. Providing answers to such questions would help matters immensely. The statistical evidence set out at the start of this book supplies only the bare bones of what being a man entails: if individual men are unaware of, or ignore, such evidence, then it might as well not exist; if they interpret it in such a way as to provide further support for a macho way of life, then it will not have served its purpose. More knowledge is needed and only research can supply it, but that research needs to be much better focused than it is at present and tied in closely with potential policy prescriptions.

Without being fully aware of the facts, there will be little incentive for men to desire and work for change, so effort must be put into getting research findings across to men. Although it might be advisable to target the younger age-groups (15-25), the reality of being a man should also be brought home to older men. Health and education agencies could play a major role in disseminating such knowledge and helping men to begin to change their life-styles. Annual compulsory health checks could be instituted for all; indeed, these could be carried out with one's partner or even be family checks. Obviously, such a campaign would require money and political will, neither of which is probable with our present political masters, but even they might be persuaded of possible benefits. Certainly, the financing of such initiatives should not be at the expense of taking money away from resourcing policies for women.

On the education front, one possible initiative which might have long-term pay-offs would be actively to encourage young boys and girls to play together. Pre-school children tend not to mind too much whether they play with children of their own sex or not (at least as far as observing my own four-year-old daughter goes). They tend to play the same kind of games and do the same kind of things whether they are with boys or girls (though I still occasionally hear complaints such as that the boys will not let the girls play in the castle at nursery). At primary school, however, same-sex groups begin to predominate at play; boys increasingly move towards the more physical games, while girls shift towards the less physical. I would not wish to suggest that such behaviour is encouraged by teachers, but it is unlikely to be discouraged. The longer boys and girls could be encouraged to play together, the better it might be for both groups, and it is surely not beyond the wit of teachers to be more proactive in this direction; joint games, indeed joint activities of all kinds, should be developed.

Education has a more general role to play. It is imperative that strategies are worked out to make schooling more relevant to boys so that they will stay on and achieve more in academic terms. The present situation, where girls are doing better than boys, can only lead to further deterioration in the position of men, with the consequent possibility of a male backlash against women. The needs of Afro-Caribbean children are even more pressing in this respect. The content of what is taught may also need to be re-evaluated. Stereotypes of men and women could be questioned in lessons on almost every subject; gender issues could be brought into play more often. Teachers may complain that this would involve them in a great deal of extra work, which might open them to ridicule and attack and which should be left to families. But families cannot do this on their own; it is precisely the job of educators to help to open minds to new ideas and to begin and encourage the questioning of dubious stereotypes.

In the field of crime, we have known for many years that men are far more likely than women to commit offences, but, in dealing with such men, the role of masculinity has, until quite recently, largely been ignored. Slowly, more and more probation officers and prison workers are recognising that they should try to take account of masculinity in their dealing with male offenders. Various educational programmes have been developed to try to do this[5], and such initiatives are very much a growth area in probation work. While these programmes should be encouraged, criminal justice workers should be warned that they are unlikely to provide the definitive answer which they often seem to expect from the latest flavour-of-the-month idea. Assessing the impact of probation programmes is difficult enough without having to take account of the effects of a masculinity module as well. A good deal of research will be necessary before the effectiveness of programmes which focus on masculinity and crime can be assessed.

There is also the question of gender imbalance in the criminal justice agencies. Both the police and prison services have far more male staff than women, and both can be accused of relying heavily upon macho notions of dealing with offenders. The attitudes of police and prison officers towards women are notoriously condescending. Initiatives to increase the number of women in both groups should be undertaken immediately — and not just at the lower levels. This would almost certainly contribute to a more humane atmosphere towards prisoners and suspects, which can only be a good thing. Interestingly, the Home Secretary's new proposals for probation training (essentially, no training at all) seem to be posited upon the desire to increase the number of men in the probation service, thereby toughening up probation supervision. This would be a retrograde step, which should be resisted at all costs.

Next, in terms of what might be done for men, are three points which could be instituted by employers who, we might assume, want to get the best out of their workers. First, a statutory limit on working hours should be instituted. This might have to be on the high side, but would serve at least a symbolic purpose. It is clear that too many men work longer hours than is good for them (in a variety of senses), and a statutory maximum might help to signal that this is not desirable. Second, the statutory annual health checks for all, that I have already mentioned, could also be a condition of employment; this might help to encourage men to see their own GP's more often, and would help pick up early signs of illness. And third, given the significance of childcare in the life of many women, increased paternity leave over the pre-school years at least should help men to get much more involved in what Connell[6] refers to as 'the sensual pleasure' involved in childcare. Each of these three steps would, of course, have financial costs in the short term, but would lead to a healthier, more satisfied (and perhaps more productive) workforce.

Education and employment are two very obvious areas where substantial changes could be made. A third area would be the rather more nebulous, but no less important, matter of culture — and particularly the images of men and women in advertising and the media. Without getting into the swamp of political correctness, it is all too plain that such images are, for the most part, crude stereotypes. They — like all stereotypes — are based on culturally grounded images, but go on to reflect, disseminate and affirm these images more widely. Some clear guidelines on how men and women might be portrayed in advertising and the media are needed. No doubt, any such initiative would be greeted with outrage by some sections of the media (remember the furore when Clare Short tried to have Page Three girls banned), but that would only go to show how important such a step would be.

In concluding this essay, I should draw attention to some of its shortcomings.

In the first place, I have treated men as an undifferentiated mass. I am only too aware that this is a dubious assumption, but, in the space available, it would be impossible to try to take account of the various kinds of men and masculinities which might be covered. In particular, I would especially note my failure to address the issue of young black males, a group which is seen by all too many as posing a serious (though undefined) threat.

Secondly, I have not addressed the issue of responding to unemployment, where it should go without saying that more jobs should be created, especially for young men — and women (although the preponderance of jobs offering low wages in the service industries raises interesting questions for young men, who may be more interested in more typical male jobs).

Lastly, although I have tried to keep my prescriptions in touch with reality, they may well seem naive and idealistic. I have, for example, scarcely touched upon the issue of power.

One might well inquire where are the mechanisms for change, where is the money to come from, where is the interest in change, and where is the political will? Such questions certainly need answers, but the first step is surely to decide on what might be done and then focus on how to do it.

ENDNOTES

1. I would like to thank Tim Newburn and Shirley Rawstorne for their support while I was working on this essay. They and Trefor Lloyd offered helpful comments on the first draft.
2. Newburn, T. and Stanko, E.A. (eds.) 'Just Boys Doing Business: Men, Masculinities and Crime', London: Routledge (1994).
3. Boone, J. "Of me(n) and feminism: who(se) is the sex that writes?" in Porter, D. (ed.) 'Between Men and Feminism', London: Routledge (1992).
4. Connell, R.W. 'Masculinities', Cambridge: Polity Press (1995).
5. Newburn, T. and Mair, G. (eds.) 'Working With Men', Lyme Regis: Russell House (1996).
6. Connell, R.W. ibid. (1995).

Keeping Men Mainstream
(An interview with Herman Ouseley)

Herman Ouseley is Chairman of the Commission for Racial Equality (CRE), having previously worked continuously in various areas of the public services since 1963. In recent years, he has been Chief Executive of the London Borough of Lambeth, Chief Executive of the Inner London Education Authority and Head of the Ethnic Minorities Unit at the GLC. He has written extensively on local government and race equality issues, as well as on managing institutional change in public and voluntary organisations.

What concerns me about the situation men find themselves in are the global trends and the structural changes in the economy which suggest that more women than men are going back into work; the world of work is changing to low-paid part-time work and the growth in the economy relies on low pay. As we speak, there is the global conference taking place in Asia, looking at the Asian economy and how that effects the world markets. The big issue there is the way that international companies are under-cutting each other on pay for production, and here more women are taking up the slack in the economy. The new jobs tend to be part-time jobs, and men haven't altered their outlook sufficiently to take up those part-time opportunities, which has led to a real problem of culture and perception about what jobs are for whom. This means that, in the medium to longer term (if structural changes are going to mean that women are often going to be the breadwinner in many households, particularly relatively poorer households), men's role in families, where they are looking after the children, doing the shopping, doing domestic tasks, is a fundamental issue.

The specific area that concerns me is education and boys, and men's academic achievement. Girls and young women are achieving better qualifications than boys and men, and, whilst there are more men going back into further education, they are having to catch up, in terms of basic achievement. When we look at black male under-achievement in education, it's certainly to do with exclusions, lack of enough successful male role models, the way the 'macho' culture impacts on how they see themselves and what leads to the problems they experience at school. That also links into crime, because, if you're out of school, you're much more vulnerable, much more likely to be led into situations that bring you into contact with the police, and evidence suggests that younger children are now being lured into the criminal situation much more easily.

The prevalence of domestic, racial and sexual violence, abuse, suicide, all impact on young people's lives at a stage when their behaviour is affected. They go to school, and, if they are withdrawn, are seen as slow learners and lagging behind, or, if they express themselves in boisterous ways, the school sees them as aggressive; they are quickly labelled as disrupters, and eventually disrupters get thrown out of school.

The last issue is fatherhood — not so much the drop in the sperm count, but really fatherhood in the sense of what has been described as 'absent fathers' as a phenomenon in the black community. I don't believe men are necessarily absent. Because of the way in which single parent statistics are interpreted, it doesn't mean that the father isn't making a contribution to the children's development, but I think, as an issue, it is one in which we're looking to see greater responsibility being exercised by fathers for the development of their children in terms of leadership, guidance, education, training and going into work.

You've described external factors that impact on people, such as employment, and the changes necessary in men's minds.

I think there's one other factor which is important in my perspective, and that's discrimination.

Interestingly, talking to a number of large employers recently, one of them very casually made the remark that there is a big problem with the black male and how the black male is perceived in the workforce. What he was saying was that black men are seen problematically, and, in certain situations, it's hard to employ them because they are perceived as representing a threat because of their physical presence, their appearance or just because of the psyche of race. Very often we've heard women teachers say they feel intimidated by the presence of black boys, and so there's a real issue there about perceptions and appearance and presentation that locks into racism and has a negative impact, particularly on black males. That has an impact on race relations, because how black males see themselves being treated and how they interface with the rest of the community — with their own adults in their communities, with younger children, with white people and white males — are all part of that psychological interaction that determines how people see and treat each other; it's a very important factor.

Would you see that as a factor in the difference between the educational achievement of young African-Caribbean women and men?

Yes, particularly in terms of the young women having better employment prospects. There's quite a difference, in fact — some of the statistics suggest that young black women are doing better than quite a lot of young white men, so the gap is quite considerable and growing between young black women and young black men. Part of the problem is that employers can see the black woman as a more acceptable person who can blend in: it enables some employers to attract diversity, and gives them the opportunity to say, "Hey, we're not a bad employer — look at all these ethnic minorities we're giving jobs to". At the same time, it gives black women the opportunity to see that there is the scope for advancement. That brings us back to the shifts taking place in the economy and how black women may see their role changing in terms of being much more dominant in family and economical relationships. This is an important shift that people don't necessarily understand or come to terms with, and I think, unless it's worked through, the danger is of black men falling even further behind in the way they perceive themselves (as a persecuted species) and reacting in a way that isn't the best way of reacting, aggressively perhaps.

I think black men have become resentful over a long period of time. As second and third generations, they have tended to reject the sort of jobs that black males took in the economy during boom times, which were the low-paid, long-hour jobs, 'the shit jobs'. Even though many have drifted into not achieving their full educational potential and therefore have not been able to compete for better-quality jobs with career prospects and better pay, nevertheless the rejectionists have said, "We're not going to take a part-time job paying us a pittance — we're not gonna be slave labour". This links back to racism within the workforce and job allocation. Often these jobs are the only ones available, and women have been more inclined to take them, whereas men, to some extent, are still rejecting them.

Then there's the 'employment assistance' that's available to some employers who take on trainees (on a short-term basis), where the tendency is to casualise the labour force. They take on men and offer them an attractive sum for fairly hard work, but in short bursts (3-4 weeks), grinding them out and pushing them out, getting a subsidy from the state for taking them off the employment register. It's a very exploitative process and they come off the dole and then go back onto it and I think in the end that has a very debilitating effect on people.

Entering into work relates very much to the education output and also to the training opportunity. That's a very big area of discrimination. If you look at the statistics in regard to training outputs, black people go to training schemes in proportion to their needs, but disproportionately come out and continue to be unemployed, perhaps going on to another training scheme because they can't get a job to go with the first one. Much higher percentage of whites coming from training schemes get into jobs: irrespective of how long they stay there, they get into them.

If you look at the modern apprenticeships which came out a year ago to make sure that training led to jobs, only 2% went to ethnic minorities within that year. It's a real problem, the problem of getting adequate training that leads to jobs.

And that is a passport if you failed in formal education. It is a stepping-stone into the world of work of getting some experience of getting some education of getting some job related training that enables you to be competitive in a highly competitive situation. And that is a big area for us right now.

The employers' attitude towards black men and black men's responses to that attitude — is it similar in school? If so, when does that start?

The empirical evidence suggests that black kids are not disadvantaged educationally until about seven, then there starts to be a shift. I don't think there is a difference between black boys and black girls at that age.

At seven, you can start to see shifts, both in terms of race and sex, but, at five, all the evidence suggests that black kids don't start at a disadvantage: in other words, they don't come into the school and are behind already. It's quite clear that black boys are way behind by the time they get to the transfer from junior to secondary school. Even at primary school level, teachers are sorting out the good from the bad almost at entry. Teachers will distinguish between maybe 20 of an intake of 30 who are really into it: they're creative, they join in, they do the work. Another group of children may be more withdrawn, and are left alone and considered uninterested because they don't participate. Then there are those who just want to play and mess around, and who are very quickly identified as disrupters, the 'trouble' ones. Unless someone's been able to work with some of the more withdrawn, or those who've been boisterous and loud, and pull them back in, by the age of seven they are already being labelled as difficult and aggressive. It's partly because they have not been supported to cope with the problems that they are bringing from home. These problems may be a broken family, domestic violence, abuse, suicide, poverty, low income, overcrowding, all sorts of things. Some get help, but most don't because of the pressure on schools. Some of the ones that are in that difficult group will be black boys: a few in the withdrawn group might be seen as educationally sub-normal. By secondary school, the problems become much more pronounced.

The real problem I see is that there are not enough support structures that enable the school to be able to give sufficient attention to guide those young men who are drifting and being labelled. The home/school partnership is the problem, although in a good school you would find that the relationships are fairly good. That's where I see a missing link — where the school can't act as a bridge, or provide additional help. At this point, young men may start to drift in a direction of rejecting school: peer group pressures are also important. By about 18 or 19, most of those who have drifted into that direction will have come into contact with the criminal justice system, and some will already have been incarcerated.

So, as Minister for Men, what would you do?

I think we need to develop social support systems within those schools which are under pressure, have counsellors and therapists working with those who are either withdrawn and not participating, or are boisterous and deemed aggressive, and reintegrating them back into the mainstream. They would provide that link between school and home. They should also have an understanding of boys and the pressures that they're facing, particular from peers and macho culture. Where there are schemes such as this, the schools tend not to exclude, but manage to get most of those kids back into the mainstream. That investment enables you not to have to spend the level of resources required later on in dealing with delinquency, other adolescent problems and the drifting into criminality. That's a very fundamental part of what I would want to see. I'm not saying that will solve all the problems of boys as they go through the stages of adolescence and become young men, but I think it has the capacity to help us to hold onto more of them and keep them within the mainstream of education.

So does that mean, the earlier you get there, the quicker the fix might be?

I think so. I think you've got to get there by five, when they are starting to peel off into groups, the pressure on the classroom teacher is to identify those who are going to get you the exam results and keep your school at the level where it is not going to be at the bottom of the league table.

What about mentors?

Well, I think mentors are important, but coming a bit later on, where it becomes much more meaningful, when they're looking to someone that they can relate to. We should be putting a lot more time into developing mentoring schemes. People often ask me, "Who was your mentor when you were growing up?". And, realistically, there wasn't anyone: there was a situation in which you were looking at people and trying to learn from them, but you didn't realise there was no structured situation where people were trying to understand what was going on in your head, what was affecting you or giving you bad days or bad vibes.

In the States, there is a view that young black boys do not have role models, and some suggest we need more black men in schools. How would you respond to that?

My view is that I don't want to see artificial situations created just to say, "Hey, this is what's gonna make you tick", because we're going to put a successful black male in the classroom. I think that would be helpful in some situations. I think what is more important is recognising that successful black men have something to contribute back into the community, recognising the usefulness of that and the long-term benefits for society.

There will be successful black men who can get into schools and other places where they are seen as influential, but I think that influence must affect all other men, as well as all children, of all colours because the importance is seeing successful role models. It's like saying that we do need to have more black head teachers in our schools where there are concentrations of black kids, and more black males where black boys are failing. There aren't enough, because what we also need is successful black role models in white schools throughout the country where very often they'll say, "Well, we've got good equal opportunity programmes, we've got good multi-cultural education in the curriculum, but we never see black people": people will come through their school life and think they're well-rounded, and then someone will throw them in the middle of Brixton or Tottenham, or maybe black people become police officers or bankers in the City, and their perceptions are reinforced very quickly by the way in which society has, in a sense, created perceptions of what black people are, what they're capable of, what they're up to and what they're not up to.

Because boys tend to mature much later, I think, as we see this changing culture of women's dominance become much more known, understood and accepted, that women could also become role models for boys. The dilemma is not seeing that you've got to get the school environment right in which black boys can feel more comfortable and experience it as congenial and see themselves as equals, whilst also recognising that there are white people who can be successful in understanding and inter-relating with a culture that helps them to achieve. I'm looking more to those kids who are seen as drifting outside the mainstream of school being reintegrated because I think, as a society, we've got to try and hold together and combine in a cohesive way, and the more you separate out either on sex or race lines, the more I think it's difficult to achieve social cohesion. This isn't in any way suggesting I don't think that there is a role for black role models, black male role models, either in the classroom or outside, but I don't want to create artificial situations.

So you would envisage a series of safety nets?

It's having support systems that recognise that families in 1996 are in crisis and that we need to educate boys for the responsibilities that become theirs in a few years' time, because it is they who become the absent fathers, the people who are not able to sustain support for their sons. It's a vicious circle. You've somehow got to break that because those who are growing up now, coming through the school system (both boys and girls), need to understand the responsibilities that go with parenting, otherwise they're the ones who are going to produce the next failure of boys. They need to know what it is they are taking on, what it is they can do that helps, through their own experience, not repeating situations. You do need to have those support mechanisms that help them to understand what they're letting themselves in for.

Are there strategies you would add as Minister for Men to deal with the more structural problems?

I think there is enough policy and practice guidance around that seeks to deal with institutional discrimination, whether it's against men or women or black people or other ethnic groups, and that would have to be reinforced. The legislation itself is still weak in the way in which it enables people to be discretionary and to be cosmetic about how they institutionally apply their programmes, their resources and their responses to group needs. Undoubtedly, that has to be addressed if discrimination is going to be eliminated. Anti-discrimination has to be much more driven by those who have power; if there were such people with the determination to make things happen, then it would change. It really requires a major shift, in the same way that we were talking about a cultural shift in people's minds and attitudes about what the changes in the structure of the economy means in the labour market. Someone's got to help to make that transformation happen, and it's got to be government, it's got to be educators, it's got to be the media.

But does that mean laws?

Well, laws are already there; what it means is that people need to take greater responsibility at a political level. Laws need to be strengthened and be much more explicit, accompanied by the drive to change the attitudes that underpin behaviour, and this can only be done by leading public opinion. Public opinion on racial attitudes is not currently being led by anyone in this country. You are not hearing it coming from the Government, you are not hearing it coming from the Opposition. There is no-one saying we've got black achievers, we've got ethnic minorities contributors, we've got a lot of positive things happening, we're doing this for young men who are in difficulties. Instead we hear they are a bunch of criminals, they're thugs, they go around beating people up, wrecking the joint. You've got to build a positive profile, and you've got to be influencing public opinion as well as doing things. I think the way in which shifts have taken place in people's perception about the world of work and competition and individualism over the last 15 years has been driven by government, it's been driven by an ideology. You can only transform thinking, by driving that through government policies, the corporate sector, local authority leadership, influencing people's thinking through the media. So that's what you would have to do.

How, as Minister for Men, would you deal with major employers' perceptions of black men?

You would use legislation to ensure that greater pressure is being put on those discriminating employers. Look at the patterns where they are saying they are doing well in terms of ethnic appointments: why is it that only black women are getting jobs, and not young black men? But also, if you're seeking to change the culture, then part of what you're doing is looking at the examples where black men do not represent a threat and are succeeding. Where are those successful role models that you hold up to other companies? British companies are highly competitive. If a big company is doing something and it involves ethnic minorities, and it's looking as though it's being successful, it's increasing its market share, it has added profitability, the other one wants to know about it and do it too. It's about how you build on success, however limited it is. People often say, you know, "The guy who reads the news now — he's just a token, they don't have anyone else to put on the TV screen". But, that one token has led to a lot of other black people coming through in terms of features, newscasting documentaries and serious issues. That now needs to multiply in similar ways in other professions and opportunities.

So it's about the strength of the black pound?

No, I think that's only from the aspect of the corporate sector. They recognise, where there is a market, they've got to get to that market, and, clearly, if there is spending power in the black community that's been tapped by one producer or manufacturer or retailer and you're in competition with them, you want to get in there and get a piece of that action. In America, marketing is very targeted and you've got to target your product. Increasingly, you will find that some of the big players recognise this and you'll start to see more black faces featured in advertisements, although it hasn't happened significantly as yet.

What about fatherhood?

Parenting in the curriculum is very important, as are support programmes for those parents who are experiencing difficulties.
Fatherhood is all about the responsibility of being a parent. It's not necessarily being in the home, but recognising responsibility entails supporting young people (particularly as a role model for young boys) and being part of the partnership — helping with their development, understanding their problems, sharing and seeking to help to find solutions both within the home and school. The notion of sending the kid to school to get educated is so outdated. School can do so much, but learning is from the moment you wake up to the moment you go to sleep, from the moment you are born to the moment you die. I want to see young black males (particularly through adolescence) learn about relationships through education, through information, through knowledge of what responsibilities go with being a father

and how you translate those into practice. Nothing is going to change in the longer term unless everybody plays their full part. If people say that the system has screwed them, the police are chasing them, if they are unemployed, under-educated, a failure, there is still no reason why, as a father, you couldn't be a success. Because it is within you to become a success and we can encourage this as part of the whole process of change within the context of the changing structure of the world at work. The most important role young men can have is being good, responsible parents, producing the next generation of responsible and contributing adults.

Boys Won't Be Boys:
Tackling the Roots of Male Delinquency

Sandy Ruxton

Sandy Ruxton is a freelance researcher and policy analyst. He worked for 10 years with young men in education, community work and the penal system. He has written extensively on children and young people, especially in the field of youth justice, and is a regular contributor to 'Working with Men' magazine. The author of an innovative research study of men working in childcare settings, 'What's He Doing at the Family Centre?', Sandy has two publications due in 1996 — 'Men and their Children: Proposals for Public Policy' (co-authored for the Institute for Public Policy Research) and a book on children's issues in the European Union.

Robbery, mugging, battering, burglary, joy-riding and rioting are almost always male activities. Undoubtedly, men commit more crimes of all types (and proportionately more serious and violent crimes) than women. In 1994, of the 524,000 known offenders found guilty or cautioned for indictable offences in England and Wales, 81 were men. Furthermore, most crimes are committed by young men; the male peak age of offending is 18. And, of those born in 1973, one in 10 young men will have had a conviction for a serious (non-motoring) offence by age 17, compared with one in 100 young women[1].

Of course, care must be exercised when studying figures such as these. According to the Home Office, they reflect the fact that more men than women are detected by the police and prosecuted, and not the precise extent to which involvement in crime differs[2]. There is evidence from self-report studies which indicates a much higher involvement of young women in offending than officially-recorded data, especially for property offences[3]. Nevertheless, the figures do reflect a real divergence between the sexes, not least because the gulf has been consistent over time and because other countries' statistics all show similar patterns[4].

Juvenile crime is also overwhelmingly non-violent. For all age groups, theft and handling stolen goods is by far the most prevalent offence, reaching 47% of offences for 14-18-year-old boys. The highest figures for offences of violence against the person are found in the same age group, but still only make up 13% of all offences. Sexual offences represent only an additional 1% of the total.

Conversely, young men are most frequently the victims of the most serious forms of crime. The recorded rate for violence against the person from 1990-92 shows that those in the 16-24 age group were at by far the greatest risk, with 1,180 offences per 100,000 population. These figures are twice as high as for young women in the same age group, and far higher than for the elderly, who are, in contrast, very rarely victims[5].

It is important to keep statistics about levels of crime in context. Not all young men are criminals, far from it. In fact, official rates of known offending show a substantial fall over the last decade. The number of male juveniles found guilty or cautioned per 100,000 population fell by 47% and 38% respectively for the 10-13 and 14-17 age groups between 1985 and 1994. Meanwhile, there was an increase of 10% for adult males. No doubt the fall for male juveniles is partly explained by the increased use of informal action, as a result of which the vast majority do not come to the notice of the police again. Nevertheless, the discrepancy between the directions taken by the figures for juveniles and adult males is striking.

So, contrary to the opinions of politicians and pundits, official crime rates — the most accurate statistics available — show little evidence that crime rates have suddenly taken off among young men. Such perceptions must be located within a very long-standing tradition of 'respectable fears' of lawless, violent young men whose behaviour threatens social order.

In the 1950's, for example, whilst Britain sought to come to terms with Teddy Boys, France faced the 'blousons noirs', and even countries such as Russia and Japan experienced disturbing youth revolts[6]. Looking further back, Graham Greene in 'Brighton Rock' described the activities of 1930's razor gangs; 'Hooligan' street gangs were a common feature of turn-of-the-century England; and 'garotting' — a form of violent robbery involving choking the victim — frequently took place in the 1860's.

One well-established research tradition suggests that apparent upsurges of law-breaking are essentially 'moral panics', recreated for each generation largely by the media, and echoed by the establishment. Such panics, accompanied by a nostalgia for a return to the stable values of a previous 'Golden Age', are then translated into controlling strategies for curbing the excesses of youth. These, in turn, can lead to more crime being committed as a response to the intensity of the new measures[7].

This analysis clearly has relevance to the contemporary identification of young men as the main deviant group within society. In the wake of the horrific Bulger case, the media have stepped up their sensationalised coverage of youth crime, even attaching animal epithets — 'Wolf boy', 'Spider boy', 'Rat boy' — to individual members of the new deviant group, 'persistent offenders'. Government has responded predictably to media demands that 'something must be done', issuing condemnatory calls and initiating a series of measures designed to 'crack down' on juvenile crime. It is no doubt likely that these will, in turn, lead to increased crime by these children in the long-term as they become increasingly segregated and alienated from mainstream society.

The 'moral panics' approach remains a useful tool with which to examine societal reaction to specific aspects of delinquency.

Nevertheless, it fails to provide a complete explanation of the immediate social reality of crime and violence. Nor does it explain why it is predominantly young men who are involved. Moral panics do occasionally surround the activities of girls, as was evidenced by the spate of articles about girl gangs following the street robbery of Liz Hurley. Yet, with notable exceptions, they almost always arise from male delinquency.

This reflects the fact that young men are directly responsible for a considerable amount of serious damage to property and violence to people. Doubtless too, the indirect effects of their activities are dramatic. The court and prison system remains hopelessly overloaded as they return with exhausting regularity; insurance premiums spiral ever higher, especially in inner-city areas; fear of crime keeps many people, particularly the elderly, imprisoned in their homes; the drain on the economy is huge, and has been estimated as comparable to the costs of running the entire National Health Service[8].

So why is it that young men are more involved in crime than young women? The most obvious explanation would be to regard crime as biologically predetermined. For example, studies have suggested that, when injected into a wide range of animal species, the male sex hormone, testosterone, increases their tendency to violent behaviour. It has also been found that the existence of an abnormal chromosome pattern in males (XYY instead of the normal XY) can been linked with violence. However, such arguments are not convincing. It is dangerous to draw strong conclusions about human behaviour from animal studies. And the contribution of individual XYY males to the total picture of male violence is tiny, and has little bearing on male-female comparisons.

One recent review of the evidence on the links between gender and violence concluded that there are good reasons to think that the differences are largely determined by social influences, and not by physical factors. First, one can point to — admittedly unusual — societies in which the biologically normal females have shown a greater tendency to violence than the biologically normal males. Secondly, we know that boys living in non-violent neighbourhoods, and brought up in non-violent households with parents providing good quality care, show levels of violence that are very little different from girls brought up in the same circumstances. Thirdly, there is evidence that the levels of testosterone in young violent males are no different from those in non-violent males[9].

A more widely-accepted attempt to explain crime by young men has centred on the ill-defined notion of 'underclass'. According to the American 'New Right' commentator Charles Murray, the underclass is composed of people with deviant behaviours and lifestyles and characterised by "illegitimacy, violent crime and drop out from the labour force". Murray singles out young men — the 'young male barbarians' — for particular criticism and suggests that, for them, marriage is an indispensable civilising force[10]. In the 1990's, others have followed Murray's lead and argued that the predominant cause of anti-social behaviour on estates is fatherless families[11].

Yet these claims are questioned by the most recent self-report data. These indeed suggest that children who have no father, or have one but never see him, are more likely to offend than children in intact families. However, they are much less likely to offend than those who have a father but get on badly with him (this is particularly true for young males). Similarly, those who either have no mother, or never see her, are also less likely to offend than those who get on badly with her[12]. These findings support the body of research on crime and the family which consistently shows that, for boys and girls, it is primarily the quality of relationships with both mother and father which is one of the most important influences on offending[13].

Although the impact of disrupted family structure on offending should not be underestimated, it appears that it should therefore be considered less fundamental than the nature of the relationships between parents and children. At this stage, it may be as well to conclude — as Home Office research on parental supervision did in 1985 — that it is unwise to assume that more one-parent families must mean more delinquency, or that they are necessarily more lax in their supervision, or less able to provide support or affection, than two-parent families[14].

This is not to suggest that the role of the family in preventing delinquency is insignificant; indeed, parenting styles appear to be of critical importance. For example, the seminal Cambridge Study in Delinquent Development of over 400 working-class boys, mostly born in 1953, found that experience by age eight of harsh or erratic parental discipline, cruel, passive or neglecting parental attitude, poor supervision and parental conflict, predicted both convictions in general and predictions for violence in particular[15].

Useful though they are, many studies in this area are, however, flawed in that they generally focus only on boys. There are some exceptions. The 1985 Home Office study mentioned above found that girls who broke the law appeared, in particular, to suffer from a range of communication difficulties with their parents. Boys, on the other hand, were found to be less well supervised than girls, and delinquency was less common among teenagers whose parents kept a check on their various activities[16]. Another failing is that studies have also tended to concentrate on supervision provided by mothers, rather than fathers. It is therefore hard to identify from research the particular influence on boys' and girls' delinquency of having a committed father.

It is not just the family, however, which impacts on male juvenile delinquency. What is often relegated in importance, or overlooked completely, is the potential contribution to offending of the wider social processes involved in learning to be a man. These are, to a large extent, explored in predominantly male peer groups in a range of settings (including schools, pubs and workplaces) and reinforced by advertisers and the media.

The dominant view of masculinity is that a man should be tough, strong, aggressive, independent, rational, intelligent, and so on. But the dominant image of children and young people is that they are vulnerable, weak, immature, passive and dependent. This creates a particular contradiction for boys, which is heightened as adulthood gets nearer, simply because, within the construction of childhood, being a man cannot be achieved[17].

Although the increasing focus of research on the links between offending and the construction of masculinity is often regarded as a novel avenue of enquiry, re-reading long-standing research shows that the identification of such processes is not new. As far back as 1955, criminologist Albert Cohen identified that delinquency was a solution to problems of adjustment which were "primarily problems of the male role"[18].

In the same year, 'Street Corner Society', a classic sociology study set in Chicago[19], showed too that there are subtle variations in masculinities. Whilst all men are affected by the dominant image, it is mediated by other influences such as class, race, disability, and sexuality. The text explored the way in which working-class men are encouraged to learn their masculinity out on the public world of the streets. It showed them drinking, swearing, gambling, standing on street corners, watching the girls and fighting. It identified how standards of masculinity are set up which members are expected to meet, limiting their behaviour to narrow categories, and portrayed men's attempts to gain, and maintain, power in a variety of formal and informal settings. More sensitively, mutual concern and tenderness for other members of the group were shown to operate under the surface. Many of these conclusions have resonance for young working-class men today.

In contrast to the working-class boys, the college boys in 'Street Corner Society' manifest ambition to succeed, to 'get on'. Lloyd has similarly argued that, in contemporary society, middle-class boys are expected to be good with their brains, to be self-reliant, to compete, to think rather than to 'do'. Upper-middle class boys, often sent to boarding school from an early age, are expected to be aloof, to be separate from the 'others', to rule[20].

These class variations have implications for how the offending of different groups of young men is seen by society at large. As Winston Churchill once pointed out in a speech in the House of Commons:

"(Imprisonment) …is an evil which falls only on the sons of the working classes. The sons of other classes may commit many of the same kinds of offences and in boisterous and exuberant moments, whether at Oxford or anywhere else, may do things for which the working classes are committed to prison, although injury may not be inflicted on anyone."[21].

Similarly, there is considerable evidence that the behaviour of male Afro-Caribbean youth is more readily defined as 'problematic' — and therefore in need of intervention to control it — than that of their white counterparts. The recent Home Office self-report study found that these groups have very similar rates of offending, and that whites are slightly more likely to use drugs than Afro-Caribbeans[22]. Yet, although there is no evidence that young Afro-Caribbeans commit more crime or more serious crime than young whites, they are significantly over-represented in the prison population.

Whatever the particular influence of different masculinities, it is clear that peer influence exerts an especially powerful influence on the behaviour of young men. And, whereas young women tend to grow out of offending, the same pattern is not evident in the case of males.

The Home Office self-report study referred to above identifies the main factors in young women growing out of crime as leaving home, entering into stable relationships with the opposite sex, forming new families, and eventually becoming economically independent, socially responsible and self-reliant individuals. For young men, none of these factors were found to be statistically associated with giving up crime. Instead, avoidance of a delinquent lifestyle, including heavy drinking and drug use, was paramount. Moreover, desistence was more gradual and intermittent, with attempts to stop often thwarted by events or changes in circumstances. The positive effects of personal and social developments tended to be outweighed by the more powerful, but largely negative, influences of the peer group.

Despite Home Secretary Michael Howard's dismissal of 'trendy theories' which seek to attribute delinquency to socio-economic conditions, his own Department's research has indicated there is also a link, albeit a complex one, between economic circumstances and crime. For example, crimes against the person, largely committed by young men, were found to increase as their personal consumption grew. Conversely, property crime increased as personal consumption fell[23].

Unemployment has risen dramatically since 1979 to over 3 million at times. Amongst 16 to 24-year-old white men who have no qualifications, one in five is unemployed; amongst young black men, one in three.

Box, in his 'integrated theory of recession and crime', argues that, during economic recession, when unemployment soars and income inequalities widen, crime rises, particularly among those experiencing thwarted ambition or relative deprivation. The cutting edge of recession is sharpest in inner-city areas where there are problems such as poor housing, high unemployment and dwindling public services. The impact is heightened if individuals suffer from discrimination or are marginalised or alienated from the police[24].

In the UK in recent years, this explosive cocktail has been more applicable to the circumstances of young men than to those of any other group. In contrast to the fall in male employment, especially in sectors such as manufacturing, mining and the army, female employment (albeit often temporary, part-time and low-paid) has grown to the point where it has overtaken male employment for all age groups. The gap is most clearcut between male and female teenagers.

Events have shown the effects of the increasing marginalisation of young men from employment. The relatively recent phenomenon of 'joy-riding' has been linked to social deprivation, with young men venting their boredom and frustration by stealing cars. It has been suggested that riots on the Blackbird Leys estate in Oxford in 1991 were linked to job losses at the nearby Cowley car manufacturing plant[25]. Cars are a symbol of wealth, marketed in aggressive terms of power, status and style — an image especially resonant for young men, whose masculinity is often constructed from these same elements. Denied legitimate access to these goals, they have increasingly turned to car crime in response[26].

During the 1980's, riots have taken place in inner-city areas such as Brixton, Toxteth, Broadwater Farm and Handsworth. In the 1990's, this pattern has been broadened by similar events on run-down estates, such as Ely in Cardiff, Meadowell in Tyneside, and Marsh Farm in Luton. If poverty, unemployment and marginalisation have not been factors, why have similar riots not occurred in Hampstead or Tunbridge Wells?

The precarious position of young men in the labour market has serious implications for society. In 1992 in Manchester, 85% of those dealt with by the Probation Service were without jobs, and this trend was confirmed a year later in a survey by senior probation officers which found that, nationally, 70% of serious offences were committed by the unemployed[27]. But these young men are not just the casualties of recession, for whom new opportunities may arise as the economy picks up. They are the victims of a fundamental process of economic restructuring in industrial countries, and the evidence suggests that there will in future be fewer and fewer jobs available for men.

Whereas men's traditional role as breadwinner has fractured, young women have been able to add the role of wage-earner to their traditional role of home-maker and carer. It is anticipated that eight out of 10 new jobs between now and the turn of the century will go to women. And, even in communities where there are no jobs for either sex, young women have a route to adulthood by becoming mothers.

Paid employment has traditionally been central to a man's identity, conferring status, success and material reward. However, we are now looking at a situation where the traditional routes to adulthood, to being a man, have been cut. Without paid work, young men are struggling to find alternative sources of self-esteem. It appears that one effect of the economic crisis in disadvantaged areas has been that young men have often re-asserted their identities in highly destructive and criminal ways.

An increasingly common response among young men has been for them to get involved in the informal economy of the drugs market. In 1994, recorded crime figures show that, after theft and handling stolen goods (36%), drug offences were the most frequent (22%) for young men in the 18-21 age range[28]. Whilst most of these relate to unlawful possession of cannabis, the sharp rise in the overall figures in recent years suggests a significant shift in behaviour among young men. This is confirmed by the Home Office self-report study, which found that involvement in offending and drug use accelerates dramatically for 18-21-year-old men — 47% participated, compared with only 17% of women of the same age. Yet, for ages 14-17, the figures are the same for both sexes[29]. The study concludes on the bleak note that, where young male offenders indulge in heavy drugs (and similarly, alcohol misuse), they are likely to become "embedded in a criminal lifestyle from which it becomes increasingly difficult to disengage"[30].

It has also been argued that another response to the current economic situation has been that young men from the lowest income families, with lowest educational qualifications and the least prospects of employment, have taken refuge in siring children — one remaining way in which their manhood can be proven. Unfortunately, they frequently do not have the financial or emotional stability to support their offspring and their partners, and are often rejected by young women, who feel they will be better off without them[31].

Any serious attempt to tackle male delinquency must engage with the realities of young men's experience. Yet, paradoxically, the official responses of male-dominated institutions, such as the police force, judiciary, and prison system, frequently serve to reinforce, rather than undermine, such a culture.

Young offender institutions, for instance, often only brutalise young men and make them tougher than they were before, distancing them further from the private world of their emotions and removing all responsibilities for decision-making from them. This approach can prepare them admirably for a long-term offending career on release. Government initiatives to introduce 'secure training centres' and army-style glass houses for young men, and to encourage ex-military personnel to join the Probation Service, can confidently be expected to further this process.

What is less understood is how the responses of welfare agencies can similarly shore up macho values. Hudson argues, for example, that male youth justice workers also need to re-examine their own values, motivations and practice[32]. Working with young male offenders can sustain the worker's own masculine image as 'strong' and 'tough'; as a result, he can avoid challenging, or easily reinforce, the macho behaviour of the young men he works with — and, at the same time, marginalise the needs of women workers and offenders.

More fundamentally, although the diversionary approach of the dominant 'justice' model of youth justice practice has largely proved effective in recent decades, it is possible that its focus on the offence has inhibited exploration of how the construction of masculinities influences the nature and form of male juvenile delinquency. From this perspective, treating male delinquency as just part-and-parcel of 'normal' masculinity, of 'boys will be boys', has helped to avoid pathologising the offender as 'sick' or 'bad', but has simultaneously shifted attention from crucial components of male offending. As Hudson puts it:

" ... practitioners involved with young men in trouble with the law need to consider, firstly, the extent to which the form of a young man's delinquency is connected to his socially-constructed self-identity as a man, and, secondly, the extent to which such behaviour serves to express, legitimate and even encourage a disposition to dominate and maintain power over women and other social groups"[33].

These are important issues for criminal justice agencies to address, especially at a time when the latest research suggests that young men are no longer 'growing out of crime' as they did in the past — even by their mid-20's[34].

At the same time, the British Crime Survey shows that, for every 100 crimes committed, only 41 are ever reported, and just three result in conviction. If we are to have a real impact on the root causes of male delinquency, we need not only to develop initiatives within the justice system, but also to recognise the limits of the system and the additional need for a comprehensive prevention strategy. A positive programme is needed which would address the needs of young men, and remain sensitive to the needs of young women. The key elements should involve:

● Establishing a positive, non-violent ethos in schools. In particular, methods of discipline should promote pro-social, anti-violent attitudes; participative decision-making and teaching styles should be encouraged; pastoral care should be developed; equal opportunities should be made integral to the curriculum; parents should be involved as far as possible in the life of schools; and democratic approaches to school organisation should be fostered. Particular attention should focus on tackling the causes of high levels of truancy and exclusions, especially among Afro-Caribbean boys.

● Developing education on relationships and responsibility. This relatively unexplored area should become a central element of the education curriculum. Boys may be best taught in single-sex groups: working in mixed groups may make it more difficult for boys to express enjoyment of caring for young children, or to say that they might want to be a parent who stays at home with young children. Issues to address should include experiences of being parented, expectations for the future, discussion of what responsibility is and what a responsible father might be, managing conflict, coping with stress, finding help and support, and looking after oneself and others.

● Expanding youthwork services. Expenditure on youth and community services should be made a statutory duty on local authorities. Specific initiatives should be designed to engage 'hard to reach' young men. A particular aim should be to protect young men from the influence of high-risk activities, such as drinking and drug-taking, and from the negative influence of offending peer groups.

● Establishing pilot programmes to encourage young fathers' paternal involvement. Programmes have been initiated in the US which seek to de-emphasise the immediate implications of not being able to assume the breadwinning role, and provide fathers with alternative avenues for demonstrating responsible behaviour (eg. participation in a jobs training programme, involvement in an education course). Similar initiatives should be tested and evaluated in the UK.

● Encouraging fathers to attend parenting classes and family support services. Appropriate recruitment strategies and activities should be developed, and father-friendly environments established. The existing network of pre-school provision and family centres should also be expanded, and family preservation services made available to provide intensive short-term support to families experiencing difficulties.

● Investing in a jobs, education and training programme for young people. Young people (and young men in particular) are dramatically over-represented in the most insecure parts of the labour market. Although expenditure on a high-quality labour market programme to tackle youth unemployment would initially be costly, it would result in significant net savings after four or five years as the benefit bill fell. Raising the status, quality and attractiveness of vocational training should also be a major policy goal.

● Encouraging young men to work as carers. This would particularly require appropriate recruitment and careers initiatives in areas which have traditionally been dominated by women (eg. nursing, social work, early years education). In the same way that women have increasingly entered areas previously dominated by men, it is time that the obstacles to men working in 'women's jobs' should be removed. Such a strategy must also maintain appropriate emphasis on widening the range of opportunities for women to work in areas where they are currently underrepresented.

● Setting up pilot projects designed to explore with male offenders the links between masculinity and crime. Of the agencies involved in the criminal justice system, it appears that the probation service has developed the most innovative responses[35]. These fledgling initiatives require greater financial support and in-depth monitoring and evaluation, and the findings should be disseminated widely among agencies.

●Targeting resources and effort on tackling the apparent rise in numbers of 'persistent offenders'. This should involve local multi-agency strategy groups reviewing policy and practice and ensuring that all concerned are prioritising those at the heavy end of the offending spectrum.

● Updating and widening cultural images of masculinity. At

present, young men are often surrounded by images of brutality and violence. All media should be encouraged to discourage interpersonal violence, to promote non-violent conflict resolution, and to portray men in caring roles. Through public awareness campaigns, Government can initiate public discussion of these important issues. Attention should also be directed at ensuring balanced, non-sensational coverage of youth crime issues.

REFERENCES

1. Home Office. 'Criminal Statistics England and Wales 1994', London: HMSO (1995).
2. Home Office. 'Gender and the Criminal Justice System', London: HMSO (1992).
3. Graham, J., Bowling, B. 'Young People and Crime', Home Office Research Study No. 145, London: Home Office (1995).
4. Home Office ibid. (1992).
5. Home Office ibid. (1995).
6. Fyvel, T. 'The Insecure Offenders', Harmondsworth: Penguin (1963).
7. Pearson, G. 'Hooligan: A History of Respectable Fears', London: Macmillan (1983).
8. Home Office Standing Conference on Crime Prevention. 'Report of the Working Party on the Costs of Crime', London: Home Office (1988).
9. The Commission on Children and Violence. 'Children and Violence', London: Calouste Gulbenkian Foundation (1995).
10. Murray, C. 'The Emerging British Underclass', London: Institute for Economic Affairs (1990).
11. Dennis, N., Erdos, G. 'Families without Fatherhood', London: Institute for Economic Affairs (1992).
12. Bowling, B., Graham, J., Ross, A. "Self-reported offending among young people in England and Wales" in Junger-Tas, J., Terlouw, G.J., Klein, M.W. (eds.) 'Delinquent Behaviour Among Young People in the Western World: First results of the international self-report delinquency study', Amsterdam: Kugler (1994); and Graham, J., Bowling, B. ibid. (1995).
13. Graham, J. 'Families, parenting skills and delinquency', Research Bulletin No. 26, London: Home Office Research and Statistics Department (1989).
14. Riley, J., Shaw, M. 'Parental Supervision and Juvenile Delinquency', Home Office Research Study No. 83, London: HMSO (1985).
15. Farrington, D.P., West, D.J. "The Cambridge Study in Delinquent Development: a long-term follow-up of 411 young males" in Kaiser, G., Kerner, H-J. (eds.) 'Criminality: Personality, Behaviour, Life History', Berlin: Springer Verlag (1990).
16. Riley, J., Shaw, M. ibid. (1985).

17. Lloyd, T. 'Working with Boys', London: National Youth Bureau (1985).
18. Cohen, A. 'Delinquent Boys: The Culture of the Gang', New York: NY Free Press (1955).
19. Whyte, W.F. 'Street Corner Society', Chicago: University of Chicago Press (1955).
20. Lloyd, T. ibid. (1985).
21. Churchill, W. House of Commons speech of 20 July, 1910.
22. Graham, J., Bowling, B. ibid. (1995).
23. Field, S. Home Office Research Study No. 119, London: HMSO (1990).
24. Box, S. 'Recession, Crime and Punishment', London: Macmillan (1987).
25. Wilkinson, P. 'Deadly Obsession', The Times, 1 November, 1991.
26. Parker, H. "Locking up the joyriders" in 'Youth in Society 96' (1984).
27. Holman, B. 'Children and Crime': Lion (1995).
28. Home Office ibid. (1995).
29. Graham, J., Bowling, B. ibid. (1995).
30. Graham, J., Bowling, B. ibid. (1995).
31. Coote, A. (ed.) 'Families, Children and Crime': Institute for Public Policy Research (1994).
32. Hudson, A. "Boys will be boys: masculinism and the juvenile justice system" in 'Critical Social Policy 21' (1988).
33. Hudson, A. ibid. (1988).
34. Graham, J., Bowling, B. ibid. (1995).
35. Jenkins, J. 'Men, Masculinity and Offending', London: London Action Trust (1994).

Turning the Clock Forward

Clare Short MP

Clare Short has been Labour MP for Birmingham's Ladywood constituency since 1983 and is currently Shadow Secretary of State for Transport. Prior to entering politics, she was Director of YouthAid. Opposition Spokesperson of Women from 1993-95, Clare is Vice-President of Socialist International Women and chairs the NEC Women's Committee.

It is, I think, fair to say that the Women's Movement of the 1970's was broadly anti-men. Women brought out into the open the frightening scale of domestic violence and the way in which society simply turned the other way. Women felt angry that rape in marriage was not a criminal offence. Women were missing in all the major institutions of power — politics, the judiciary, business, the Church. Women had massively less income and wealth than men. Women raged at the fact that they were second-class citizens.

In the 1980's — the heyday of Thatcherism — the media launched a crusade against feminism. Feminist women were stereotyped as ugly, man-hating, bra-burning harridans. The Right has an instinct for social forces that threaten it. It went in with steel toe-caps to destroy any women who came to prominence and dared to appear sympathetic to such ideas. Although the media assault on feminist thinking spread and strengthened, the power of the social forces that were leading to a major change in women's views and expectations was unstoppable.

As we moved into the 1990's, clever commentators started to write about postfeminism. They could not see women in dungarees, burning bras and attending women's groups, and so they assumed that the movement was dead. They were profoundly wrong. Feminist ideas had, in fact, entered the mainstream. Women no longer gravitated towards special conferences and women's groups in university towns because the demand for change was everywhere. Women of all ages and backgrounds were included. Older women who found the ideas a challenge to the pattern of their own lives understood that all had changed for their daughters. Middle-aged men who resented younger women challenging their position at work were absolutely clear that they wanted an equal world for their daughters. The forces of change proved invincible and began to worry many men who felt the issues arising everywhere, but did not know where they were supposed to fit in.

The old model — which was being overturned so comprehensively — divided the world into two parts. Women ran the home and did the caring, and men ran the world of work and public life. Thus women had to fight to gain access to any skills and powers that had relevance outside the home. Women were expected to be pretty and feminine, to be able to sew and cook, and to care for children. Women were expected to try to be attractive to men, to flatter them and care for them, but never to threaten their sense of leadership, confidence and power, at home or in society. Thus women had to struggle to be educated. Primary education would enable them to read shopping lists and cookery books and help their children, but beyond this there was no point: it was considered unfeminine and ridiculous to want a university education. Similarly, when the great democratic battles for the extension of the franchise were fought, women were left out. The Labour movement in Britain, dedicated to the equal rights of all men, simply assumed that women should not have the vote.

Obviously, women throughout history have struggled to be allowed to develop their human talents. In each generation, in each family, there are stories to be told. But whilst there have been periods of great advance, there have also been other times that were more stagnant. The time of struggle for the vote was a time of advance, and then things went quiet. Women experienced an enormous advance during the Second World War, when the men went off to fight and women went into work. Crash-courses in skills from which they had been excluded were organised, and nurseries were opened throughout the land. The end of the War drove women back into the home, but families felt the benefits of the new welfare state. Girls were given equal educational opportunities. It was the girls of the post-war welfare state that formed the women's movement of the 1970's, which led on invincibly to the social revolution of the 1980's and nineties.

There is no going back. Women expect to enjoy all aspects of their humanity; they want to love their families, succeed at work and be equals in public life. In the seventies, women simply said they wanted the same rights as men. Now, as the reality comes closer, we realise it means change for everyone. Women cannot have equal rights at work and in public life and continue to take overwhelming responsibility for the family: trying to juggle everything imposes terrible stress on us and leaves more and more men muddled and confused about how they are supposed to fit in and how they are supposed to be.

Statistics on boys' achievement in school are very worrying. Girls are out-performing boys by increasing margins at every level. I feel certain that the gross figures hide a class division. Upper middle-class boys are still performing well. The educational attainment of other boys is very worrying indeed.

There is also a major change taking place in the labour market which is further undermining men. The early 1980's saw a decline in jobs in manufacturing — two million full-time jobs, overwhelmingly occupied by men in traditional skilled and semi-skilled work, were destroyed. The new jobs of the late eighties were in the service sector — low paid, most often part-time and largely taken by women. At the other end of the labour market, the old management hierarchies went out of fashion and men in their 50's were made redundant. New management systems stressed flatter management structures, lower pay and more 'people skills'; in the new management ethos, women were better than men. The result is that one in four men of working age are now outside the labour market, more than half the workforce is female, and many men are finding their wives, sisters, lovers and daughters doing better at work than them.

All of this change has, in my view, produced a crisis for men — a crisis of masculinity. We all live rationally, but we also live in a culture that gives us ideas about ourselves that we simply absorb without thought. Men are still bombarded with images of tough guys, who are adored by gorgeous bimbos and who sort out the baddies with the necessary violence. Society is saturated with pornographic images of women who make themselves available to be used and disposed of by tough, all-conquering men whose appetites must be pandered to. In the real world, women are getting on and men are being left behind. Women and their friends and magazines talk about friendship, sex and emotions. Men who cannot cope have nowhere to go and no-one to talk to. Women complain about the fact that men simply cannot talk about emotional issues. Women read about health and change their diet and decide to exercise. There are no 'well men's clinics', and men continue to die much younger than women. Men are the overwhelming majority of those involved in crime and large numbers of men continue to behave with extreme violence to the women they claim to love and the mothers of their children.

In America, there is talk of a 'men's movement' and a 'backlash.' In Britain, we have increasing numbers of confused men. Very large numbers of working-class young men are unemployed; work fails to give them status and no-one wants to marry them. Too many fall into a lifestyle of drink and yobbo masculinity. They are unhappy and insecure, but cannot discuss it with anyone. Large numbers of men continue to be made redundant before retirement age. They are not counted in the unemployment figures and feel increasingly irrelevant and lacking in status. (Some years ago, a redundant draughtsman came to my Advice Bureau. He handed me an envelope and I read a reference which said that he was a fine and reliable employee.

I said how impressed I was. He burst into tears. He had been unemployed for some years. His wife had a part-time job, and his Unemployment Benefit and redundancy money had run out: he could not claim benefit because his wife was working. She occasionally gave him money. They had been married for 25 years and the marriage was about to end. He felt rejected and useless and unwanted by everybody. He said he just wanted me to read the reference so that someone important would know that he used to be good).

The answer is not to turn the clock back. Those who claim men's jobs can be restored if women leave the labour market are not making a serious analysis. Men's and women's aspirations have changed, and we need a labour market, a benefits system and a framework of public services which can adapt to the positive aspects of this change. Women part-time workers have been used to drive men out of the labour market only because it has been possible to exploit them. It becomes uneconomic for good employers to retain permanent staff on decent wages if they are constantly being undercut by the worst employers. Legislation can deal with this. We need to ensure equal rights and fair hourly pay for part-time workers, so removing the incentive to exploit them. Many women, and increasing numbers of men, want to work part-time. British men currently work the longest hours in Europe and miss out on the pleasures of involvement with their children. Encouragement of quality part-time jobs and the loss of low-pay low-status stigma would allow both men and women to enjoy their families and their work.

For, aside from employment issues, a major social revolution is taking place which is transforming the lives of men and women. It is in tune with the values of the women's movement, and therefore women are comfortable with the change. They want to have it all — to be equal at home and at work and in public life. Men find it very difficult to understand what is happening. They hear the rhetoric of the women's movement and it appears to threaten them. They read the media's denunciation of feminism and they agree that these man-hating harridans are vile. Then they find that their mothers, sisters and lovers seem to think these things. They feel increasingly insecure and therefore feel they must prove their manhood by showing that they can be violent and domineering. But then the women walk away from them. Men feel increasingly miserable, but it is not manly to whinge, so they bottle it up and become more 'masculine' and less attractive.

This is, of course, a stereotype. Not all men are like this, and not all men are a failure. But there is a big worry in the minds of many men. I find, as I meet 'successful' men in the course of my MP duties, that they increasingly talk about how well their daughters are doing and how their sons are less certain. Of course, the great change in life opportunities for women comes when children are born; it is not true that women have become more than equal, and that all the problems lie with men. But I do believe a great sea-change is taking place, and many men do not understand it and feel deeply threatened by it.

All that women want is to enjoy every aspect of their humanity. They want to love their families and be happy at home, use their brains and creativity and be valued at work, and to involve themselves as equals in shaping society and participating in public life, but they are demanding progress and are certain that it will be achieved. At home, it is more difficult. If women work, men should share the domestic work as equals. But most men won't and can't. They see it as women's work; it is feeble and weak for men to clean and shop and change the nappies. Men have traditionally neglected the upbringing of their children, and, although older successful men often say how much they regret not being involved with their children when they were small, younger men still feel that caring for babies is not masculine. Their partners want them to, but know they cannot cope. Many men retreat to the pub or club and leave it to the women.

We are now addressing the frustration that results from women being missing from positions of power. It is widely accepted that men and women should share power. What has not yet been addressed is the frustration created by men being missing from caring roles. Traditional notions of masculinity have denied men the opportunity to develop this side of themselves, and our social structures have reinforced this. Freeing men to be involved in caring is the unfinished part of the social revolution.

At the most unspoken cultural level of sexual relationships between men and women, there is also a growing malfunction. Men feel masculine when women are weak, clinging and dependent. But, increasingly, women are strong and assertive. They are looking for strong and equal men, but cannot find them, and more and more relationships end in unhappiness. One in two of recent marriages has ended in divorce, and most often the divorce is initiated by the woman. Large numbers of couples choose not to marry, even when they have children, because they fear the old model.

The overall answer is very simple: it is for men to comprehend, and become part of, the process of change. If they see it as being anti-men and in favour of women, they will continue to be unhappy. If they understand that it is about all of us having the chance to enjoy all aspects of humanity, then they will see that there is lots in it for men. The notion of masculinity will be reshaped; men will expect to share in caring for children and elderly parents, and will not feel ashamed to expect employment arrangements which enable this to occur; men and women will work together as equals, and men will begin to understand women in roles other than mothers, sisters and lovers. Then men might begin to feel more comfortable with the special qualities of their sexual relationships. If they cease to feel they must dominate and control, they and their partners will be much happier. And, when men are allowed to be honest about their fears, hopes and emotions, they — and those who love them — will be much happier people.

The Unsentimental Juggler
(An interview with Blake Morrison)

*Blake Morrison is the author of two collections of poems, 'Dark Glasses'
(1984) and 'The Ballad of the Yorkshire Ripper' (1987); a children's book,
'The Yellow House' (1987); critical studies of The Movement and Seamus
Heaney; and the award-winning memoir 'And When Did You Last See
Your Father?' (1994). He also co-edited 'The Penguin Book of
Contemporary British Poetry'. Formerly the literary editor of the Observer
and Independent on Sunday, Blake teaches part-time for the University
of Greenwich and is currently working on a screenplay, a libretto and
a new book of non-fiction.*

The evidence looks pretty convincing that there is currently some
kind of crisis for men — in everything from employment trends
to falling sperm counts. It's probably a turning point, but what
I'd want to say is that this could be a positive thing. It faces men
with the prospect of change — we are going to have to adjust
our thinking, and our assumptions may have to alter, but where's
the harm in that? Men's bodies tend to be a bit stiff compared
to women's. We need to learn flexibility. At present we are
intellectually lagging behind women, who have had to re-consider
and re-develop their roles in society during the last 20-25 years.
It's partly because they have done that that this male crisis has
occurred.

This is particularly the case in employment, where women have moved into areas that were once occupied exclusively by men. Many men feel redundant. Many men are literally redundant, and this requires a rethink about what it is to be a man, what contribution we can make. I believe that the contribution which involves working from, at, and with home, with a more domestic life for men, is no bad thing. I suspect that there is a sort of demoralised generation at the moment, because men measure themselves against their fathers and their grandfathers, whose assumptions were very different. If we started measuring ourselves against what's happening around us and against other men in the West, we might feel less disenchanted and demoralised than we do.

So that's one general point — that it ain't all a bad thing. The other point is that perhaps the changes aren't so dramatic as some of the statistics suggest. If I look at the workplaces I know, they still seem to be male-dominated, even if there are now more women in them. The key positions in most industries, companies and professions are still male. Really, at the top, the crisis isn't evident: men are in command and clinging onto old privileges and old bits of power. There are many more changes yet to come. There's still some usurping to be done.

You're saying that men need to rethink their role in a number of areas. What areas do you have in mind?

Let's take two for the moment. First of all, employment. We seem to be moving towards a culture of short-termism; there are no jobs for life now. Our fathers and their fathers might have had a reasonable expectation — certainly within the middle classes, if not for factory workers or miners — that they could stay in one post or firm for the whole of their lives if they so chose. There was a pretty large degree of security. I take my own father as an example: he was a GP who stayed in the one place for 35 years. It's not like that any more, and it's not just at the level of people losing jobs and redundancies — it affects the way in which people are hired in the first place. We are moving into a world of short-term contracts, and I think, in time, we will be moving (though there is very little evidence of this yet) into a world of shorter working hours. Britain is reactionary in this compared to the rest of Europe: we're still resisting even a 48-hour maximum week. But this seems to me almost a last despairing blast of male workaholism against all trends.

Professions are reluctant to give people jobs for life (or even for more than a year), and I think women, without the example of their mothers or previous generations of women being at work, are more flexible about this, more able to cope with this than men, who seem affronted by it. Men feel that they are being deprived of some sort of ancestral right: redundancy means demoralisation and failure and uncertainty. It is deeply threatening, but I think that's one thing that we're going to have to learn to cope with, because, at the moment, that's the way the world's going.

I do see shorter working hours as a good thing. I think it is right that jobs are spread to alleviate unemployment; that more people be given chances, rather than have individuals hogging power and taking on more, when, with a bit of thought and flexibility, another person might come in part-time and take some of the work on. This requires some active surrender from men which we've not been trained to perform — some magnaminity, even. It's in our interests, too: if we have more hours to ourselves, it's going to improve our lifespan, our health, and, potentially, our cultivation of self. Whether it's through sport, or through meditation, or writing, whatever it is, self-cultivation is very important. It can get eroded and driven out, particularly when men are very absorbed in their work. We should have a slightly more detached attitude to work, since work seems to be more detached about us: we've got to learn to let go of it and to see whether there isn't more to us than absorption within an institution or workplace.

The other area is home life. I think it is important to cultivate the domestic part of oneself. Traditionally, our fathers did not perform domestically, either with childcare or menial tasks about the house. Those tasks seem to me to be a valuable part of life, particularly involvement with one's family and kids. It's not a loss for men to be doing more there. We can learn things about ourselves; we can control some of the darker, more aggressive forces, and can dissipate those feelings, if only through exhaustion.

There is no point being sentimental about it. I think the 'New Man' thing was sentimental. It was rather like the natural childbirth movement, again a good thing, but, in the early days, the Natural Childbirth Trust was romantic about childbirth and how wonderful labour could be without drugs. In fact, for many women, giving birth is immensely painful, immensely difficult. It's been rather similar with 'new' men — there's been an element of denial, a sentimentalising of how wonderful it is to be at home and completely equal, performing domestic tasks, sharing childcare and so on. In fact, a lot of that work does feel like surrender, it does feel like having less of a life, less freedom and so on. A lot of men weren't prepared for that and just find it much more difficult than they'd imagined.

I look at my father and think, he didn't have to do any of this stuff, and sometimes I envy him that; I feel jealous of his freedoms. He never emptied the dishwasher, or the washing machine, or cooked supper, or hoovered, or did the ironing, or the other things that I have slowly learnt to take for granted. You measure yourself, not just against your partner if you're in a relationship, but also against your father and other men, and that old culture is still there.

There is a lot of peer pressure to keep in line.

Perhaps. But I tend to find in the world in which I move — which is diverse at present: newspapers, publishing, theatre, television, teaching, a bit of this and that, roughly speaking a media world — that there's very little male peer group pressure to be a lad. If anything, the pressure's the other way — to demonstrate quite clearly that you're not.

But I guess that, earlier in your life, it was different...

Yes, it was. When I was younger, say 16-30, it was a real battleground inside me. This was the time of feminism becoming a force in Britain, and of my subscribing to it intellectually. But,

103

equally, my father and his generation and my peers formed an emotional pressure the other way — to assert your dominance, or freedom, not to be under the thumb of a woman. With my father, there would be pivotal things like going to the pub: my girlfriend and I would be visiting my parents, and my father would want to go off to the pub with me, leaving the women behind at home. I found myself horribly torn between what I felt was right and partly wanted to do, which was for all of us stay at home, and what I felt was wrong, but also partly wanted to do, which was to go off to the pub with my dad. So, yes, there have always been peer group pressures, although I don't feel them as much now.

I suspect the pressures on young men have changed quite a bit. Women, or girls at school, really now have as much, if not more, expectation of going on to college or university and having a job as do men. It was different when I was growing up; women then might think they would get a job and work for a bit, but, in the long run, they would assume they'd be having a family. In my day, fewer people went to university, and, since then, the numbers of women students have risen much faster than the numbers of men. These things have an effect, and I would have thought that it would be difficult for young men now to be quite so condescending or patronising towards women as we were. Women used to think that they had to find a man, rather than a job — that was their half of the bargain. The man's half was, "They're not going to get me, but I'm going to have sex with them" — you would score, but you'd escape the net that they were trying to throw over you. That was the old, horrible collusion and struggle, but I think it must have changed: if women are now equals in terms of their job expectations and economically, then it can't be so unbalanced as it used to be.

There seems to be some growing evidence now that a lot of boys are just letting girls get on with it, in the sense that they don't see the education system as relevant to them, possibly because there aren't the jobs at the end of the line anyway. It's the old attitude towards swotting — they just don't see it as part of what

they ought to be doing, they'd rather hang out on the streets or do more exciting things than sit behind a school desk. They find in their late teens that the women are just miles ahead of them, and then you've got the problem of women looking for male partners and not having many to choose from because of that. Some would say it's about the education system not responding sufficiently to boys' needs.

I think there's something in that. In the old system of 11-plus, you were divided into 'pass' or 'fail' categories. Even if you passed, you went on (as I did) to a grammar school, and there were three streams, and, if you were in the bottom stream, you didn't have huge expectations. Already there was a feeling of, "Oh, it's not worth trying", and presumably through the secondary modern there would be that same feeling. In some ways, that's always been there. What's different is that, in the old days, there were probably more jobs for the unskilled, for those that didn't have qualifications, than there are now. There were always things to go to, bits of industry that have disappeared now. In the old days, you could muck about knowing there'd be a job afterwards; now boys muck about because they know there won't be a job.

One of the big changes has been the growth of the service industry: that must account for a vast percentage of new employment opportunities and jobs, but they tend to be taken by women and are seen by men as 'women's jobs'. Men should be equally well-equipped to do these jobs. But it takes a lot of time: it takes almost generations of example. Until we've seen more and more men doing these jobs, then the next generation of boys are still going to find it 'unnatural'. So much depends on precedent, I think — what you're seeing in your own home or around you.

The media have got an important role to play in that, and I think a lot of the media images of men are the same old images that they've been churning out for 30-40-50 years. Maybe that's an area where things could change a bit more.

Yes. If you take an ad that's showing a lot at the moment, the

Coke ad with the group of women office workers who come to the window to look at the guy who's a builder and his male torso: 20 years ago, it wouldn't have been allowed for women to be shown to be openly lusting after and enjoying a male body like that. That would have been considered unseemly. Yet, in other ways, the ad is still a reinforcement of stereotyping; that's what a bloke should be — he should look like that, he should be physical, he should be a labourer.

The media reinforces stereotypes, but I don't know what you can do about it. One has also to acknowledge that there are essential, or habitual, male characteristics. It's like the idea that, if you don't give your boys guns as toys, then they won't be aggressive; that somehow, through choice of toys, your children's gender can be eroded. I think that's sentimental, romantic and wrong. My children, without particularly being encouraged to do so — in fact, in some areas, in spite of being actively discouraged — have assumed some very traditional stereotypes currently. My two sons are obsessed with football, and my daughter is very keen on riding. You see it with five and six-year-olds in the playground: the girls are standing talking, while the boys are out there with the ball. You can say that it's television and that it's the media, and so on, but I suspect it's not, that these are really gender instincts. But men can still look at themselves and ask, "Does being interested in football mean that I can't empty the dishwasher?". To acknowledge that we have a bundle of old-fashioned male assumptions, attitudes, interests, hobbies, whatever, does not mean that we can't also perform in new male ways as well.

It's about acknowledging our male strengths and passions, but also having a much broader picture of what we're capable of and what we should be doing.

Yes. I think men are more obsessive than women, but the passion itself is the thing that matters and the obsession, as long as it's not socially harmful, can even be a good thing. 'Hobbies' seems a very old-fashioned word now, but I don't think hobbies, though much derided, need be unattractive — a passion for something outside the workplace, at a time when the workplace is shrinking, can't be a bad thing. I think the kind of intellectual and emotional energy that can be invested in a hobby — whether it's football, photography, dancing, hang-gliding, trainspotting or whatever — is valuable, and better expressed that way than through workaholism.

If you were Minister for Men, what would you be doing to address the kind of issues our evidence has thrown up?

I've got to say that I'm not terribly keen on the idea of a Ministry for Men. But, if there's one place where they need to start rethinking all of this, it's the House of Commons. The example set there seems almost completely reactionary: the noise, the loutishness, the backbiting, the plotting, the career desperation, the fact that most of the things that happen in the House of Commons take place after 6 o'clock in the evening. There's a place that needs to do some rethinking about what it is to be male... and to make room for more women.

The post could be a vehicle for encouraging the disempowerment of men from the top of professions, while empowering men in more traditional 'feminine' ways. If there is a ministerial role in this, it can't be artificially worked up — there can't be a 10-point programme that everybody will agree to, because they just won't. It's a matter of slowly changing things, and already there are some signs of that — individual adverts, individual articles and programmes, and so on.

One issue that can be addressed is health. Work might be done to overcome the resistance of men to seeking help when they're ill — emotional and psychological help, as well as physical. The resistance stems from a fear of appearing weak and dependent, of intimacy, of admitting that something's gone wrong. There are still a lot of unnecessary early deaths, not so much because there are not the doctors to address men's problems, but because of the reluctance of men to go and admit that there's something wrong.

What do you think would help make men come forward?

I think we just have to be battered — there has to be a campaign, a lot of billboards, more concerted and direct nagging at men. There are adverts that make men go out and buy particular brands of beer, so let's have adverts that make them go out and do this as well. It means changing attitudes in schools, at home and within hospitals, which need to become more user-friendly.

Somebody was telling me that systems are now being developed where, in effect, in 10 years' time, if you were worried about something, you could go into a computer room in a hospital, log on and look up the relevant stuff. This would remove the problem of actually going to sit in a room with someone and say, "I've got something wrong with me", which men find so difficult.

Why is life expectancy for men so much shorter? All those early deaths seem a lot to do with a culture of heavy drinking, but also of danger, risk-taking. We could address that, in schools particularly, and point out to boys the risks they run and the potentially self-destructive activities that seem to attract young men. Boys like, and I suspect will always like, adventure films in which there is danger. But the whole basis of reading fiction, whether it's crime or romantic fiction, is voyeuristic; it's not that we are ourselves going to do the things we enjoy watching or reading about. There is currently a particular sort of male culture which seems to want to connect seeing these dramatic, exciting things being done with having to do them oneself.

I think some of that is that men have the impression, as they grow up, that they're in the world to do important things, and some of it is about proving you're a man through risk-taking and bravery.

Yes. 'Bravery' always means physical bravery, and I think to teach boys that there are other kinds of bravery — intellectual bravery, emotional bravery (which doesn't mean not crying) — would be worthwhile. There are different kinds of courage.

Going back to the health information on computer idea, I could see the usefulness of that in terms of linking into things that men enjoy doing and giving them information, but it doesn't

get men talking. What could you see happening to improve that? If you take the Dunblane tragedy, for instance, when you read about the background of the guy who did it, here is someone who was obviously behaving very strangely and yet people stood back from it and didn't seem to engage with him. You see that pattern time and time again with men who eventually just break. They're not truly communicating what's going on inside for them, and, in a sense, people don't seem to be that interested either partly, I think, because of the effort of trying to communicate properly with men or getting them to talk.

It's difficult, because it's a pretty ingrained instinct: men don't like to feel under this pressure to talk. There's this terrible resentment at being told, "The trouble with you is that you don't discuss your feelings". But you're right — male suicide rates, mental breakdown, and so on, all seem to have risen, and I would guess that, with men, such crises are much more likely to involve violence to oneself and others. So we are talking dangerous stuff here; we're talking about men's capacity to destroy themselves and other people at a moment of crisis. Undoubtedly, the lack of somewhere to go at a crisis point, or somebody to turn to, afflicts men more than women. Women do seem to be better at talking to each other, at having someone to ring up, somebody to go and see, somebody to share problems with. Men are not necessarily more private than women, but what they speak about when they're being sociable is much more neutral, public domain stuff.

Men's groups might be an answer. But their image badly needs to be changed: at present, they either seem like work-out sessions for aggressive men who are afraid of their waning power and masculinity, and who want to get together and work out the old tribal stuff; or they seem a little bit precious, for a select group working on the soft end of things. Ordinary blokes don't identify with either of these. So the image needs to be changed to put across the idea that men meeting together, other than in pubs or at a football match, is not necessarily either following Robert Bly or being a wimp — there's nothing disgraceful about it.

Men are always being accused of not talking enough about their feelings. Their accusers are usually women. Ironically though, when it comes to exposing their inner selves and their worries and anxieties, men are much more likely to talk to women than to other men.

What could you do about this?

I'm not sure what you can do, except keep battling away at what 'male' and 'female' mean. Over the last 25 years, there've been times when women and men have tried to pretend there are no gender differences really — "We're all equal now" — and then found that wasn't so. Sometimes, couples have swung back the other way, reverting to a strict gender division of roles. I think you've just got to go on struggling to find the right way for all that to work, and there's no point pretending you can standardise this. Couples, partnerships, homes are about finding out what works best, and you can't have some kind of blanket rule about how it should be. Nevertheless, we're right to try and move away from the old ways towards more equality, both at home and in the workplace — that's got to be right, just as a more democratic society is right. It's a very slow, hard battle. There have been periods when everybody's pretended it's easy, and that it's just a matter of goodwill. Well, it's not just a matter of goodwill — you've got to actively make changes, too.

I think there are ways of encouraging this process. With schools, for instance, there are issues about how often boys get the chance to talk together about emotions and non-laddish things. There are issues about preparing boys for real life, as opposed to just work. So there are things which could be done to help the process, which wouldn't be seen as too interfering or constricting.

Yes, that's certainly something a Minister for Men could do, look very hard at male employment conditions, and what the likely prospects are over the next 10 years, and address that, and, with boys from the age of 13, not rely on the home and parents to deal with that question of expectations, but have schools face it head-on. That would be a good use of resources — it could be a special part of a budget within the education programme. There is no point in training and fitting people for jobs that don't exist and in creating attitudes and assumptions that are meaningless. We have also to see whether certain kinds of work — for instance, in the service industries — might not be more acceptable to boys if presented in the right kind of way.

How do you see women in all of this? Do you see a role for them in addressing the problem?

Yes. I think much of men's awareness that there is a problem has come through women — it's women who have faced us with it, not in any hostile way, but usually with a desire to help. So I think women do have a role. It is they who, traditionally, have encouraged men to talk, to explore their more private, vulnerable and emotional selves. Publicly, they're playing a much larger role now, too. I've found myself in the last couple of years working a lot more with women than I ever did — women directors, women publishers, women editors, organisations run or staffed by women.

Have you found it enriching?

Yes I have. Women moving into what used to be male territory has made that territory a more interesting place. They bring different approaches, assumptions and ways of looking at solving problems. All the juggling they do with home and work is part of this. Why can't we be jugglers as well? Can't we learn to juggle? It's one of our problems, that we haven't been brought up to be as flexible as women. There was an old male idea that you went out, you did your work, you came home. Now, even when that's not the case any more, there are still attempts to reproduce or replicate that. But why does it always have to be the one thing? Let's see if we can't be more 'two hours of this, four hours of that', juggling like women have had to do. It means perhaps spending less time with male colleagues, or at the company, and more time with children, or going around supermarkets, or emptying the washing machine, but is that necessarily worse? A degree of drudgery and self-sacrifice, yes, but is that such a bad thing? Has there been perhaps a touch of hubris about men, a sort of vast ambition? Really, not to be driven in that way — or to be driven, but have a more rounded sense of oneself, of that drive having to take place within this much larger set of things happening — would be so much more useful.

Schooling from a Masculinities Perspective[1]

Victor Jeleniewski Seidler

Victor Jeleniewski Seidler is Reader in Social Theory at the Department of Sociology, Goldsmiths College, University of London. He is the author of 'Rediscovering Masculinity: Reason, Language and Sexuality', 'Recreating Sexual Politics: Men, Feminism and Politics', 'Unreasonable Men: Masculinity and Social Theory' and 'Recovering the Self: Morality and Social Theory'. He also introduced and edited 'The Achilles Heel Reader: Men, Sexual Politics and Socialism' and 'Men, Sex and Relationships: Writings from Achilles Heel'. He also edits the 'Male Orders' Series for Routledge.

How are boys to be schooled in relation to their masculinities? This is a question that is coming into prominence in the 1990's from a growing recognition that boys (particularly boys from working-class backgrounds) are not doing as well as girls at school, even in traditionally-defined 'boys subjects'. This is a significant change, since the concerns used to be predominantly with the performance and choices that girls were making. Those concerns have informed feminist work in education, established in the context of boys having power in the classroom to take more than their fair share of time, space and attention. It was girls who were so easily silenced and marginalised within the conventions and practices of traditional teaching.

Teachers were anxious (especially women teachers, who could recognise the issues involved) to limit the boys' troublesome behaviours. Sometimes this involved taking girls on their own in order to help them establish a clearer sense of self-worth and self-esteem. The issues were rightly seen in terms of providing increased support for girls, but sometimes this meant not fully recognising what was going on for the boys.

In these feminist discussions, boys were largely seen as part of the problem, and rarely as part of the solution. For boys were too readily identified with the power that a dominant white heterosexual masculinity had within a patriarchal society, and masculinity was often construed almost exclusively as a relationship of power. So it was that, in education, boys were viewed as obstacles that stood in the way of girls getting the time and attention that they were owed.

There seems to be a perception that, if we argue for policies specifically related to boys, then we have to be suggesting a false parallelism between the experience of boys and girls, so losing a grip on the ways in which society is still very much shaped in the image of a dominant white heterosexual masculinity. There has been some resistance to the arguments for policies specifically related to boys because they are seen as linked to the views that, after 20 years of feminism, it is now boys who are 'oppressed' in the ways that their experience has been derided by women teachers, who supposedly only recognise boys as 'problems' who need to be silenced and disciplined to give girls a chance for equal attention.

But, if we can sense a backlash against feminism not far from the surface, we still have to be careful about how we evaluate these concerns. At some level, we have to recognise the anger that some men feel at the power which they see feminism as having acquired. For some men, there is a desire for revenge and a wish to reclaim a power that men have lost and which they feel is 'rightfully theirs'. This makes it crucial for other pro-feminist men to engage with these arguments, whilst at the same time recognising critically some of the failings of the sexual politics of the 1970's, which, in many ways, failed to enumerate positive visions of how boys might move towards manhood, and too often left boys feeling unsure and confused in relation to their masculinities, with no way through to more emotionally-fulfilling visions of themselves.

We can acknowledge that girls need a different kind of support to grow up with a clear sense of their self-worth within a patriarchal society which still so often diminishes, devalues and trivialises their experience as young women. But, at the same time, we can recognise that we have to address more directly what has been going on for boys from different class, ethnic and racial backgrounds. We also have to recognise the workings of relations of power between different masculinities (also between sexualities and able-bodiedness) and the different structural and cultural worlds into which boys are growing up and the diverse pressures they are under. We need to listen to what boys are saying and also to what they are not saying, recognising how they might be feeling lost, but also unsure about how to express what is going on for them without threatening their sense of male identity.

In many ways, young men from diverse class, racial and ethnic backgrounds are carrying the anxieties and insecurities of the larger culture, which is no longer sure what it means to grow into manhood when war and the breadwinner role no longer seem available as sources for a male identity that boys can grow up feeling good about. Sometimes, the strains and pressures created by these unresolved crises in masculinity show themselves in depression and self-harming, and, in extreme circumstances, in the very high rates of young male suicides. Something is going badly wrong. One way of dealing with it is to think more creatively about what is going on for boys in school.

Masculinity is something that can never be taken for granted; it is something that always has to be proved and affirmed. This builds its own tensions into boys' lives, as they often feel that they have to prove themselves. This shows itself in primary schools, particularly around the ages of 9 and 10 when there is often a sharper gender division that takes place in the classroom and when girls often withdraw from any contact with boys. In the earlier years, in more liberal schooling, there is much more active encouragement of mixing across gender lines and less demarcation about what boys can play with. Often it is the boys who have felt easier relating to girls, and who might still be more emotionally connected to themselves, who can find themselves isolated and stranded in the top junior classes. They can become targets for bullying, especially if they do not readily conform to the macho cultures that many of the boys are in.

When boys feel threatened in their male identities, they often withdraw into traditional macho styles. They can be made to feel that they are not 'man enough' and that they have to forsake the softer and more emotionally nourishing aspects of themselves. What we find reinforced is an identification of emotions with the feminine and a construction of homophobic feelings as a form of self-defence. It is in the junior schools that boys can begin to call each other 'poofs' and 'gay', and this becomes a form of self-policing which works to foreclose the possibilities of different ways of being for boys. As the peer culture grows in strength, it becomes important for boys to be accepted and they often learn to judge themselves according to a dominant masculinity, even if, at some level, they do not go along with it.

Often the transition to secondary school is particularly scary for boys, who are unsure how they are supposed to be in this larger context. It comes at an awkward point in boys' development, just as they are beginning to establish more of a sense of themselves in relation to their male identities. They have to prove themselves through putting down others, for it is only in relation to others that they can traditionally feel good about themselves. Boys feel that they have to show that they can handle the new situation on their own, and often that the insecurities they feel are not shared with others. Needing the help of others is a sign of weakness, and the showing of emotions, especially of vulnerability, serves to prove that you are just 'not up to it'. So boys learn to be independent and self-sufficient and that, to have emotional needs, just shows that you cannot make it on your own.

As boys are finding ways to affirm their masculinities, they also have to deal with the feminist challenges to notions of gender equality. At an intellectual level, some young men in schools with strong anti-sexist policies might affirm the equality of women, but, emotionally, they might find it more difficult to handle. This is because, traditionally, in diverse cultures, a sense of masculinity is so often constructed as a relationship of superiority in relation to women.

Because they have learnt of the inequalities and oppressions that women face, young men can feel torn between affirming a traditional masculinity and feeling unsure about themselves as men. It can seem as if masculinity is exclusively a relationship of power, so that it has to be given up, or forsaken, because there seem so few affirmations of the ways men can change. Masculinity defined as the problem can serve to silence boys and make it difficult to share what they are feeling, because it might just prove their sexism. And so boys withdraw into themselves, and there is a sharp divide between the uncertainties and anxieties they might be feeling in their inner lives and the ways they feel obliged to present themselves in public, where they might be tempted to act out a harder notion of masculinity in order to be accepted as 'one of the lads'.

With the growth of lad culture in the 1990's, there is a sense of release as boys no longer consider that they have to feel guilty about the ways they behave, but can feel affirmed in their sexism. This is a regressive development, but it does serve to show up the distance between how men were supposed to feel and behave (a set of moral imperatives) and what has been going on in their inner emotional lives. This is a conflict that has been there since the beginnings of lad culture in the 1980's, which — affirmed in the 'loads of money' ethos — was so much a part of Thatcherism: if you earn enough money, your behaviour is beyond moral reproach.

But some of the difficulties that boys are having need to be placed historically within a culture that in so many different ways already makes boys feel bad about themselves. At some level, we all learn that 'boys are bad' and that you cannot expect anything but animal behaviour from them. This leaves its own marks, as boys are often left feeling 'good for nothing' within a Protestant moral culture, as I have previously explored[2]. This adds to the pressure that boys feel to prove themselves and to be constantly on guard against the attacks of others.

In school, boys often learn to protect themselves through withdrawing emotionally and presenting themselves as cool, detached and uninvolved. Often, they do not want to deal with gender issues, either choosing to believe that these issues have nothing to do with them but with girls alone, or else that it will turn out as a way of getting at them. Feminism has made a great deal of difference to the culture of many classrooms, and boys have often withdrawn, rather than risk sharing feelings or emotions that might be deemed oppressive to girls. Boys find they turn in on themselves and feel 'unsafe' in expressing themselves, for they do not want to 'lose face' in front of their mates. It feels too risky to speak, or at least to speak seriously about oneself. Rather, there is a withdrawal into humour and irony as forms of self-protection.

The ways that boys are feeling about themselves as boys cannot be separated from the ways they are learning. For, if boys are taken up at some level with these emotional challenges and feel they have few spaces in which they can explore them, then it will be harder for them to focus upon their learning. They will be more likely to opt out and they might find it harder to express themselves in their learning. They will avoid forms of self-expression that have become so important in contemporary pedagogues, not wanting to expose feelings that might only make them feel worse about themselves. What becomes more important is keeping face in front of your peers and not showing any signs of weakness. Boys then get so used to suppressing what is going on in their inner emotional lives, not wanting to connect to parts of themselves that can leave them feeling exposed and vulnerable to the ridicule of their peers, that they cut off and split from their inner lives and it becomes a habitual pattern that is almost impossible to recognise.

Some of these patterns are taking shape within primary schools. My daughter Lily was immediately able to recognise in her primary class of eight-year-olds that the girls talk, but seem able to get on with their work at the same time. The boys seem to find it more difficult to do this, and they spend more time mucking about. Boys already know that they are not supposed to cry and that they have to be 'strong' and keep their feelings to themselves. This creates different kinds of tensions in boys' experience that they often learn to work through in the playground. However, there are also significant changes in that a wider range of masculinities is available, especially in the earlier years of primary school, when boys are given permission to play with dolls in ways that earlier generations would have been denied. There is a welcome fluidity in gender relations, but this seems harder to sustain in junior school years.

We still have to acknowledge what socialisation means in the growth and development of boys and the particular needs that they might have as boys and the kind of nourishment and support that they might need from relationships with older men. In this context, there is a great deal to be said for the importance of mentoring that was introduced most clearly by Robert Bly[3]. He has helped us to recognise the contact that boys might need to have with men and the ways they can be supported through such relationships. This is something that has been tried with African American boys in the United States but can be more generally applied. It does not need involve a father, but there should be a man — even an older student — who can be respected for his personal qualities and ability to share his life story and experience. Where there is uncertainty about what it means for boys to grow up into manhood, we need to open up a conversation between different generations in a way that can help boys feel good about themselves as young men.

Traditionally, we have wanted to separate out emotional issues that have to do with personal and family life and the learning that takes place within the context of schooling. We want to think that learning has to do with intelligence and with application, and that these qualities have little to do with emotional life, which teachers are not in any way skilled to deal with. But we might have to challenge some of these demarcations, as we have already begun to do with girls, where there is more appreciation that issues of self-esteem impact upon the kinds of choices girls make for themselves in education, and the ways they learn, and cannot be separated from gender concerns.

Of course, some boys will learn regardless of the emotional and gender issues they face. As boys, we are often taught to put our emotional lives aside to get on with the tasks at hand. This splitting is one of the ways male identities are affirmed. But learning is easier to do when boys feel validated and affirmed in their gender identities. If we leave boys feeling bad about themselves so that they turn in on themselves, or else act out their conflicts in anti-social ways, they will be left feeling that these are personal issues that they have to deal with on their own, and they will not grasp how their unease is tied in with larger cultural unease and a crisis in relation to masculinities.

Within the West, we have few ways of marking a transition in boys' lives so that, in the early years of secondary school, they can be left feeling uncertain: "I am not a boy ... but I am not sure that I am a man either" or "I'm not a child, but I'm unsure that I am really an adult, even if I am on a path towards adulthood". These are difficult days, and heterosexual boys unsure of their sexual identities can act out in all kinds of homophobic ways as a form of self-protection. They can be tied into competitive relations with each other, unsure of their friendships and whether it might be their turn to become a target of abuse.

In the 1950's, we were as uncertain in establishing our sexual identities, but we could be confident in a different way because we were not open to the charge of sexism in our relations with girls. Nowadays, sexual relations across genders seem more fraught and tense, and it seems as if more teenagers are content with same-sex friendships. Possibly relationships with the opposite sex have become just too fraught with complications. Boys often deal with this through opting out; they withdraw into their own groups and some take refuge in traditional sexist behaviours.

School is often not a safe place to explore sexual identities, and boys who suspect that they are gay can have a difficult time sharing their feelings with their friends. In the early years of secondary school, it is so important to be accepted by your friends that people do not want to say anything, or do anything, that risks rejection. Often, young men who recognise their attraction for the same sex will keep these feelings to themselves, for there is so much homophobic feeling around and 'gay' is frequently used as a term of abuse.

There is a kind of double-consciousness that emerges in which young gay men are careful about what they say and the ways they behave. They might do a lot of sport as a form of self-protection, or some might lead the gangs in the playground, even accusing others of being gay as a way of deflecting attention from themselves. Young gay men carry considerable inner tension about with whom they might be able to share the knowledge of their sexuality, and this probably has a bearing upon the high suicide rate for young men. Though work still needs to be done to investigate these figures, they do reveal a silent desperation and a widespread feeling that appropriate help is not available.

It is very important for boys to be able to keep face, and they do not want to take unnecessary risks in front of others. Boys who have been brought up in anti-sexist families often find they behave differently at school from the ways they can be at home — and often feel bad about this. Teachers, especially male teachers, have been reticent in exploring their inherited masculinities in a way that would be helpful in opening up conversations about what boys are going through. This should form an important part of teacher training.

Greater sensitivity to issues of class around masculinities is needed also. For many working-class boys, it used to be possible to feel that working in school did not matter that much because your dad could guarantee you a job. This was important in sustaining the relationships between fathers and sons, and it meant that fathers could feel good about being able to offer their sons a future. This made it easier for working-class boys to deal with not being able to do well at school, for they still knew that they had a future to look forward to and that, if they could scrape through, they would still get the apprenticeship that was waiting for them. But, with the breakdown of apprenticeships and with high levels of unemployment, there has been a dislocation with the past. All of a sudden, there is no future, little sense of what there is to work for. Rather than young men being motivated to work hard at school to be in a better position to compete for the few jobs available, they can feel, "What's the point, if the chances are that I am going to end up on the dole anyway?".

We have to realistically face the new realities of the job market and the changed situation that confronts young men in education. If your dad is unemployed, or only in irregular work, boys can feel in conflict with the predominantly middle-class values of the school, which might think this was a mark of personal failure, and perhaps feel forced to reject the school so that they do not have to feel bad about their fathers.

Working-class boys often feel that, if you do not compete, then you cannot be said to have failed. If schools are to become more competitive institutions, this will lead to even higher rates of truancy and boys just withdrawing. It is often easier for boys to drop out, rather than feel that they have failed in front of their friends. At some level, there is already tension between making it academically and dominant masculinities, though the opening up of the curriculum to give more recognition to different learning paths besides the strictly academic would help (in Holland, vocational education seems to have a status that it has never had in England, and there seems less stigma attached to choices made). Within the changed worlds of new technologies, there are different arenas in which male identities can be played out and negotiated. Many of the video and computer games tend to reinforce macho conceptions of masculinity: here there are virtual spaces to which boys can withdraw when things are not going well at school. These games give boys a sense of competence and power that can easily compete with the kinds of affirmations they might get at school.

In some ways, boys in the early years of secondary school are learning to relate to each other through these new technologies. These discourses help them sustain their relationships, completely independently of what is going on with girls. As the arena of sexual relationships with girls becomes too contested and risky; as boys are forced to recognise that their traditional ways of acting out their male superiority are a turn-off which leaves them open to ridicule and rejection on the part of the girls; so boys often find it easier to withdraw into a world of their own. At some level, boys have frequently found the arena of relationships difficult to navigate, partly because the emotions and feelings that might help them monitor what is going on have so often been interpreted as signs of weakness that threaten male identities. In contrast, you know where you are with the computer images, and this can be reassuring in uncertain times. Boys can develop relationships with their computers that seem far less threatening these days than relationships with girls. The new technologies can help boys create new senses of identity which feel far less risky and where boys can feel that they know where they are with themselves.

Recognising the distances that separate generations, it might be important to acknowledge that adults live in a very different world from their children. Some of the qualitative shifts mean that there has been a breakdown of communication. This is clearest in the area of drug education, where the kind of statements adults make, say about ecstasy, only confirm to a younger generation that they do not know what they are talking about. The fear tactics used in the wake of Lia Betts's tragic death showed the breakdown in communication across the generations. This can make it important to open up a conversation between different ages in a school, as has effectively been done in relation to bullying. Where there is a 'whole school' policy which has been able to demonstrate that it is the coward who bullies, and where children have felt empowered to share their experiences with other children, rather than feel forced to keep it to themselves, there have been significant changes. (It is not only boys who bully, but again there are important connections between bullying and the culture of dominant masculinities). Projects, such as those organised by the Pop Up Theatre group, which goes into school to work in different groups with students and with teachers around emotional issues such as bullying, help to shift a school culture in crucial ways.

Boys need to learn to deal with a variety of cultural, ethnic and class differences that they might not know from home life, and they need to learn how to respect and honour differences, rather than to fear them. There has been a sense of equality that has informed comprehensive educational practice that needs to be valued. This has helped students coming from different backgrounds feel that they can be accepted for who they are, so that they do not have to feel shamed or that they have to become 'like everyone else' in order to be accepted by their peers. There are many conflicts in liberal schooling between the individualistic focus that can so easily separate people from a sense of their histories and cultures and the ways that collective identities can also be honoured. These issues are not easily resolved and they intersect with issues of gender and intimate relations. With the breakdown of traditional forms of family relations, we have to recognise the diverse forms of personal relationships and family forms as a critical part of issues that children are having to deal with. While it is important not to extend expectations of what we can demand of schools to alleviate the crises of the larger culture, we also have to rework our visions of education. For it might be that, as children learn to be more literate emotionally, they can also cope better with the demands of traditional education.

If boys are to learn to draw support from each other in the process of redefining their masculinities, then they must be helped to value developing an inner relationship to self (this is something that feminism has already helped girls to do, though we should not underestimate the difficulties they still face). We need policies which will relate specifically to the experiences of boys and which appreciate the diverse backgrounds they come with. This should help boys find ways of accepting their masculinities, not exclusively as relationships of power and superiority, but as sources of strength, insight and wisdom. These policies are necessary not only in schools, but also in the youth service, where we have been slow in developing positive images of manhood which can allow boys to feel good about themselves. There is a responsibility that boys have to learn in relation to women, but one of the first lessons is for boys to take more emotional responsibility for themselves, for, traditionally, men have looked to women to do the emotional labour for them. As boys learn to affirm their masculinities, so they will be more ready to struggle for greater gender equality. As long as they feel guilty and ignored they will not feel appreciated and recognised, and this is a source of bitterness that can so easily be used as part of an anti-feminist backlash. Changing our schools in the ways they deal with boys is an important step on the path towards greater gender equality.

To conclude, I would suggest the following steps should be taken to improve boys' schooling:

- We should learn from the experience of Denmark[4] about the importance of decent nursery provision which allows boys to experience a whole range of activities. It seems as if co-education from an early age helps establish easier gender relations. At the moment, the lack of provision of nursery education in Britain is putting four-year-olds into reception classes in schools. This leads to early institutionalisation which means that, by the time boys are 12, they are often sick of school and develop an anti-school culture. It might well be that we send boys to school too early and for too long hours — and then get surprised when they truant;
- Teachers need to feel validated for the work they do, and male teachers need to be encouraged to think more about issues in relation to men and masculinities, so they might have more sympathy for what boys are going through;
- We need to think about mentoring (where older pupils might also take on the role of mentors) because of the gulf that separates generations which can mean that teachers have little sense of what boys are experiencing and feeling;
- It might be helpful to bring groups into school that can help provide a space for more open emotional exploration, so that boys are given a chance of working through some of the issues that are so often bottled up and which can block learning;
- We need to find ways of validating the diversity of subjects that are available at school so that they are not, as at present, evaluated against a single standard of academic performance. So often, this leaves boys with a sense of failure, which could

get exacerbated with the increased competitiveness in school cultures;
- We need to think of positive ways of affirming male identities in school, so that we challenge the homophobic culture that develops in many schools;
- School is often a hard and brutal environment in which boys are expected to put up with things and prove themselves through not complaining. We need to develop a shift in school culture, in which secondary schools begin to learn from the more open methods employed within primary schools (often, boys feel betrayed as the recognition they have enjoyed in their primary schools is no longer available in the more formalised secondary school setting);
- We need to think again about the size and impersonality of secondary schools, which were formerly developed to sustain a viable sixth form: with the establishment of sixth form colleges, we need to rethink what size of schools we need, especially given the fragmentation of communities within the inner cities;
- At the moment, we are failing too many boys, and we have to be ready to listen to them more in order to learn how we can best begin to change schooling.

FOOTNOTES

1. This article is an edited version of a longer paper titled 'Boys, Schooling and Masculinities'.
2. Seidler, V.J. 'Recreating Sexual Politics: Men, Feminism and Politics', London: Routledge (1991).
3. Bly, R. 'Iron John: A Book About Men', Reading Ma.: Addison-Wesley (1990).
4. In Denmark, children do not enter school before the ages of six and seven, and then attend small co-educational schools where relationships between the sexes can be formed.

Moving Away from Power: Family, Care, Sexuality, Violence and Organisations

Jeff Hearn

Jeff Hearn has been involved in men's groups and anti-sexist activities and in researching and writing on men since 1978. His publications include 'Sex at Work' (with Wendy Parkin), 'The Gender of Oppression' and 'Men in the Public Eye', and he has co-edited 'The Sexuality of Organization', 'Taking Child Abuse Seriously', 'Men, Masculinities and Social Theory', 'Violence and Gender Relations', and 'Men as Managers, Managers as Men'. He is Professorial Research Fellow in the Faculty of Economic and Social Studies, University of Manchester (based in the School of Social Policy), and is currently researching violence and organisations.

There are two paradoxes that currently beset men. First, men's power and dominance remains virtually unchanged, and may even have become intensified in some respects; yet men's power is constantly being challenged, fragmented, and even transformed. And second, men are more than ever being affirmed as 'men', whilst, at the same time, the experience of being a man is subject to questioning and acute fracturing[1]. Men's situation

— and particularly men's power — is a complex mixture of change and no-change.

The maintenance of men's power, and men's use and abuse of power, is purely and simply unjust. It exerts massive damage on women and children in terms of direct and indirect controls, removal of options and opportunities, use of violence and abuse, more subtle definitions of their realities, and so on. In a different, and certainly lesser, way, some men — perhaps all men — may also be damaged by competition between men, hierarchies of some men over others, their treatment as boys and self-violation. In the light of this, what is to be done about men and men's power? What are men to do — or not do? How are men to move away from power? Towards what do men need to move? What is next for men?

Well, perhaps the first thing to say is that we need to be careful of falling for instant panaceas or simple solutions or over-insistent grand plans. Just as men's relationship to feminism is likely to remain problematic[2], so it is probably accurate to foresee men's movement away from power as problematic and uneven. It is highly unlikely that a radically new 'sexual contract', or 'gender contract', will suddenly arrive; rather, we can expect a series of temporary 'settlements' or 'truces' within a difficult long-term process, burdened by the weight and oppressions of history.

Secondly, there is a need to say something specifically about the changing context of 'the world' for men's lives and power. While, for most men, life remains local in the way it is lived, the forces that affect it are certainly becoming more transnational in character; globalisation is in place. This is a very complex picture, and one that is often contradictory in its effects. At its simplest, it means that the fate of men and women is increasingly in the hands of social and cultural processes that transcend the nation. These processes often involve racialisation, sexualisation, and the reproduction of other massive inequalities between 'North' and 'South' and between various 'cores' and 'peripheries'. The idea of the self-contained 'unit' — be it the nation or the individual man — is breaking down.

The third thing to say is that, whatever change in men and men's power is needed, or is advocated, or, indeed, occurs, it can be usefully seen as affecting all areas of social life. These include: education, class, work, employment, race, sexuality, violence, the family, childcare, the state, personal and private life, sport, care, health and illness, age and ageing, birth and death, the body, and so on. Everything, from the most mundane activity — who does the washing up, who answers the phone, who drives the buses — to the most global and international of issues, is up for grabs, is relevant when seeking to move men away from power.

In being asked, "What next for men?", we are being invited to consider how men need to change in order to really make a difference. We are not just concerned with change that is going to produce more of the same; we are interested in ways that men might develop that would bring a substantial change in relations between men, women and children. In this contribution, I shall focus mainly on men's changing relation to the body, their bodies, our bodies. The body is a very important reference point for defining men — indeed, arguably the body is the most important aspect of both formal and informal constructions of gender. Yet, while the body may be the defining feature of men, embodiment is being transformed and challenged through globalisation and new technology — for example, through virtual sex, electronic intimacy, and trafficking of women on the Internet and elsewhere.

A first and fundamental aspect of the politics of the body is men's relationship to fatherhood and 'the family'. Although patriarchy has certainly changed in form over the last century or more, especially through the growth of the state, men's power still resides, at least in part, in the institution of fatherhood. Historically, fatherhood is both a means of possession of, and care for, young people, and an arrangement between men. It has also been, and still is, a way of men living with, being with, being violent to, sexually abusing, caring for and loving particular young people (those that are called 'your own'), and a way of avoiding connection, care and contact with other young people more generally. Above all, fatherhood is an assumption of rights and authority over others — principally women and children, but also other men. Even nice fathers can switch to become nasty ones.

All this has been complicated by increased state intervention in the rights and responsibilities of fatherhood — most obviously through the Child Support Agency and the Children Act, but also, more subtly, through state control of Insemination by Donor. Indeed, the last few years have seen signs of an increase in the rights of fathers, as well as in the assumption that such power and authority are 'natural' and 'normal'. Even a glance through history and across cultures will show this to be extremely problematic.

A man should not have automatic rights in law 'as father' over children (and, indeed, women) simply by virtue of having passed a bit of fluid into the woman's body some years previously and almost regardless of what he does afterwards. Instead of such 'rights', men should have responsibilities toward, and responsible relationships with, children and young people.

These issues become more complicated as men's relationship to families develops over time — how to be positive and responsible to others in families, without asserting the power and authority of the father. This is important in different ways in both short-term and long-term relationships (whether within or without marriage) and with the increasing number of men involved in separation, divorce and reconstituted families of various kinds. There is a clear need for a 'post-marriage' ethics for men. So, a challenge for many men is how to respond to these difficult questions — to love, care for and be friends with young people without drawing on the power of the father — and even to work toward the abolition of that power of fatherhood whilst recognising the reality of responsibilities in our own lives[3].

A second and closely-related aspect of the politics of the body concerns the question of care and caring. The central issue here is how are boys and men to change their practice of caring for others, both physically and emotionally — how are boys and men to be more caring and to do more caring? So often, men's avoidance of caring has been the defining feature of 'being men'. This is clearly structured very much in terms of women doing more caring work, both in private and in public. Boys and men learn not to care for others, and changing this is an important part of the project of socialisation, for example, in the education of boys at home, in school and elsewhere. This should be a major policy development — in nurseries and schools, by government and education authorities, and in higher education — not as an afterthought, or something left to the whims and wishes of individual teachers. Like fatherhood and the family, caring is both a very personal issue and one that is built into wider societal structures and political institutions. It is not 'solved' by increasing day care provision, vital as that is — the problem goes to the very structuring of how men behave, feel, are. It is an area of life that can bring fundamental change for men in the way we experience ourselves; it can also bring about both direct antagonisms (for example, deciding who will stay in or look after someone who is ill) and direct improvements in the quality of relationships. The question of caring also raises the challenge of how men become and do more caring, without just taking over.

A special challenge is how to encourage boys and young men to become more used to the bodily care of others in a way that does not lead to further dominance. I think this has to be attempted, yet with great care and caution — perhaps initially by the encouragement of care in their own families, and, in schools, by the teaching of safety and first aid, and the care of pets and animals, and then moving on, under supervision, to the care of babies, young children, older people, those with disabilities elsewhere. This entails redefining nurturing as normal for boys and young men. More specifically, it involves teaching to boys gentleness and non-erotic forms of touch. However, we need to be alive to the problems with this scenario, for example, in terms of potential abuse. It is not enough to just leave the dominant forces to define boys and men and then pick up the pieces later on. There is an urgent need for positive initiatives that assist the redefinition of boys and men towards care and nurture as central defining features[4]. Thus boys should be taught in schools how to care; caring should be expected and rewarded, and it should form part of the normal National Curriculum.

The next aspect of the politics of the body I want to focus on is sexuality — men's sexuality. This has continued to be severely neglected as a focus for change, except as a reaction to the initiatives of the Right. The central problem is that 'normal male sexuality' is itself highly problematic. In 'The Sexuality Papers'[5], Lal Coveney and her colleagues characterise it in the following ways: power, aggression, penis-orientation, separation of sex from loving emotion, objectification, fetishism, and assumed 'uncontrollability'. These features are not the way men's sexuality is, or has to be, all the time; they refer to the dominant ways in which men's sexuality is represented and reproduced now.

Of all these elements of the politics of the body, sexuality may feel to be the most personal, the most 'one's own'. Yet it is also structural. For example, heterosexuality is as much a social institution as marriage. Heterosexist culture and homophobia continue to abound. Men's domination of sex and sexuality, and the reduction of sex to intercourse, to ejaculation, to orgasm are again, like fatherhood, "just normal, aren't they?". Heterosexual men may often be misogynist: the object of love can be the object of hate. Gay men are not necessarily pro-feminist. Homophobic men may inhabit homosocial pubs, clubs, organisations and workgroups — so what exactly are these sexual loyalties between men?

More broadly, the pressures on the construction of men's sexuality seem to diverge more — the forces of reaction, of the glorification of sexual violence, of Internet sex, of anti-gay politics (most obviously around HIV/AIDS) are ever stronger — while, at the same time, there is a gathering public confidence around sexual progressivism, queer politics, lesbian and gay rights, and even a small anti-sexist politics of heterosexuality.

Furthermore, anti-gay politics can damage gay men, bisexual and heterosexual men, as well as women. They can be physically dangerous and personally undermining for gay men. Heterosexual men may come out or change to being gay; less obviously to some, there is the gay part or gayness of heterosexual men. So heterosexual men need to support gay men, partly for political principles of equality and justice, and partly for self-interest.

Again, in all of this, there is a need to develop an important educational debate and practice around sex and sexuality. This has to affirm different sexualities, work towards non-oppressive sexualities, support young gays, and engage with the real dilemmas that young people face in their everyday lives. For young men, this means promoting — in schools and elsewhere — intimate and sexual relationships that are non-threatening, non-oppressive and responsible[6]. More generally, men need to change our sexuality, both individually and collectively. There is, of course, an urgent need to abolish discriminatory legislation against young gays (around the age of consent), same-sex sexuality more generally (Section 28), and older gays (around pensions, property rights and so on). A major challenge is to acknowledge our sexuality, and even be proud of it, without being oppressively sexual or sexually oppressive. There should be 'zero tolerance'[7] of sexual violence, sexual abuse and sexual harassment. We have to move towards non-oppressive and non-violent sexualities. What chance is there for real change in men without that?

This brings us onto the next arena of the politics of the body, and in some ways, the most difficult — violence, men's violence. As will already be apparent from the previous discussion, it is not possible to make a strict separation between men's sexuality and men's violence, in this society at least. A lot of what men do needs to be re-labelled as violence. This would include child abuse, child sexual abuse, domestic violence, rioting, crime, pornography, policing, soldiering, wars, football hooliganism, public disorder. Similarly, a lot of violence needs to be understood as men's conscious, deliberate actions and as forms, or examples, of particular masculinities. Men's violence to women, children, young people, and each other — what is seen as the 'normal' behaviour of certain men and boys, as fathers, teachers, workmates, school colleagues and so on, in reproducing ordinary, everyday violence — needs, indeed demands, not just patching up the problem, but the changing of men and 'normal masculinity'.

Men's violence is about both violence to women, children, young people, and each other, and, often less obviously, violence to the self — in self-brutalisation and the denial of and 'victory over' the non-violent parts of ourselves. Violence doesn't do us any good! Violence may bring power and dominance, but it can also bring unhappiness and self-destruction. We need to recognise our own violence and potential violence, whilst opposing and stopping violence — in war, armies, initiation ceremonies, bullying, unsafe working conditions, personal relationships, and being on the street. Campaigns against such initiations, lack of safety at work, bullying and violence at work, are good ways of bringing together boys and men concerned to work against sexism, as well as trade unions, anti-racist and other interested groups.

In reducing and opposing men's violence, a necessary first thing to do is to make a national commitment against violence. This should be an absolutely central plank of the policies of the national political parties. The recent Gulbenkian Foundation Commission Report, 'Children and Violence'[8], made as its first priority recommendation:

"Individuals, communities and government at all levels should adopt a 'Commitment to non-violence', of similar standing to existing commitments to 'equal opportunities'."

The Report continued:

"The aims of the commitment are to work towards a society in which individuals, communities and government share non-violent values and resolve conflict by non-violent means. Building such a society involves, in particular, reducing and preventing violence involving children, by developing:

- understanding of the factors which interact to increase the potential for violence involving children, and those which prevent children from becoming violent
- action to prevent violence involving children in all services and work with families and children
- consistent disavowal of all forms of inter-personal violence — in particular by opinion-leaders."

Thus governmental and other policies and strategies should tell boys and men not to be violent, should advocate policies that encourage men to behave in ways that facilitate women's equality, and make it clear that the realisation of such changes depends partly on men in politics and policy-making, and their own understanding of their gendered actions.

More specifically, there is now increasing interest in policies that try to stop men's violence directly, such as programmes for men who are known to have been violent to women. Such programmes remain controversial in terms of underlying philosophy, methods of change and resource basis. In recent years, there has been a developing critique of approaches that are narrowly psychological or focused on anger management, and, instead, a movement towards those based on a 'power and control' model that is pro-feminist in orientation[9]. The latter kinds of programmes can be a significant and effective initiative, especially when linked to wider educational and political change. A crucial and current issue is whether such programmes should become Court-mandated and a responsibility of the Probation Service, rather than accessed on a voluntary basis. Any such development needs to carefully screen out men who have no interest whatsoever in change and who may even use programmes to learn new forms of violence and control. Even more importantly, any innovations for men have to be supplements to broaden major public policy changes, including consistent police prosecution policy and practice; inter-agency work for women experiencing violence; improved housing provision for women; and full state support for Women's Aid and other projects for women.

Finally, I want to say something briefly about organisations and institutions, and men's place within them. The politics of the body is not just conducted in private, in the home, in the domestic sphere — it also operates very much in the public world of work and other organisations. When men are in organisations, we continue to have a relationship with families and domestic lives; similarly, workplaces are, or can also be, places of nurture, sexuality and violence. In particular, men remain in control of most powerful organisations, whether state, capitalist or third sector; this is especially so in terms of men's continued domination of top management[10]. There is a long history of men in management being uncaring, sexually oppressive and even violent and abusive, without much comeback. Such managerial men also have the task of overseeing and underwriting the behaviour of other men in their charge. Whether men are interested in reproducing or challenging sexism, organisations are major arenas for the future of the politics of the body. Transforming organisations involves transforming management, and that, in turn, entails transforming men and masculinities. It is in organisations that the public doing of gender, the public politics of the body, is predominantly done and re-done. Furthermore, organisations and their control are fundamentally important — and becoming even more important, with the development of globalisation through multi-nationals, transnational governmental institutions, worldwide media and information networks, and so on.

Accordingly, changing men's place, position and power in organisations, and particularly management, is a necessary priority for the politics of the body on a world scale. It is also vital in the changing of men's relationship to fatherhood and the family — and so this brings us back full circle to the private, the domestic and the personal.

All of these issues are important for what it means to be a 'man' in this society. However, they all remain neglected in what is generally defined as 'politics'. Transforming what we understand by politics is part of transforming men. All of the issues are both profoundly structural and intensely personal. Each can prompt great depths of negativity — feelings of hopelessness, terribleness, desperation — as well as being arenas of possible positive change and hope. Each is a way of unifying men as a class, with different interests to women, and dividing men from each other — old from young, heterosexual from gay, healthy from unwell, and so on. Each is a means of oppressing women, children and young people, and a way of relating to other men. And each represents an avenue for men opposing oppression, supporting feminist initiatives, and changing ourselves and each other.

REFERENCES

1. Hearn, J. 'Men in the Public Eye', London and New York: Routledge (1992).
2. Hearn, J. "The personal, the political, the theoretical: the case of men's sexuality and sexual violence" in Porter, D. (ed.) 'Between Men and Feminism', London and New York: Routledge (1992).

3. Hearn, J. 'Birth and Afterbirth: A Materialist Account', London: 'Achilles Heel' (1983); "Childbirth, men and the problem of fatherhood" in 'Radical Community Medicine, 15' (1984); 'The Gender of Oppression', Brighton/New York: Wheatsheaf/St Martin's (1987).

4. Jackson, D. and Salisbury, J. 'Changing Macho Values. Practical Ways of Working with Adolescent Boys', Basingstoke: Falmer (1996).

5. Coveney, L., Jackson, M., Jeffreys, S., Kaye, L. and Mahoney, P. 'The Sexuality Papers', London: Hutchinson (1984).

6. Jackson, D. and Salisbury, J. ibid. (1996).

7. Zero Tolerance is a media, poster and advertising campaign against men's violence to women and children, originally sponsored by Edinburgh City Council, and since adopted in other parts of Britain.

8. Gulbenkian Foundation Commission Report 'Children and Violence', London: Calouste Gulbenkian Foundation (1995).

9. Adams, D. "Treatment models of men who batter: a profeminist analysis" in Yllo, K. and Bograd, M. (eds.) 'Feminist Perspectives on Wife Abuse', Newbury Park, Ca. and London: Sage (1988); Edelson, J.L. and Tolman, R.M. 'Intervention for Men who Batter', Newbury Park, Ca. and London: Sage (1992); Caesar, P.L. and Hamberger, L.K. (eds.) 'Treating Men who Batter', New York: Springer (1989); Pence, E. and Paymar, M. 'Power and Control: Tactics of Men Who Batter. An Educational Curriculum', Duluth, Mn.: Minnesota Program Development (1986); Gondolf, E.W. and Russell, D. 'The case against anger control treatment programs for batterers' in 'Response, 9, 3' (1986); Fawcett, B., Featherstone, B., Hearn, J. and Toft, C. (eds.) 'Violence and Gender Relations', London and Thousand Oaks, Ca.: Sage (1996)

10. Collinson, D.L. and Hearn, J. "Naming men as men: implications for work, organization and management" in 'Gender, Work and Organization, 1, 1' (1994); Hearn, J. "Changing men and changing managements: social change, social research and social action" in Davidson, M.J. and Burke, R. (eds.) 'Women in Management — Current Research Issues', London: Paul Chapman (1994); Collinson, D. and Hearn, J. (eds.) 'Men as Managers, Managers as Men', London and Thousand Oaks, Ca.: Sage (1996).

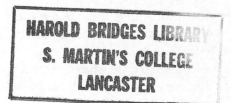

Sharing Our Powers and Aspirations

Lindsay Neil

Lindsay Neil is a freelance consultant working mainly in the sexual health field, both in the UK and overseas. She was previously Director of Sexual Health at the Health Education Authority, and, before that, worked on a national strategy for post-16 education at the Further Education Unit. With a son and daughter both now in their early 20's, Lindsay has a longlasting interest in the impact of gender on people's lives.

What is a middle-aged wife and mother doing writing in a book about men? This is a reasonable question, and, indeed, typifies my self-questioning whenever I'm tempted to comment on anything to do with men. After all, how do I feel when men presume to comment on women?

In this essay, I am not setting out to present a well-researched and argued case for anything. What I am setting out to do is air some of the things that have been troubling me, in the hope that these will act as a useful irritant in the current debate. I want to declare my interest in men, and use my own experiences and understandings to pose yet more questions — and some of them will be put quite starkly in order to emphasise the points I'm trying to make.

I have a bold answer to the question posed by this book title: that we closely investigate how 'masculinity' develops, or we do nothing at all (if we choose the latter, then it will mean more of the same dismal statistics about men's health, levels of criminality, educational achievement, domestic and sexual violence, and the generalised view that men don't make good fathers).

I am interpreting 'masculinity' as the catch-all term which covers the many and varied influences which create the expectations we all have of men. I want to concentrate on drawing attention to some of the more awkward questions about where many of these influences come from. These are questions which have not always endeared me to my female friends and colleagues, and which have often caused my male friends and colleagues to wonder if I've left my feminist principles on the bus.

I'm emboldened to say all of this because I'm rather tired of being invited to anguish about why men eat and drink (in kind and quantity) more than is good for them; grow up not being able to remember their collar size or their mothers' birthdays; occupy so much police and schoolteacher time; or comprehensively 'fail' to be good fathers.

There are personal and professional reasons why I'm in this book, and, as with most people, these cover some common ground. While I'm clear about the boundaries, I know there are times when I wander over them.

The most public of my 'boundary wanderings' was at an international AIDS conference. I was sitting in a workshop which was titled 'Women'. I listened to a series of presentations where men — particularly young men — were, at best, blamed and, at worst, ridiculed for the state of the world's sexual health. I could sit still for only so long before I felt the need to stand up and comment on the many and varied reasons why men behave in the many and varied ways that they do in their sexual relationships with women — and I quoted a few bits of research. So, for instance, we have a conventional belief that men do not use condoms because they think it de-sensitises their sexual experience, when, in fact, research has suggested that, at least for some men, it is their fears of losing an erection that are paramount, and fussing with a condom adds to these fears so much that they do not use them. Many men will not acknowledge this fear to others, so they say what they have said about sensitivity and everyone then takes this without question. And I said to the assembly, "I am the mother of a young man, as well as the mother of a young woman. I know something of the struggle they both have in their relationships — he no more, and no less, than she".

I wince at the attacks on young men, which are so often made without any apparent attempt to understand why they behave as they do. There is also a willingness among women, and men, to collude with these negative attitudes, and a reluctance to stand up and say, "Yes, but hang on a minute, it isn't quite that simple ... ". I return to this notion of collusion later.

I have the same hopes and aspirations for my son as I have for my daughter. I want them both to have long, happy and healthy lives — and I'm well aware of the evidence that suggests my daughter will outlive her brother. Like many women, I'm living with a man already older than me, who is likely to die when he is younger than I will be when I die. And so I can look forward to at least 10 years of widowhood — and widowhood doesn't appeal to me much.

The personal is really very basic stuff about the people I love, and I admit there are few insights to be gained from any of it. I do, however, think it's useful to remind ourselves of simple feelings like that when we move into the area of the work we're paid to do. What can those women and men have been thinking about at that AIDS conference — did none of them have sons, husbands, brothers; had the men never considered themselves as human beings, as well as health workers?

I am not suggesting that we should muddle our personal and our professional lives. That, in itself, is a constant issue for the 'caring professions', and there is very proper concern for such things as co-dependency between workers and people in vulnerable situations. What I am suggesting is that, in our reasonable professional pursuit of the scientific and objective, we don't ignore the obvious, which is all around us. It is one thing to quote from research on the impact of homelessness on young men, but don't forget that the guy selling the *Big Issue* is at the more confident end of people in that situation. The well-researched connection between low expectations, poor self-esteem, youth unemployment and some highly anti-social behaviours, is also the stuff of our local concern for safety on the streets, disruption in schools and, in extreme cases, the flight of the middle classes from certain residential areas and certain schools.

I appreciate that making the connection between poverty and social disturbance is not currently fashionable. It's also worth remembering that, if they ever were, the middle classes are no longer protected from low expectations, poor self-esteem, unemployment or anti-social behaviour; and that the bad behaviour of young, affluent men is more often the subject of tabloid newspaper reports than social research. One has to wonder why that is the case. Anyway, I've never been a fashion follower.

My point is that we risk missing both the very obvious and the very subtle if we totally disconnect our professional lives from our personal experiences, and the reasons any of us behave the way we do are both obvious and subtle.

I have a somewhat literal turn of mind, typical of my star sign, and the evidence that women live longer; have physically and emotionally healthier lives than men; and, generally and relatively speaking, stay out of big trouble, simply shrieks at me. I am equally struck by the well-researched evidence that much of this is open to change; the potential individual and collective gain in shifting men's lifestyles is massive (for instance, when men give up smoking, there is an increase in their general well-being; they feel healthier; they have more fun with their kids; they feel better about themselves; everybody benefits). So what's the problem, or, more to the point, why does there remain a problem?

After all, for men themselves, the cost/benefit analysis must be favourable. For a slight shift in your behaviour, you can live longer, healthier lives; have warm and loving relationships; make strong and life-enhancing contributions to society; stay in work and out of prison. In that wonderfully simplistic view, I'm even allowing for the structural changes which affect all our job prospects. If it's that obvious, how come things are getting worse and not better?

My adult years have seen major global struggles to balance up society, as various as Martin Luther King's dream, Nelson Mandela in a Springbok rugby shirt, abortion reform and the decriminalisation of homosexuality. And yet, despite legislation, equal opportunities policies galore and even quotas, how come there have been so few sustainable gains? In addition to disappointment about the effort and relative benefits of all this, I am dismayed by the antagonism towards equal opportunities, caught up as it now is in the gimmicky phrase of 'political correctness'. Even before the dread term gained such currency in the UK, I had been searching, with others, for some answer to the questions — how come so little changes? is this a life's work? can I be bothered? — and a dozen other related worries.

Clearly, power in its many forms has played, does play and will always play a part in the social behaviour of people. However, it seems to me that we have sometimes taken a too simplistic view of this as it influences relationships between women and men. I would go so far as to suggest that we have played down, or even ignored, or denied, that most women do have considerable power. In the same way as we know that, for men, there are significant differences between the public and the private in terms of their behaviour, I would argue that men have public power, while women have private power. This is not to discount the misuse of power in private by some men, which includes physical violence towards women and children. But I think we cannot afford to reduce the analysis of power down to saying that men have all the power, and women have no power.

With hindsight, I can explain how I arrived at my suggestion that we start with masculinity. In the mid 1980's, I read a slim booklet from the Further Education Unit, which reported on a very modest piece of work which looked at young women and their images of themselves. They had used social construct theory to describe the inevitability of what the predominant image was. Now, that may have been glaringly obvious to others, but I have to admit it was novel to me. If it was so obvious to others, then how come the piece of work, and subsequently the slim booklet, attracted so little attention from people who were, in theory at least, concerned about these sort of things? Therein lies a clue.

The second influential bit of reading came shortly after that. I can no longer remember how I came across 'Jocasta's Children'[1]. I do remember how uncomfortable it made me feel, to the extent that, although compelled to read and re-read pages, I was reluctant to turn pages over for fear of reading more that disturbed me. The principle point that I took out of the book is very simple: how come we bring our little girls up so differently from how we bring up our little boys?

Obvious isn't it — but just like the FEU booklet, how come nobody takes any notice of it? The only people I know who've read 'Jocasta's Children' are the people who have borrowed my copy.

The third influential piece of reading was Joan Smith's 'Misogynies'[2]. (An interesting bit of information: the spellcheck on my personal computer didn't recognise 'misogyny' or 'misogynist' — it does now. Funny that). Smith's essays are about appalling attitudes, some of which made my hair stand on end. No doubt she went looking for stories that would do just that, and she found them from a wide range of places and times. *The Observer* review correctly said, " ... this disturbing collection of essays ... convinces and chills".

To mention three pieces of writing is to simplify a complicated, and sometimes harrowing, process of realisation. Part of the process was examining my own attitudes, assumptions and expectations. It was fortunate that I happened across an admittedly small collection of people who were doing the same thing for themselves at that time. It was very helpful to share, and it was also very helpful that we were both women and men.

So, what is it that I'm suggesting? I'm suggesting that, nature apart, society places strong constraints on the way we all live out our lives. This is not a new thought, and it is popularly and relatively harmlessly termed 'social expectations'. However, in my view, these constraints also carry potentially oppressive and corrosive elements, which we are reluctant to 'see'. An example of this is our general acceptance as the norm the way that (particularly young) men abuse alcohol and drugs. By not acknowledging these elements as harmful and negative, we are colluding with them.

I'm also suggesting that there are two 'facts' which we hold at one and the same time, and which point up, starkly in my view, a major (but largely unspoken about) causal link. On the one hand, it is widely accepted that the early years of childhood are hugely influential in establishing our attitudes. It is also widely known (but little spoken about) that a significant proportion of men grow up dreading, fearing or hating women, at worst. At best, another significant proportion grow up refusing to take responsibility for remembering their collar size, their mother's birthday, and so on.

My point is that you cannot accept the first without accepting that the second is, at least in significant part, a consequence. And here is something which rubs uncomfortably on my feminist principles. By far the greatest influence on the early years of our sons, are women — the mother, her mother, sisters, aunts, and her female friends. These sons then spend most of their primary school years in the tender loving care of female teachers, dinner ladies and the school nurse (ever come across a male school nurse?). Unless we look at what this community of women is doing, we will make little progress in understanding why men are as they are.

I'm driven to the conclusion that there is collusion going on in the raising of our sons. We don't seem to raise our daughters to hate/fear/dread men, although many women develop some or all of those feelings as a result of their experiences of men. And this could be circular — if we didn't raise men to hate/fear/dread women, then, probably, women would not have cause to hate/fear/dread men.

We also cannot go on ignoring the influence of gender on the professions. We would not dream of suggesting that the experience of being a teacher, doctor, health worker or police officer in this country is not influenced by also being black. Not being white is a significant factor on the way you are perceived.

Given how obvious this is, how come we don't also consider the impact of being male, or being female, on some of those roles? For example, how come so many men completely disregard what they are allegedly 'taught' in personal and social education? How come the vast majority of our personal and social education, both formal and informal, is carried out by women?

To take another example, we would agree, I'm sure, that, at the very least, it is unusual to find a male nursery school teacher. What is it about that that we are not saying — do we fundamentally believe that men are unsuitable, untrustworthy, even 'un-natural' to want to pursue such a line of employment? Or is this fundamentally about the power of women?

We know statistically that, if a man has an overwhelming desire to be a head teacher, he'd do very well to start off as a primary teacher — the odds are extraordinarily favourable to him. But again, I must question whether this is entirely due to the character of man, or whether there might be something going on here which is about the character of woman.

Even accepting the very real political and economically-driven changes of recent years, the questions just tumble out. If the questions are obvious, which I think most of them are, then I have to report that they aren't always welcome, and I have to ask why I'm still asking them.

Are we serious about wanting to understand why our young men growing up seem to be struggling? How serious are we about shifting the power relationships between heterosexual men and women? What are the real vested interests operating here; and what would the actual consequences of major changes be? How honest can we be?

What is the power shift that would be needed to make the changes that so many of us, personally and professionally, feel are so strongly needed? Perhaps we should reconsider whether a shift in power is what is required after all. My own view is that we all have power and that, too often, we misuse this. We need to be less concerned with shifting power, than ensuring that power is not misused by women or men.

Another way of viewing this is to consider how we can shift the perception that, for men's circumstances to improve, women's must have to deteriorate. Instead of describing things in terms of a battleground, we should be explaining them in a win/win way, that enables women to acknowledge that it is in our interest for men to get special attention, at least for a while. We may then find that it is never in the interests of women that men should get that kind of special attention — but I think that is unlikely.

I think we can apply some 'science' to all of this, which may help us reach some conclusions about what we should be doing, what we can do, and crucially, what we are prepared to do.

We can start by challenging all the assumptions we're currently working with and designing a new set of screens to filter our perceptions through (for example, the assumption that marriage is good for men's health — is that the case, or is it just that a warm and caring physical and emotional relationship per se is good for men's health? Other examples would be the assumptions around condom use and the misuse of drugs stated earlier — let's ensure that these assumptions have some grounding before we base our actions on them). We can remind ourselves how much we already know, personally and professionally, about collusion and complicity in behaviour patterns, both good and bad. And we can look critically at how we can apply that to how we are raising our young.

This is why I make the plea to look very closely at social constructs of masculinity and also of femininity. But we can only do this if we are seriously interested in turning the vast knowledge we actually have into the necessary changes to men's behaviour, in order to make the desirable change in men's lifestyles. I'm suggesting that we need to re-draft the social rules which determine what is, and what is not, a proper way to behave, and, recognising that previous approaches have had only limited success, to approach this in a novel way. One central 're-draft' is that we stop confrontation where it is unnecessary: we have based too much on a hierarchy of need ("Men's gains are women's losses"), we have become very sophisticated in 'the sex war', but we have driven underground some of the important and difficult issues because of this basic assumption about the relationship between the sexes.

It is difficult to know how to get through the conventional ways to think about our behaviour, and I can only think that we should review, with a view to discarding, the ideology which has got us — and then kept us — in a state where the relationships between women and men are described in terms of relative power.

I don't believe I am naive. I spent many exciting years when I saw myself as an activist, and my daughter and I rattled the fencing around Greenham Common more than once. But, working as I do in sexual health, I've long since passed the point where I can sit and listen to snipes about men's behaviour, and suggestions that 'they' need more information or extended opening times for the family planning clinic. As I said earlier — "Yes, but hang on a minute, it isn't quite that simple ...".

I want to end on the personal. How could I possibly want my daughter to have more out of her life, than I want my son to have out of his? How can their father possibly want more for one than for the other? How can anybody want more for one than for the other?

REFERENCES

1. Christian Olivier. 'Jocasta's Children — The Imprint of the Mother', London: Routledge, (1988).
2. Smith, J. 'Misogynies', London: Faber and Faber, (1989).

Changing the Way Men Lead

Michael Simmons

Michael Simmons is the founder of Simmons Consulting and Training and is a total systems consultant, working with a wide variety of organisations on developing new approaches to improving their effectiveness. His work includes preparing senior women and men to become 'leaders of transformation'. He is the author of 'A New Leadership for Women and Men — Building an Inclusive Organisation', to be published by Gower Press in July 1996.

I have spent my working life as a management consultant, working with people in organisations towards the stated goals of improving how they manage their business, whether they are in the private or public sector. It's been a good life, and, whilst I would not claim that I have really made much of a difference compared to the vagaries of government policy, the market place or the irrational whims of senior people, I have had the opportunity to work with a lot of people in a lot of different organisations and their underlying desire to do things well, and their care and compassion, have always shone through.

Most of the people that I have worked with have been men. Actually, I would say that, up until 1980, almost everyone I worked with was male, and it was only when I began to work more in the public sector that I came into contact with women in middle and senior positions. Currently, I am working with two organisations in the private sector — one in manufacturing and the other in computer software development — and, in both situations, there is not one senior woman anywhere to be seen. So much for the advancement of women!

In the early 1980's, this led me to the conclusion that I should begin to pay attention to the issue of men and leadership. Since men occupy the great majority of key leadership positions in our society — in fact, it is mostly white, heterosexual, able-bodied men who occupy these positions — I realised that, if I was to contribute something useful, I would have to place the issue of how men lead at the forefront of my work.

This seems to me to be doubly important, because I'm personally not very impressed with what we men actually do with the leadership we have. The quality of the decisions that we make, the way we treat the people who work with us and the effects of the role upon our own lives are not impressive. So much power in the hands of people who function so poorly seems to me to be dangerous in the extreme.

I began to look at the men I worked with, particularly those in senior positions, to identify the core attitudes and behaviours which could be described as 'masculine'. They had a number of characteristics that I liked — the ability to develop a vision of how they would like things to be, a high commitment to achievement, a determination to get things done whatever the costs, and enormous intelligence and skill. However, in discussions with them, it became clear that the way in which they had been brought up and the pressures placed on them as adults, including in their role as leaders, led them to lead in ways that I would consider less than fully functional.

The most important of these are:

— a desire to win at all costs (beat other people), which leads to the setting up of every situation as a competition;
— a need for control and a fear of ambiguity, which leads to a command and control approach to leadership;
— a fear of intimacy with others which leads to disconnection and separation from the people they lead;
— a self-centredness which means that they tend to leave other

people to get on with it: men don't seem to know how to create a climate in which other people can grow, develop and improve;
— a willingness to mistreat themselves, ranging, for example, from overwork to heavy drinking, rather than knowing how to put themselves at the centre of their own leadership.

By comparison, women tend to be 'people orientated'. Judi Marshall, in a paper entitled 'A comparative study of gender and management style'[1], writes:
"The most frequently reported difference (between women and men) is that women managers sometimes scored higher on the supporting dimensions of leadership than do male colleagues and showed a greater concern for relationships".

In a new study[2], she found that women were considerably stronger than men in styles that emphasised teamwork, structuring the situation and consideration for others, while men were more laissez faire in their approach.

To me, it seems clear that this 'masculine' approach to leadership is a direct consequence of the way in which we are brought up as young men. The underlying basis for this appears to be a general and almost universal anti-male conditioning, which, I believe, is evident in all western societies. It portrays men as less than fully human, and therefore expendable and exploitable — 'beasts of burden' to be used by society for its own purposes. We are expected to be breadwinners, trained as warriors, and thought likely 'to go out of control' at any moment. We are brought up to consider our sisters as less important and end up becoming the agents of sexism.

My discussions with the men I have worked with have made it clear that this has been the result of a systematic 'gender conditioning'. I believe that people begin life completely 'satisfied' with themselves and 'expect' others to be completely 'satisfied' too. As the excuse for conditioning men for their future role in society, therefore, it is necessary to establish a number of attributes and behaviours that describe a 'real man'. This masculine stereotype is then used as the basis for comparison with the way men actually behave — and men are always found wanting.

I have learnt that the process of conditioning occurs in a number of very specific ways. Some of the most important of these that have a bearing on leadership are:

- We are conditioned not to value our own or other people's feelings.
- We are threatened with, and are often the victims of, violence and abuse, particularly if we show signs of weakness.
- We are told that females are inferior, and are ridiculed if we have close relationships with them.
- We are made frightened of close relationships with one another by the fear of being accused of being gay.
- As a consequence, we become isolated and replace our natural desire for close loving relationships and co-operation with the pursuit of achievement and a willingness to put work ahead of our own needs.
- When, finally, in our teenager years, close relationships with women become acceptable, we are taught that their primary role is to provide us with sex and to look after us.
- In our adult years, we are often separated from our own children by our work and the urge to 'get on'.

By the time we are adults, the accumulative effect of this conditioning seems to be to 'booby-trap' us for life, with few of us ever feeling that we make it as real men. Underneath the veneer of confidence and pretension that many of us adopt, we are insecure and uncertain. It is apparent that the men I work with who lead organisations nearly always have a very strong dose of this conditioning — indeed it seems almost a pre-condition for success. (Interestingly enough, the few women I have been able to work closely with at the top of our large enterprises also seem to have been gripped by this training — since they are generally appointed by men in the first place, the men appoint women with a chunk of male gender conditioning to join them in leadership).

The biggest change in relation to these processes in my working lifetime has been the shift towards a global economy and the economic crisis which accompanies it. In a global system driven increasingly by the need to accumulate capital and the constant pursuit of profit, governments and organisations in every country are faced with the need to expand their markets, or reduce their costs, or both. The competitive imperative dictates that the choice between economic growth or failure is built into the system, and, as long as the system is constructed in this way, organisations will have to compete.

The post-war social democratic consensus, with its commitment to a welfare state, a significant range of public services in state control and a level of nationwide planning, has been shredded in the face of such an attack. The solution, advanced mostly by men, is to build a culture which is individualistic, materialistic and 'enterprising'. The attitudes and behaviours which characterise men's leadership are apparently being magnified into statements of government policy and rhetoric — it seems that laissez faire has become the norm, not only in men's general leadership, but in the way men run the world.

This is having a major impact on the lives of ordinary people, and on men in particular. Full-time jobs traditionally done by males have faced a big decline, whilst there has been a huge increase in part-time work aimed at women. Most people now appreciate that no job is secure, and, as a result, the morale of people is low and an underlying climate of fear is common. Moreover, the elimination of many jobs in the name of cost-saving and efficiency has placed huge pressures and increasing stress on those who remain in the workplace. As a consequence, many men seem increasingly uncertain about their role and defensive in their relationships with women. These tensions show themselves in such diverse events as outbreaks of violence by young men at sporting events, the organisation of a backlash against legislation designed to improve women's situation and calls for a return of the family to its 1950's status.

Moreover, the sexism and racism of men in leadership means that these tensions come down with particular force on women and black people. The advancement of women into the workforce has been very largely into part-time and lower-paid jobs, and women remain largely at junior levels and in particular skill ghettos. The constant attacks on particular groups of women (such as young single mothers) provide a cover for the inadequacy of policy and its implementation to resolve fundamental problems. Similarly, black people face a general level of exclusion from the workforce, and are rarely found in middle and senior leadership roles. This has a particularly vicious effect on young black men, who hit back and are then blamed in outspoken terms for their behaviour which, actually, should be seen as a system problem, and not a race or gender issue.

However, as the years have gone on, I have had the opportunity to work with a number of men who have aimed for a fundamental transformation in how they go about their leadership. They are not large in number, but, because of the significance of their position, they have been able to make a real difference to the lives of the people that they lead. This has enabled me to develop my own understanding and thinking about leadership in general, and about how to give men a hand to change in particular.

One chief executive, Ralph, whom I worked with over a period of five years, was an extraordinary man. I believe that he had two or three very important characteristics which all of us need to develop. The first was that he was driven by a deep sense of love. He was a working-class Jewish man and, in everything that he did, he brought a passion and deep joy that was compulsive and energising for the people around him.

A second important characteristic was that he had a high level of self-awareness and knowledge. In a previous job, he had felt himself unable to cope and had decided upon a series of work-orientated sessions with a psycho-therapist. This led him to a profound understanding of his own motivations, which he then used to check his own behaviour. It also meant that he was deeply compassionate towards the difficulties of the people he led.

A third characteristic was his commitment to developing his people. He met each manager who worked for him on his own for a day every three months. He spent a half-day preparing, and then talked through every aspect of their work. He wasn't afraid of talking honestly, and he understood that sometimes he himself was causing the difficulties.

Another old friend, Cliff, led a local government training organisation. I remember him talking about a situation where he was completely out of his depth and unable to think out a correct way forward. Rather than keeping up appearances and pretending, he pulled his management team together and asked for their help. This was an important decision to be vulnerable, and he discovered that they thought all the more of him and gathered round to work out an excellent solution to which they could all be committed.

A white man, Cliff has always made anti-racism a priority in his leadership. He has always had close relationships with black people in his life, and, in the two organisations I have known him lead, he has worked energetically to make sure that black people figure in a significant way. More than that, he has called on the assistance of expert black trainers to increase everyone's awareness about the importance of racism and how to tackle it.

Yet another powerful man, Mike, is the director of a social services department. His strongest commitment is about putting people at the heart of everything he does. He cares passionately about public services and making them work well. He has written: "Management and leadership boil down to working with and through people" and "The best policies, practices and induction programmes are worthless if the people using them are not committed to delivering good services. Failure to work co-operatively and flexibly will lead to services failing users".

He builds close relationships with everyone who works with him. He is open and honest and big-hearted, and he defends people from attack, whilst putting his foot down with 'tough love' when things need to change.

I recall Simon, the director of a research agency, taking his first steps towards understanding the situation the women in his organisation face. After attending a training event with me for women and men on developing a new leadership initiative, he returned to work and began a series of weekly afternoon meetings with small groups of women to give them the opportunity to talk about their experience of working in the agency. In one session, he was told by one woman of how she had faced sexual harassment over a lengthy period of time, but had kept it hidden because she was frightened of what would happen if she spoke up. He was absolutely flabbergasted and appalled — he took immediate action to put the situation right and then instituted the development of an agency-wide policy on harassment, including counselling support for those who were victims.

One of the most important issues is sharing childcare. Traditionally, women seem expected to take on 100% responsibility for planning and resourcing childcare. However, in meetings with Alan, chief executive of an NHS trust, we have twice transferred meetings from his office to his house, as he was staying home to look after his son who was ill because his wife needed to be at work.

The costs of taking on this kind of leadership are considerable. Such men are often viewed with some cynicism by colleagues. Refusing to tread the path of competition and aloofness can look weak in a culture of rabid individualism. It can be judged as reason to not offer promotion and as explanation for mistakes or occasional failure. Even many women like men to appear strong and dynamic, and the decision to be vulnerable risks people slipping into complaining about lack of leadership.

Building close, dependable relationships is a road that always carries some dangers. If a male leader gets close with women colleagues, he risks rumours about having an affair. If he builds a close relationship with the men he works with, he risks being described as gay.

Some 10 years ago, I created a little organisation called the Network for a New Men's Leadership to develop policy and provide development in this area. We have offered at least two training courses every year, and people have come from all over the world to attend; there have rarely been less than 20 participants, and, on one occasion, we had 80 men present. We have had specialist workshops on eliminating racism for black men and white men, on eliminating anti-Irish prejudice for Irish men and others, and on eliminating homophobia and anti-gay oppression for gay men, bi-sexual men and straight men. We have had some five or six workshops for men who are active in the labour movement. We had a workshop for men in Scotland with 50 men present, and many men came from Northern Ireland to our workshops in England. At one point, we had small groups meeting in many different parts of the country.

Nevertheless, the numbers of men who take on this new approach to leadership, especially at senior levels, remains small. My long-term vision that we would develop a new leadership for men within all kinds of organisations, ranging from government to the private sector to the trades union movement, has not been fulfilled to my satisfaction. Moreover, we have been unable to create a widespread understanding amongst the people (particularly men) who have responsibility for the systematic development of leaders of the importance of working with men on these issues. A number of us have worked hard, some progress has been made, but much remains to be done.

The priority is still to assist men in key positions to develop a self-consciousness of their own approach to leadership. Secondly, to help them understand that their approach is very likely to be the product of how they have been brought up and the conditioning they have received as men. Thirdly, to show them that their approach is neither the only way, nor, often, the best. All in all, I am optimistic that we can get men to take these steps — despite the difficulties, the times require men to develop a new leadership, and I am sure that, although our numbers are small, there are enough of us with a sufficient comprehension about the direction we need to go in to lead the remainder.

REFERENCES

1. Marshall, J. "A comparative study of gender and management style" in Management Development Review, vol 5, 1, (1992).
2. Marshall, J. ibid.

Overturning the Cruel Joke
(An interview with Malcolm Wicks MP)

Malcolm Wicks is the Labour MP for Croydon North West and the member of the Opposition's Social Security Team with responsibility for the Child Support Agency and family benefits. He is also Labour spokesperson on family policy. His Private Members Bill, now the Carers (Recognition and Services) Act 1995, came into force in April 1996. Before the last Election, he was Founder Director of the Family Policy Studies Centre.

Let's start generally: how do you understand the evidence presented at the start of this book?

The first thing to say is that much of the debate — whether it is around family, children or care — sooner or later is translated into a debate about women's roles. I have always thought this unhelpful and that we also need to discuss things in terms of men. Clearly, if we are to build a better society, whether the subject is work, or care, or whatever, we need to talk in terms of both men and women. It is very difficult to know absolutely what is going on because, on the one hand, you have a changing relationship between men and women in society, and, on the other hand, you have profound economic and employment changes which are impacting sometimes differentially on men and women. Also, we have a great revolution in our understanding of the welfare state. Many of the big challenges facing us, whether it is how to invest more in our children (both financially and in terms of time), or how we truly create a community care system for old people, have profound consequences for men and women.

Let's get more specific; let's take employment trends.

If the role of women is changing in society (sometimes for the better, but not always), then the question for men is, what is their role? I don't think we should over-exaggerate this, because there are many men who are still in fairly conventional employment, so some of the analysis about globalisation and flexible labour markets, I suspect, has a kind of exaggerated tinge to it. Nevertheless, many men don't have the role that they used to have.

Take, for example, young men. For both young men and women, life is tougher than it used to be, and it is not so clear now what you do when you leave school. Nevertheless, there is a lot of evidence that, for some disadvantaged males, there is an absence of a role now (this may also be true for some of the young women, but I think it is more of an issue for young men). I would point to a sort of two-way pull on adolescence. Once upon a time, adolescence was thought to last for a few years: now, for some men, it may last almost a decade or more. I say it is a two-way stretch because, on the one hand, young people have, for example, sex earlier, and they might meddle in drugs at young ages. They experience aspects of adulthood earlier than previous generations. Adolescence used to last for a few years and then young men would get a job or an apprenticeship. In the early 1970's, 60% of 16-year-olds left school and got a job. A boy working as an apprentice alongside men would soon be knocked into shape, would be introduced into an adult world.

Now what happens to those who leave school at 16 on training courses? They don't get apprenticeships, they don't get jobs — what is their role? It is visible; you see kids hanging around on street corners, they are not 16 or 17, they are 22 or 23, and they are still acting as adolescents, at risk of getting involved in criminal behaviour, vandalism, drug addictions or whatever it may be. I think, for some men now, there is this extraordinary problem of not being able to grow up.

What about young women?

I don't think we have clear enough evidence yet, but one hypothesis is that, for some young women in very adverse social and economic circumstances, either in a planned or probably unplanned way — or somewhere in the middle — some of those young women see that the only 'career' available to them is to become a mother. Some might argue this is one bright spot in an otherwise dreary world. With no jobs, no good training, a child gives them a role and status.

Public opinion is, of course, pretty hostile — the view that they get allocated a council flat and obtain Social Security entitlements. I suspect that, for every one young woman who plans this, there are about 20 or 30 who will stumble through a casual relationship in a much more unplanned way. The evidence from the sixties shows that a young woman who became pregnant would have married the man. Now she doesn't — in six out of 10 cases, she has the baby, while in three or so out of 10 cases she has an abortion. But where are the men in all this? It may be that part of the answer to this is that no sensible young woman will marry the man, because he is not a good prospect, he hasn't got a job. Especially if the man is still in the middle of that prolonged period of adolescence and hasn't got any prospect of housing and still prefers to go out with his mates and hang around, how attractive a figure is he really?

Are you arguing that this is an issue of transition — if boys moved out of school into a job, that this would knock them into shape?

Yes, we have certainly lost it for some, although, when I talk about this group, I am not saying 100% of young males. A vast percentage of young males are in education, higher education, some are getting decent training and some are getting jobs, so we are talking about a minority, but a significant minority.

The recent Demos Report[1] suggested that what was a comparatively small minority of alienated young people was rapidly growing.

I haven't got a figure in my head, but one's instinct suggests that it is growing and that it impacts, for example, on school exclusions, as you mentioned in your evidence. At a time when politicians and the Press are demanding higher performances from school, my instincts tell me that schools are becoming less tolerant of the disruptive child, less willing and able to invest resources in that child and more willing to exclude that child. With the growth of grant-maintained schools, they are in the happy situation of excluding children, but not having to take in some of the exclusions from other schools.

So, what is the cause and what is the effect? Does it stem from unemployment, or from that lack of transitional opportunities?

It stems partly from economic insecurity, and a feeling among some young people who will say, "Look, my brother is out of work, although he has some GCSE's. The teachers tell me I should work hard, but why?". For some kids, that economic insecurity is compounded by family insecurity, because, if a successful transition from childhood to adulthood depends on security, then two of the foundation stones are family security and economic security. While I am not trying to paint a picture of a golden age, in the fifties many children had the security of a family and dad in work. Now, many children have got neither of those things going for them, and I believe the ones most at risk are more often victims of those two things.

These are also problems for men at the other end of the age spectrum, those in their 50's. The retirement age for men is 65, but, if you look at the evidence, you see this is a myth. If you look at men aged at 60 to 65, just over four out of 10 are in employment — so a majority are not working. There may be a very few who have chosen that, but others (such as white collar workers) have taken the retirement package because there is no alternative, or they've been made redundant. Suddenly, the social security system has really found itself providing support, either through the Income Support scheme or invalidity benefit, to many men who, a generation ago, would have been in employment. If you look at the age group 55 to 59, supposedly a long way away from retirement, once upon a time virtually all of these men would have been economically active, but now one in three are not in work. This is a huge proportion: there is a crisis about the role of these men. Increasingly, we have an economy which wants to become more efficient; the private company wants to increase its profits next year, and they weed out men over 50 to save money. The public cost of this is enormous because, not only are these men out of work, but, at the very same time, they are going to live longer than previous generations.

History and demography are playing a cruel joke on us. Once upon a time (while this wasn't particularly good news), men worked until they dropped. We introduced a pension, but many men would have died within a few years of getting their retirement and pension: now they are out of the labour market at 50 or 55 and they might still be around 30 years later. We are moving to a situation where you could spend a third of your life as a retired person, and that is just crazy.

And we don't have wars to rebalance this.

No we haven't. I think it is all short-termism: companies and public agencies are being told that, to be efficient, you should cut back on staff, and no one is thinking of the wider implications of this.

So, with men being forced out of the labour market at both ends, what do we then do about it?

We do two things. The first is to recognise that we have to move back to full employment. We have just celebrated the 50th anniversary of the defeat of fascism and Nazism, when people came back from the War and wanted to build a better peace, and all the thinkers and leaders at that time recognised that full employment was crucial to that. Whatever your goals — whether they are to tackle poverty, or to create better education — Beveridge and Keynes said full employment was crucial. Nowadays, too many people are giving up on full employment and even kind of sneer at the concept; it is somehow unmodern to suggest the idea. While there is globalisation, there are flexible labour markets, but the idea that you can't run an economy which would enable all men and women who wanted to work to work, I think is wrong. We need a modern statement about full employment in a different and maybe more difficult time than in the 1940's. I am convinced that, if we maintain an economy whereby two or three million people are out of work, and therefore some people have lives where it is the exception rather than the rule that they are working, I think in a real sense all is lost.

The second thing we do is to foster a greater equality between men and women, both in the formal economy and also in the informal domestic economy. So it is about work and home.

Let's go back to these one at a time. With the trends suggesting that there is growth in women's work and a decline in jobs with a big enough wage to enable a family to live, what have you got to say about the nature of that full employment? Careers officers are reporting that young men are saying, ''I don't want to do that — it's women's work''.

I think we need to question what is men's, and what is women's, work. I take the point that the shipyards have closed, the iron and steel industries are in deep trouble and the mines have closed down, and that these were associated with men's employment, and that we have built more offices and there are more computers and jobs that require keyboard skills, and that these have been associated with women's employment. I also take the point that to suddenly expect a 53-year-old man who has worked in the shipyards to immediately become proficient in these new skills is asking perhaps too much of someone. While I understand that,

I certainly don't accept that the future is for one gender, rather than another.

So, how do we de-gender work? A lot of research, particularly with 14-16-year-old men, is saying that they want jobs like their granddads', so clearly a change in minds is needed.

That is not easy, but it clearly has to happen, both within the home, and within schools. I think, in some areas, it is already happening, but it's rather a slow train coming.

Do we focus on employment, create the jobs and let everything trickle on behind, or are there ways to accelerate this change in mind-set?

Although I have never taught in a school, I think that schools should be far more involved in preparation for adulthood. I don't feel a great authority on how you do that, but I think it is important. I think the pressure on the national curriculum is clearly enormous. I would question, however, whether we are leaving enough time for this rather difficult territory of teaching children to be more rounded citizens and properly focusing on issues about sex education, drug concerns and real life. I take the point that most of the evidence I have seen is that the home is rather more important than what happens in schools, that parents, for good or ill (and often both), can be more influential than teachers — thankfully in some ways — so it is a twin-track approach, but I am also aware of the fact that there are some families who are in a total shambles and disarray, so one has to counter-balance the other to some extent.

The second area you mentioned was equality at home. How can we impact on that?

It's the women who have the babies, so there will always be differences. We are seeing the rise of the dual working family, with every new group of mothers returning to the labour market more quickly than the group before, but what we are not seeing much of is the rise of the dual worker within the home. While the British Social Attitudes Survey shows some improvements in the trends towards greater equality, it is still basically the women doing the ironing, the nappy-changing and the rest.

So again, how do we change those mind-sets?

Pessimists would say look at the hard evidence, forget the fascination of 'New Man', because there are few sightings of him really. The optimists say, hang on a minute, compare what many men are doing now with what their fathers or grandfathers were doing.

And where would you fall — in the pessimists' or optimists' camp?

Well, in both camps, of course! In the long term, I think I see the improvements. My son, when he is at home from university, does rather more cooking than I ever did. More men are interested in their babies upbringing nowadays than were their fathers, so the long-term trends are encouraging. However, I am also impressed, and rather saddened, by the fact that, at the moment, there are many women who have rather tough part-time jobs or full-time jobs and who still come home and do the work around the home, which men don't expect to do.

To be honest, I don't think the state can do much about it. I don't know what the state should, or could, do — I think we need more confident women to sort those things out. It may be they are. Why is the marriage rate declining? We musn't exaggerate that either, because there are still 70% of all women and men who will marry, but it is rather less than it was, and more women are now postponing the age at which they get married (and that is not just because more are cohabiting). Women are deciding to live as single for longer. We have the high divorce rate, and, while this is not solely explained by women being fed-up doing their own and their men's ironing, clearly women are less tolerant of unhappy marriages than they were. I do think more and more men and women are in the middle of negotiating these things, although these negotiations will not always be successful or happy.

More and more women are not tolerating the nonsense, and so some of the pressures are on men — and rightly, I think. Some men don't like this. The campaigns against the Child Support Act — while the Agency hasn't worked properly, has made terrible mistakes, and has victimised some individual men — are about men paying maintenance for their children at adequate levels and some men not liking it.

The CSA is an example of state policy that is saying to men, ''You should be taking responsibility for your children, and, if you don't, we will ensure that you do''. How much do we need to use 'sticks', and how much do we need to use 'carrots', in changing men's attitudes?

Well, we certainly need to be teaching our boys, and some of the men, that gone are the days that, if you have a baby, it's the woman alone left holding it. I am absolutely convinced we need to move towards a situation where boys and men realise that, if they take the enormous step of having a child (even if they do it accidentally), in a very real sense they are also left holding the baby, certainly in terms of financial responsibility. Now, that might add to pressures on men, but tough really, because otherwise the alternative is often poverty for the mothers and children. It is a major cultural revolution in terms of attitude.

Some would argue that, if men are going to have responsibilities, then they should also have rights, and that the Courts deal with men at the moment as though they do not have rights.

We have certainly got to move away from a position where the Courts assume that, barring major evidence to the contrary, women should be given custody. We certainly have to move away from Courts and lawyers assuming that it's women's right, or indeed their responsibility, to provide the main care for the children. We may expect in the future that, if this is working well, rather more children will end up living with their fathers, so, yes, you have to balance responsibilities and rights.

Returning to full employment and equality at home, how do we help those things happen?

Certainly, what is not helping at the moment is that, over the last 10-15 years, unemployment has tended to be concentrated in certain kinds of families and households, so, if your dad's out of work, it is likely that your mum's out of work too, and your big brother, so you have a concentration of worklessness. But, alongside this, you have a concentration of work in other families. Men who are in employment often have to work harder than ever before: once upon a time, there were 20 of you in the section you are working in, and now management have got it down to 12 or 13 and you're just having to work harder and harder. That is the paradox — you have the rise of worklessness in certain families and the rise of overwork in others. In difficult financial times, to earn more money, particularly in low-wage sectors, people are looking for the overtime; if you are a security guard being paid £2.50 an hour, you just have to work 70 hours a week to bring in the bacon.

Also, a lot of successful people nowadays are not getting established until their mid-20's, so, from their late 20's to their mid-40's, everything suddenly happens — they are forming relationships, cohabiting, getting married, having babies, bringing up their children — all the things requiring massive investment, emotion and energy, exactly at the time when they are building their careers. So you have the rise of what I call the over-active family, where, in a sense, too much is going on, and, although incomes are reasonably high, I suspect not enough time is being invested in children and substitutes for parental care are being found which may not be as high quality as parental care would be. Given that we are all going to live until we are 80 years old — men slightly less, women slightly more — it is daft really that we are concentrating all the things that matter into a short period of time, and therefore I think we need policies, particularly at the end of the life-cycle, that challenge the kind of narrowness of that, and the ageism of that, that throws people out of work and so on.

What would that involve?

Well, I am interested in laws to actually outlaw age discrimination. I noticed that the magazine *Management Today* said the other day that they were no longer going to feature age in job advertisements, but that is only a part of it, because actually it would be far more sensible to say that, when people in their late 20's or early 30's are having babies, then they should be able to take a year or two off, or go part-time — whether they are men or women — and then, when their children leave home or are in their late teens, their parents can actually put more time into the labour market. There are a few encouraging signs: B&Q, who deliberately hire older people in their stores, actually find people in their early 50's-60's are rather better workers than young kids.

The pragmatist would say what you are doing here is increasing the number of people out there who could potentially work, and that is going to put even more strain on the competition for available jobs.

What we need, I think, is a very strong challenge to conventional economic arithmetic, to the traditional way we draw up our national accounts. People talk about the gross domestic product, but it is an extraordinarily narrow indicator of the worth of the nation; for example, if you sell hamburgers, you are contributing to the gross domestic product, but, if you are home caring for your mother or father with Alzheimer's disease, you do not contribute. That's just daft economics; we need proper cost benefit analysis so that, when people say, "I am sorry, we are going to make you redundant" to a 53-year-old man, instead of just knowing the company has saved £20,000 and increased its profit margin by x%, we also need to know the cost to the social security system is £Y,000 a year, together with the knock-on effect in terms of health cost. We need to measure things more accurately than we are doing. I don't agree with that argument about the number of jobs available, you see. If, in my constituency, all of the families with children and all of the elderly were well-housed and there wasn't a housing waiting list, they all had decently insulated dwellings with good central heating and adaptations for the disabled — if that were true, and if all our parks were well-maintained and all of our stations had decent staffing levels so that women could travel safer at night, etc., then, yes, I might say to you there doesn't seem to be any work available, but we have high levels of unemployment and loads of work crying out to be done. It requires a certain amount of political will, but I believe it is possible.

REFERENCE

1. Wilkinson, H. and Mulgan, G. 'Freedom's Children: work, relationships and politics for 18-34-year-olds in Britain today', London: Demos (1995).

Looking for a New Balance
(The British situation as seen from Holland)

Lauk Woltring

Lauk Woltring is a consultant on work with boys/men and a Senior Lecturer on Socialization and Youth Work at the Polytechnic College of Amsterdam's Faculty of Social-Educational Services. He is coordinator of the 'Work with Boys' Project and Network in the Netherlands, editor/co-author of 'Boys Between Bravado and Timidity: Sex-specific Work with Boys' (1988) and author of 'It's Up to Me to Decide!? Work with Boys: design for a sex and gender-specific education' (1995).[1]

The first impression from the facts and figures at the front of this book is that the traditional distribution of tasks between men and women is over — in Britain even more radically than in Holland. Though we are catching up fast, it is not expected that, within the next decade, the replacement of 'men's jobs' in Holland by 'women's work' (low-paid, part-time, intricate manual work, etc.) will be as strong as in Britain. Nevertheless, things are changing. In general, male unemployment is not rising in Holland, except in specific groups with low education levels and/or ethnic minority backgrounds and among rootless men. The education level of women is definitely rising, with men lagging behind in an increasing number of sectors. In Holland, the proportion of women in middle management or leading positions is still inferior to many other western countries[2], but it is growing strongly, particularly in education and social work, in public services and health care (by 2000, most doctors will be female), and is gradually expanding over the commercial sectors as well. This change should not, and cannot, be stopped. The strategic question now is: what's in it for men?

In the UK, as well as in Holland, men are still in the transition-zone to a new situation. The old fly-wheel is still spinning round, but more slowly and with ever-louder creaking noises. Some people adopt outmoded positions which shun the facts, some embrace new ideas that there are no significant male-female differences at all and declare every differentiation pure idiocy. Like most fundamental changes, this is accompanied by a lot of turmoil and disturbance. So be it. Practical policies and strategically well-chosen initiatives can accompany and facilitate necessary changes in favour of both men and women.

The old distribution of work and caring roles arose from a mixture of biological facts and power politics around gender issues. Certainly, women can give birth and men cannot, and this gives women a special position in the reproduction of human life which should not be underestimated. Woman's role is unique from every conception, and her tasks in the child's upbringing (bonds, attachment, separation) are partially specific. In the same way, men do have particular things to offer in the reproduction of the human race and its achievements, and that is a lot more than just a bunch of sperm cells; for instance, as a father, being the first significant 'other' with which the newborn child can develop relations different from its relationship with the mother, showing the child those qualities which have, to date, generally been better developed in men and offering the child masculinity itself to relate to.

Possibly some distribution between women and men of caring and other work (hunting, fighting, defence) has been functional in past periods in the human evolution, but nowadays behaviour stemming from those roles has, to a large extent, become obsolete. Civilisation has made some progress. Women in western industrialised countries don't, on average, have more than 2-3 children; these children, and they themselves, live much longer. Potentially, men and women can fulfil almost the same tasks, yet women get double-burdened when they try to combine parenthood with paid work and a career, as is dramatically shown in one-parent families headed by mothers. Moreover, young boys in single-mother families seem to be particularly vulnerable.

Labour — paid work — has been the realm for men in which some of them grew rich and many got exploited, but from which nearly every man derived — and still derives — his significance and big parts of his identity. Certainly, work has tended to organise their life-course and the rhythm of their everyday lives. But, life-long and full-time employment for men can no longer be taken for granted.

Men may do little at home in raising their kids and taking care of the household — and are consequently secluded from a powerful source of inspiration, meaning and orientation in everyday life — but, in their paid work, they were, and still are, one-sidedly overburdened; their productivity may have been compressed into 40 hours a week, but it is nowadays much more intense, for instance, keeping pace with the work done by computers. Workers are feeling threatened by big shifts in the global economy, and managers manipulate their fears (and if they don't, the Head Office will replace them with others that will do…).

The 'modernisation' and 'flexibilisation' of labour may give new opportunities for the individual's organisation of everyday life with a partner and children — part-time 'flexi-workers', on-line work at the family home, and so on — but, all too often, these words are beautiful cover-ups for the corrosion of sound labour, satisfying positions, humane work relations and the rhythm of night and day.

The main 'problem', as I see it, is the way in which men cling to, and cope with, their restrictive role, for instance by compensating behaviour, and by fright, flight and/or fight-reactions to what they see as threats, be it women's lib demands, new work relations, new technologies, etc. These reactions are blinding them to the opportunities that lie ahead and which require new forms of organisation and initiative.

Of course, there are many rewards in the dominant male 'coping-styles': money (for some), power in the outside world, 'status' and 'prestige' (for he who needs it) and being cared for by a woman (out of date now).

However, there are more hidden aspects, especially for young men who look up to these so-called successful men. Middle-class men work too hard in order to be able to cope with, and compensate for, the pressures of their work — a symmetrical escalation leading to unhappiness and a lot of divorce — and women don't want this any longer. Lower-class men get hardly any jobs and have to fight all their lives, while youngsters with low education levels are not enabled to devote their energy to jobs and may find a way out in criminality. The same goes for many young men from one-parent families and others who have not been given enough direction and/or the right attention, love and caring, not only from their mums, but especially from their fathers and other men.

Men tend to keep each other in unduly restricted roles, using a broad range of masculinity codes and mental defence systems, each of these being an expression of how they try to survive under the prevailing conditions.

Men systematically overtax themselves and have got used to their stress, even defining it as masculine. Their 'life-strategies' are centred around:

- Compartmentalizing or segmenting their lives (feeling/thinking; doing/talking; work/leisure; body/brain; now/later; friends/strangers; wife/mistress). The underlying principle seems to be 'divide and rule', not only with regard to the (social) environment, but even their own bodies and thoughts;
- Being silent about problems: "You can't solve them, so it's no use talking about it — it'll only make things worse";
- Compensations in terms of extra money to buy the things they long for during their work; compensations in terms of their relationships (during their work in the harsh masculine world

of labour, they can dream of the evening at home — being at rest, familiarity, intimacy), or in terms of fantasies about sex or creating a fantasy world associating themselves with the images from glossy adverts;

- 'Constructing their course of life', eg "Work now, live later".

The answer of many middle-class men to National Insurance reductions is to work extra hard to put their money into an annuity. But the insurance companies win in the end: many men die soon after their work has stopped, or even before, when their bodies are too heavily affected by the stresses placed upon them.

When work is not satisfying, or even not within reach, young men in particular compensate by risk-taking behaviour as a means of 'meaningful living': as soon as the adrenalin is coursing through their veins, the problems seem to be far away. A young courier, zooming on his motorbike with his parcels through Amsterdam at 50 mph and asked why he chose to neglect every kind of safety rule, answered very simply: "It's fun, and if I crash, so what? At least I'll have no more problems. Maybe I'll try again in my next life".

Many men who cannot cope with the demands of everyday life, nor see the advantage or possibilities in sharing the burden of raising an income with a partner, tend to get isolated, depressed or (especially those with more rigid patterns) take their frustration out on others — wives, children, minorities, homosexuals.

Those young men who have not developed the necessary skills to maintain themselves in the labour market may find an alternative lifestyle in criminality in which other qualities are asked for. The proportions of young criminals with developmental problems from childhood onwards, and those who are young men from mother-only families, are remarkably high. Experiencing divorce during their childhood seems to have a particularly significant effect on boys.

As I've said earlier, the almost digitally clear distribution of care and paid work has become completely obsolete. Things are changing, albeit gradually, as the old patterns are rooted very deep. Men's coping-behaviour can be effective or ineffective, constructive or destructive, but, by and large, it is limiting and defective in the long run; men die sooner, men react (often violently) to others, rather than interact; many men are disappointed when they grow older; etc.

So, what needs to be done? If we look at the presented facts and figures, we can, at best, regard male behaviour as men's answers to the conditions in which they are brought up and to the age-old division of men and women. It is not natural male behaviour: instead we are dealing with responses shaped by our cultural environment. If we see behaviour as a response, the discussion is no longer about how men are, but about what they do. This opens up other perspectives: "Aren't there more satisfying responses to the same threats and opportunities?". Further, we must present our findings in such a way that makes the necessary changes not only visible, but attractive (this could, for instance, involve promoting the gains for men in the redistribution of paid and unpaid work between men and women through television 'soaps', videos and games). In this way, we can work on goals and motivations. Having set out the problems, the solutions follow almost automatically.

Changing men, changing ourselves, means altering our responses to changing conditions, but, first of all, changing the way we look at ourselves, our motives, goals and horizons — with an open eye for diversity, as no man is the same.

We should not condemn men/ourselves for what they/we are, but we should look at how we can learn from our experiences. There is plenty of evidence of bad role-adjustment in the presented facts and figures, with men not wanting to talk about their difficulties, settling for the known rather than the unknown... so, learning is our first main task.

In Holland, some common agreement about the necessity and value of a 'fine-mesh social network', with the corresponding social policies, still remains. This may no longer be the case in Britain — a challenge for a post-Major government?

Good social policies can enable men to learn and find new perspectives. This requires the initiation (ideally by government) of health, educational and employment/redistribution policies which address at least some of the problems which men face and where conditions, until now, have been bad. Perhaps local experiments or sectored policies enabling unemployed men (particularly the young) to experiment with part-time work can get something started?

In terms of making change attractive, let's borrow something from modern literature on management. It's nowadays common practice to make a so-called SWOT analysis for companies in the market: 'What's Strong, what's Weak, what are the Opportunities and what are the Threats?'.

The 'market' for men changes very quickly; not only the labour market, but also the market of relations and happiness. Boys and men who do not adjust to the just demands of new generations of self-assured women tend to be left alone, on the margins of society, left to obsolete masculine self-pity, ganging-up amongst themselves and revelling in 'laddish' behaviour.

Yet these developments offer not only threats for men, but also many good opportunities. Many men do not campaign against bad conditions because they regard the economic position of their household (partner and children) as solely dependant on them. But sharing their financial responsibilities (such as mortgages) with their partners, for instance, will reduce their feelings of vulnerability in their employment, and can make them less open for blackmail in their labour relations.

Sharing the work role with your wife enables the individual to spend fewer hours in the week at work, making it possible to spend more time with the kids. Caring can bring men into contact with more aspects of life itself. That may start up a sequence of other behaviours in a range of other fields (for instance, 'environment' becomes something real instead of something in the papers: the same goes for health, security, good food, etc.). A male life with a better balance between paid work, care, study, voluntary activities and recreation, is not only a healthier life, but also makes men more attractive partners.

Once the basic needs of food, housing, clothing and communication are fulfilled, lower consumption rates can offer a much better quality of life. Labour organisations asking for equal wages high enough for good living if both partners work, let's say 50-60% of a full-time job, have new horizons for fighting unemployment. There is no full employment for everyone anymore, so let's act on this problem, instead of only feeling threatened by it.

In education (in families, in schools and elsewhere), we need a more balanced attention for the specific needs, developmental tasks and motives, mainsprings and motivations of young men, as well as the dilemmas they are placed in by society (being 'a man' in the traditional way — as asked by the army, by many bosses, sports clubs, colleagues, schools, most adverts — as well as being a good partner, being wise, sensitive, and so on, required by partners, some teachers, campaigns, some other adverts).

It would be a good idea to develop exchange projects between middle-aged men from traditionally masculine worksettings looking back on their lives and boys on the verge of making choices about their study and/or career. What did these older men gain in the course of their life, and what have they missed? Research in Holland shows that lots of men, given the opportunity to do it all over again, would have preferred to have been at home more; having more contact with their children (their kids are often leaving home at the moment the fathers tire of work and spend more time in the home); investing more in their relationships; and so on.

The nature/nurture debate deserves a special place in discussions about education. Biology is too important to leave to biologists, certainly in an era where real attention and good therapy tendentially seems to be put aside and replaced by chemical steering of human behaviour, gene-manipulation and all that. Good medicines are okay, but.... I consider there should be a more balanced attention towards the biological dimensions in analysing male development from birth and male behaviour.

Facts and figures all over the world show bigger perinatal mortality, and extra morbidity and vulnerability of boys over girls under 10-12 years. In 98% of children's diseases, boys score (much) higher. 'Vulnerability' here includes boys' greater propensity for risk-taking, and their corresponding tendency to be prone to accidents in the playground, at home, etc.

We will have to look to the 'brain-sex debate', not in the reductionist approach of Moir and Jessel[3], but with more emphasis on the developmental aspect in brain differences between men and women, possibly asking for specific educational strategies. Some researchers offer fine ('transformative') models of the interaction between the groundwork laid down by our genes and the environment in which we develop our behaviour, which again influences the body and brain[4]. There is a strong need for gender-specific education for young boys, albeit with some interaction with girls. For instance, combining under-12's for speech and spatial movement education might be of great help to boys in preventing them developing their skills so separately from girls as they do now, certainly if this is combined with an increased role for men in the upbringing of children. Many boys grow up in a predominantly female environment, at home and at school, where they have little identification with masculinity. In their early childhood, they are approached in a dominant feminine way, verbally, emotionally and socially — those same skills that boys tend to develop poorly, or at a later stage, compared with girls. This, added to the fact that, until 12, boys lag behind in growth, maturity and the co-ordination of different capacities like verbal, spatial and emotional intelligence, is to a large extent responsible for the way they later turn to defective coping-strategies.

We can also look at the ways in which men and women learn to deal with (overload of) information and visuals, which call for a combination of rational and emotional skills, concentration and multi-tasking.

Turning to combating sexual harassment and violence, many men, especially young men, feel clumsy in their relations with the other sex. A lot of campaigns aimed at them call for them to respect women more. However, it might be a good idea not to begin with respect for others, but with more self-respect and self-confidence, because it is in these areas that the roots of violence often lie. For instance, in Holland, we are now developing training in self-defence techniques for boys, aiming in the long run to reduce sexual violence. The basic idea is that, when a boy knows how to defend himself, he will feel less threatened and more free to reflect on his behaviour (including any homophobic tendencies). We use Oriental fighting principles, such as 'being water' and 'being rock', along with training in feeling your own energy, in self-control (breath, body, impulse regulation, well-addressed energy), all leading to much more appropriate behaviour. It is then much easier to convey to the boy a better approach towards women. Moreover, deep-breathing boys behaving relaxedly and appropriately may become much better lovers... The same strategy, beginning with encouragement of self-respect, will hopefully soon be adopted in a nation-wide 'safe schools' project.

In confronting young men's current problems (violence, low education, bad self-organisation, etc.), there is a need also for re-evaluation of the role of fathers and other men in the raising of young men (and women too).

There is an overwhelming list of books concerning motherhood and the stresses mothers live through, which increasingly place blame on the absent father. What we need is not remorse or penance, but sound research on ourselves and other men into what keeps us away from fatherhood. Simply feeling guilty about not being with your children is rather destructive when it is hard to change the conditions of your work; feeling guilty is a strong emotion — if it can't be dealt with, it leads to silence, talking-up, acting-as-if, the construction of a tower of semi-lies and bad feeling. Eventually, it can result in resentment and even violence.

What happens with a man when he hears that he is going to be a father? What goes on inside him? How does it change his relationship with his partner? How do his colleagues react? How will his boss react should he dare to ask for a temporary shorter working week? Research shows that many men turn inside, communicate very little and work harder in order to provide their families with the necessary goods. We'll have to find other, better answers than these. Public services such as health care, infant welfare and pregnancy services could experiment with clear programmes for the young fathers with whom they are in contact.

But, first and foremost, we have to tackle the full-time work pitfall: full-time work as we currently know it cannot be combined with the demanding task of bringing up children and caring for the home environment. So, what keeps men in full-time work? 70 % of Dutchmen want to work shorter hours, even if this means a lower income (not too much lower, but even then some of them would do it).

If a woman wants to work shorter hours (for instance, because she is pregnant), she can change her circumstances, although this is very often followed by reduced career prospects. Indeed, her low payment is already an expression of the 'risk' of her becoming pregnant. Companies do not invest in women: they might leave the company for their child. But, after centuries of feminism, women have achieved something in this area (and have not yet finished their struggle).

How about men? In the traditional masculine settings of finance, engineering, construction, transport and so on, a man risks a lot when he dares ask for a part-time job. Just at the point in his life when he might become a father, competition and rivalry over positions are very high. He who does not give at least 120% is not sufficiently loyal: "Your priorities must be with the firm" (… the words "or you can go" are not said, but read between the lines). Being part of a team without communicating about the demands and pleasures of fatherhood keeps men in their (work)place.

How many men simply work until their pension comes along? The slogan should be, 'Work less hours a week, and live longer, healthier and happier lives!'. This means less costs for the company and for society as well, if you take into account health insurance costs, sick pay, poor work performance and the laying off of overstressed, 'burnt-out' staff. Talking about human resource management, a medium-sized Dutch building firm has a very experimental attitude and has offered generous leave arrangements for young fathers and part-time work, even to foremen and managers. They found out that staff turnover (many men change jobs in this sector every few years) reduced sharply, so they needed much less investment in training and teaching on the job, teamwork became much better, and, remarkably, morbidity reduced very sharply from an average of 11% (the building trade norm) to 3-4%. In the end, this firm ran more smoothly — workers knew that they could take a break when necessary, and their colleagues were glad to take the overtime work, knowing that the same opportunities would apply for them — and at lower cost.

Men do have much to offer when conditions are better ... I conclude this text by restating the title of this chapter. We need to find a new balance, and the main solution to today's problems for men and women lies in redistribution of work and care between men and women and between young and old. The dynamics in all other fields (aggression, environmental issues, security, war/peace, sexuality, health and so on) will change when this redistribution is realised.

ENDNOTES

1. Book titles are translated from the Dutch.
2. The comparative backward position of women in the Dutch labour market is remarkable compared with the outspoken position of liberal feminism over several decades. This is, to a large extent, due to a very old tradition of living in small families (instead of extended families); the role of the Catholic and Protestant Churches under specific Dutch circumstances; the fact that Holland has not been fighting 'great' lasting wars for a very long time (we got occupied, but did not lose many men in the trenches); and the domination of ideological and 'token' politics over open power politics, compared with, for instance, Britain.
3. Moir, A. and Jessel, D. 'Brain Sex', London: Michael Joseph (1989).
4. Wijngaard, M. van den. 'Reinventing the sexes. Feminism and the biomedical construction of Femininity and Masculinity, 1959-1985', Delft: (1991).

Taking Responsibility for a Healthy and Moral Society

Sue Slipman

Sue Slipman is Director of London TEC Council and, prior to this appointment in 1995, was Director of the National Council for One Parent Families for 10 years. She has had an active involvement in youth, education, training, employment and economic issues and social policy during the last 20 years and has written a number of publications, including 'The Lone Parents Survival Guide' (1990) and 'The Challenges of Social Policy' (1993).

At the start of the 20th century, women and children were the property of men inside marriage. Freud posed the question, 'What Do Women Want?', at a point where the frustration of female constraint led him to concepts about the female psyche that enraged latter-day feminists. The century has been an interesting journey for women, but what of men?

Call me jaded, but 10 years of working with lone parents and their children have left me feeling depressed about men. There are only so many stories of abandonment and betrayal you can absorb before you take to muttering the immortal words, "You'll be sorry" under your breath every time you pass a church and see a wedding taking place.

The Right-wing family lobby would have us believe that relationship breakdown between men and women is the result of the hedonistic culture unleashed in the sixties. Rampant individualism, deified over the last 30 years, has killed the commitment and selflessness required to sustain family life. We are wallowing in disgusting indulgence, seeking only instant sensual gratifications. In their world view, single mothers become the symbol of social disintegration and the touchstone of fecklessness. Given what I have seen of the very unselfish commitment of lone parents to their children, I always find this view strange. The family lobby are never clear on what they mean by selflessness and about which part of the parenting couple should make the personal sacrifice to uphold the whole. A simple plea for a return to traditional family structures that does not call for men to change, or wealth and power to be more justly distributed within the family, is necessarily misogyny.

Organised groups of men would have us believe that they have been thrust out of relationships by evil pariahs who deny them access to their children. Of course, there are women who are vindictive and who use children as battle weapons in their war of attrition against the men they feel wronged them. But they are few compared to those whose hearts ache for their children's longing for acknowledgment from their fathers.

At a recent and rather prestigious meeting of professional women, an older generation were promoting the view that men had changed, whilst those of us still actively engaged in childrearing looked on in amazement. The meeting ended in some disarray with one side — the flat earthers — concluding that what children needed was to grow up seeing their fathers actively parenting. I lead for jaded womanhood willing to settle for the lesser goal of fathers paying their child support. Sad to say, but, in the real world, we cannot seem to manage even this little commitment.

So, what is happening to men? In my view, we cannot separate this issue from the changes to the lives of women and the social and moral framework in which both women and men live.

The last 30 years have been an interesting period to live through. The 1960's were an unprecedented period of growing freedoms and individual rights, based upon strong notions of social justice with an accompanying theory that the state would take the responsibility. We took the lid off, and have spent the decades since then getting increasingly concerned about some of the strange and disturbing things that crawled out.

Now, there are no big ideas about solutions to our problems that win broad social assent. Most of us have emerged dazed and confused about where we are heading, with no clear theories and a lack of conviction about the routes on offer. We no longer know how much responsibility should rest with individuals — whether men or women, or both, should carry it — and how much with the state, or, indeed, whether this is a moral, or simply an economic, problem.

Beveridge assumed we needed a safety net for a society based on full male employment, with two-parent families with stay-at-home wives providing childcare, while the men went out to earn the bread. The system was to be based on male contributions through National Insurance taken from the pay packet. The only adjustment was to pay Family Allowances to mothers, as enlightened campaigners like Eleanor Rathbone knew that men receiving wages did not always mean mothers receiving housekeeping money to keep their children. Hence, Family Allowances (later combined with Child Tax Allowances to make Child Benefit) were a recognition of the need to transfer some wealth between men and women for the sake of the children.

Today, it is still possible to predict poverty on the grounds of the relationship to the labour market, but the picture is much more complicated. Ours is a rich, privileged world in which there is ever more choice for those who are equipped to make choices. But the gaps between the affluent majority and the poor minority are getting ever wider. The poor, poorly educated and disadvantaged cannot compete in a world requiring skills for success, and are increasingly pushed to the margins. The fear of social disintegration, crime and violence is palpable. The biggest question for the affluent majority is will we choose to create an inclusive, or an exclusive, society? Our democratic process through our political parties is not yielding answers that are acceptable to wide consensus, so individuals are being thrown back upon their own moral conscience to grapple with difficult issues.

It seems to me pointless to apportion blame to those who are seeking individual solutions, for it is demonstrably true that many of our traditional social structures have broken down, that our traditional ways of delivering services are no longer adequate and that, as a result, we are faced with an elite busily exiting from social institutions to secure their own privileges, leaving an excluded minority for whom the right to integration is the new crucial social issue.

Some argue that, in future, personal behaviour will be crucial to securing affluence. We are moving into a world in which individuals will increasingly take responsibility for their own behaviour and development. Personal choice will depend upon personal responsibility and issues of personal morality do matter. But we have stopped talking about what kind of support systems — if any — these new human beings will need. It all sounds like a convenient theory of the survival of the fittest, with morality as the test.

So far, our politicians have offered us only visions of a return to an idealised Golden Age that take no account of the underlying reasons for contemporary change in institutions such as the family. Instead of finding appropriate support systems, they proffer simplistic answers to deny modern freedoms, and, as a result, cannot help modern adults to create strategies which combine freedom with responsibility. Until we understand that you cannot turn back the clock to a simpler time, fundamentalist views and the blaming of the victims of rapid social change will remain an unhelpful feature of the debate.

In the real world, the long-term health and moral welfare of society has to be negotiated between men and women.

The death of Socialism as a practical system of social organisation — confirmed by the break-up of the Soviet Union — is of immense importance to the issue of principles of social organisation. We have now rejected the only developed alternative social philosophy, and, with it, a centralised social system — and all its many variants — that carries responsibility for the individual. We are now in favour of more open social organisation that throws individuals back upon their own resources to progress within that system.

The biggest change over this century has been in the role of women in society — the rise of female ambition. Most women now work outside the home. The accumulation of rights to education, careers, the political process, to control over sexuality and fertility have been the staging posts on that journey. It has been a slow and painstaking revolution, but its effects reach wide and deep into the female psyche and society's structure. The Beveridge model of the split between industrial and domestic spheres now applies in only 6% of households. This has a number of implications:

- Some women are now affluent in their own right;
- The gap between one and two-earner households is growing. In many families, even where the woman's wage is low and would once have been considered pin money, that wage is now essential to maintenance of family income;
- If current projections are right, the number of childless women in the population will dramatically increase. The perceived opportunity costs of being a mother are too high for increasing numbers of modern women: what slows women down in the career competition with men are the babies.

You may not think this growth in the numbers of childfree women matters, but the reason it ought to concern us is that a rapidly growing number of elderly people to keep, and a fall in the proportion of young people to work to keep us all as tomorrow's tax payers, will mean a reduction in our standard of living, as well as affecting balance in our society and culture. If the numbers grew to epidemic proportions, our society would decline and die. Other Europeans have been neurotic about the state of their birthrate for many years and made it a strong feature of their social policy. I am not saying we should become obsessed with it, but it might not look so smart to be so child-unfriendly in a few years' time.

The second major change has occurred to male employment. The job for life is disappearing, along with the decline of the staple industries established during the Industrial Revolution and the rapid growth of new products born of the Technological Revolution. Global competition demands constant change. Companies are downsizing and rightsizing, flattening out and getting leaner.

The old jobs had space for unskilled male labour, and, with trades union influence over collective bargaining and restrictive practices, provided the attainment of a family wage for those who filled them. We now have a growing gap between the salaries available to the high flyers who are trained for work skills and the unskilled. In the new, flexible, non-regulated labour market, the unskilled will rarely earn enough to sustain a family.

Family life, too, is going through dramatic changes. The majority of children — around 80% — live with both their biological parents. But, 20 years ago, the figure was 90%. This is a big change in two decades. We now face large-scale divorce, a rise in cohabitation, the growth of second families and increasing divorce on this second round too. All these factors suggest that relationships between men and women are in crisis.

There are those who believe that modern cohabitation is far more unstable than marriage — but, when you realise that the great research work that argued this was based on a sample of 25 couples, you will see that the ground of the argument is, at best, shaky. If one in two new marriages now ends in divorce, and the average length of time of such marriages is six years, compared with five years for cohabitation, it seems to me that the argument is academic.

The recent debates about the family have highlighted the nostalgia of the men in power for the days when men were the authority in the family and the breadwinners. The debate has provided few useful guidelines — and little light amongst much heat.

The big debate on the family was sparked off by John Redwood in a speech on a Cardiff estate in summer 1993 in which he remarked that it was sad that 50% of the children on the estate were growing up without the expectation of a father in the family. We might all agree with this — but he went on to blame the mothers and to promote the singular view that benefits should be cut for mothers and children, not just until fathers paid up, but until they gave loving support to their children. Then the Chief Constable responsible for policing the estate (who is not a Vulcan) commented that the last thing the police wanted was the forced re-integration of fathers onto that estate, as they had exclusion orders for violence against half of them.

The Government launched the Back to Basics campaign. Ministers attempted to make 'family values', and a return to traditional family structures the new 'big idea' of politics. In doing so, they were responding to the genuine anxieties of people in a society adjusting to structural change — but the noise of the Back to Basics campaign was finally drowned out by the sound of ministerial trousers dropping in numerous sex scandals which made the Government seem merely hypocritical.

Relations between men and women remain at an all-time low. Divorce is spiralling, marriage declining, cohabitation increasing. The number of one-parent families grows apace, still largely as a result of relationship breakdown. You can already see the signs of diminishing optimism that such relationships can work and are worth nurturing as more women decide their best — perhaps only — option is to raise children on their own.

In the early 1980's, I went to an international conference on 'Whither the Family?'. A group of equal numbers of men and women examined the issues and eventually crystallised what we thought they boiled down to to two propositions on which we voted. The first was: Will men change? The second: Will women give up the struggle and go back to the home?

On the first, all the women voted that men would change, and all the men that they would not. In the second, all the men voted that women would give up, and the women that they would not. It was clear that the pieces were in place for this bitter endgame of the 20th century.

New Man is a myth, and even Newish Man is difficult to spot. There was an amusing survey by Mintel last year in which they set out to find 'New Man', defined as he who takes an equal share of domestic tasks. They could not track him down. They then set out to find 'Newish Man', defined as he who does some domestic chores. They thought 18% of men were 'newish men'. Women will no longer take the lion's share of responsibility for making male/female relationships work and for nurturing the children. Even if women wanted to make the old compromises, the gap between being assertive at work and a doormat at home is too great for the modern female psyche.

Traditional male rites of passage are dying, along with the staple industries and the breadwinner's wage. The growth of the 'jack-the-lad' syndrome has helped fuel a curious view, that it is neither their fault nor their concern if the sex they see as purely recreational results in procreation. Unemployment and part-time, low-paid jobs are producing perpetual boys — we even spell it b.o.y.z. so it sounds cute. It might be cute to be boyz in your teens, and maybe even into your twenties — but, come your thirties, forties and (horrors) even fifties, it looks pathetic.

The description of these young men put forward by those on the Right does have a spark of truth in it. Often, they are roaming the streets being a public nuisance — condemned forever to be lads, with none of the traditional ways in which they were socialised into maturity. So far, the exponents of male interest have a point to their analysis of what is happening to young men. New power feminists also argue that, if these young men were in relationships, they would be better. For both, it comes down to being the job of women to civilise men in the family: what they entirely fail to explain is why any woman in her right mind would take one home with her!

Male identity is in crisis, and men are still stoutly resisting change. Yet, material forces and the changes in women's attitudes prevent men from playing by the old rules of family life. Over the last 20 years, they have refused to negotiate a change in the rules, and now they are withdrawing from the game. The recent battles over the Child Support Agency may have been fuelled by a shoddy piece of legislation, but their cause is male resistance to a transfer in wealth to women in the interests of children. In other words, if men no longer have the power, they will not make the wealth available to meet parental responsibilities. Indeed, they appear to have gone to the other extreme of taking no responsibility for parenting.

As a society, until the setting up of the Child Support Agency, we tacitly sanctioned the non-custodial parent abandoning their children. This was part of our view of individual rights that lost any meaningful or clear concept of a private responsibility and counted upon the state to take the strain of individual choice.

Before CSA, only three out of 10 lone parents received regular maintenance payments for their children. These were often derisory, bearing no relationship to the costs of keeping a child. As a result, 1 million of Britain's 1.4 million lone parents were trapped within the benefit system. The common experience amongst the nearly 2.2 million children was abandonment by one parent and a life in poverty with the other. We have sanctioned this state of affairs, allowing men to think that, if the first relationship does not work out, they have the freedom to go off and create another set of children without a backward glance.

What has been hidden in this process is the fact that the poverty of lone parents and their children has been subsidising a much more affluent life style for the absent parent and any subsequent family. It took many years of campaigning to get anyone in power to recognise this fact as a national scandal. The CSA was set up to right a great social injustice which has its origins within a totally unfair distribution of wealth within families, which, up to now, has made men richer after divorce and women poorer. The CSA was not only about chasing the 'feckless' men who were paying nothing — it was also about ensuring that those who paid, paid a decent amount somewhere nearer the real costs of children.

There were three principles behind the CSA — all to do with transfer. The first was to get maintenance into the hands of parents with care responsibilities (transferring wealth from men to women). The second was to provide a portable income for lone parents (transferring lone parents from benefit dependency to financial independence through work). The third was to save money for the state (transferring some of the costs of supporting one-parent families from the public to the private sphere). I see nothing wrong with these principles. Children, throughout their dependency period, should have the right to be maintained by both their parents, regardless of the marital relationship between them. In the event — as is too often the way with government — the third principle became the most important, and the Act was skewed towards the interests of the Treasury.

The Government made a pig's ear of the policy, by deciding to make it retrospective — ensuring a major backlash from men — and by refusing to allow parents with care responsibilities on Income Support to keep any of the money, ensuring less support than there might have been from lone parents. The male backlash included those who had been through the so-called 'clean break' divorce settlement. The new formula did not take things like property transfer into account and was bound to fuel an already simmering reluctance to pay and give it some justification. But you will have seen the virulent campaign of the fathers who do not want to pay. It is as if being forced to meet their parental responsibilities has stirred up all the bitterness, anger and resentment of the relationship breakdown — and something more — a bedrock refusal to countenance a transfer of their wealth. If they no longer have the power, they will not provide the wealth. Nothing much has changed, but, if the powerful voices get their way and defeat the Agency, we could see a return to the backlash against lone parents that would mean an even bleaker future. Ministers have already started to cut benefit for lone parents.

Some policy analysts have viewed the CSA as merely spreading poverty. There is a grain of truth in this, but this is as much a moral as an economic argument. Of course, if we decide the proper balance of a transfer of wealth in favour of children from the private purse, we need to find solutions to maintaining family income overall. This question of the reciprocal nature of obligation is ultimately inescapable and gives us more prospect of putting back onto the political agenda realistic strategies for overcoming poverty that we have had for some time. Besides, the argument smacks of the old view that individuals only had rights and the state had responsibilities. This may well prove to be an insidious way of further melting the glue that holds society's fabric together, and, far from being a progressive approach to social development, could be an undermining of the basis of a civilised society.

Ultimately, of course, the question of state and parental responsibility and children's rights is not only economic and moral: it is also emotional. The research, limited though it is, does tell us that many children suffer enormously from family dislocation — in health, in educational attainment and in life chances. There is clearly a lot of pain for children who go through disruptive life transitions. The proposed new divorce procedures will stop couples separating for the sake of the children, but might generally lead to an improvement in adult behaviour and relationships and in how they care for their children before, during and after relationship breakdown and transition.

If we want men to change as parents, we are going to have to tackle them on an emotional, as well as on an economic, front. Aiming for relationships based on partnership, rather than inequalities in power and wealth between men and women, requires a more egalitarian psyche in both parties. Women are achieving greater power in the public domain, but they may need to face the issue of how much power they are prepared to hand over in the domestic sphere and over children. Men are losing some of their power in the public sphere, but they do not seem to want responsibility, coupled with power-sharing, in the domestic sphere.

Educating for relationships, helping boys develop their emotional literacy and inter-personal skills, would help. They will need these people skills if they are to find alternative sources of work — for all the jobs coming on stream require them.

Taking the pressure off family life might also help. The provision of adequate childcare support might ease some of the practical conflicts between men and women in relationships. Making our working world more family-friendly and shaping it more around the needs of parents would be a boon. It would at least free up the men who are willing to be fathers to undertake the role, although it seems unlikely in a world of global competition demanding longer and longer hours from regularly downsized employees.

However, I do not have any prescriptions for tackling men. If I were made Minister for Men, I would resign. I think men have to make the choice to go for personal growth. I know too that the kinds of skills that tomorrow's public world of work will demand are exactly the same kinds of inter-personal and team-building skills that are the basic building-blocks of human relationships, and so it may well be that the impetus for personal change will come from the combination of the demands that women are making on men and the demands of that public world of work. But, like the old pyschotherapist joke says, "It only takes one to change a lightbulb — but first the lightbulb has to want to change".

The consequences of men resisting change and growth will be for them to have written themselves out of the plot in both public and private worlds. There are some things that we can do to help them make those changes — making it easier for them to combine their roles at work and in the home, and educating young men and boys to have different expectations of their role in the world — but I think the time has come to invert the big Freudian question with which we kicked off the century and ask, 'What Do Men Want?'.

Looking for Teachers, Work – and an 'Enemy'

Nick Fisher

Nick Fisher is known as the Agony Uncle for Just Seventeen and as a frank spokesman on teenage sexual matters. A freelance journalist for 12 years, he has written for a huge range of publications from the Independent to Today, from Smash Hits to Radio Times, and from Chat to New Woman. In addition to presenting television and radio series on fishing, he also hosts the late-night ITV agony series 'dear Nick'.

How do you understand the evidence? Are we in a crisis?

I don't know that we are in a crisis at the moment, but it does feel that we could be on the verge of a crisis. I think there is very much a mood amongst certain young men of, basically, why give a fuck about anything? They think that they're not liked or respected as teenage males; teachers don't want to teach them; the country is never going to give them a living; the education system will probably marginalise them and push them out in some way; and they think, if the cap fits, wear it. This is the mood amongst certain working-class groups of teenage boys: it may be different for middle and upper-class boys (who generally tend to be held in higher regard throughout their teens and are given a better understanding of what they may achieve if they apply themselves), but it feels to me like a lot of working class teenage males who don't particularly have a supportive household background, or a particularly strong male role, are simply following their closest friends, the people they get the greatest solace from, or the greatest kind of entertainment. So they hang out with their mates and don't necessarily go to school. For some, the whole ethic of studying, fitting into the system and applying yourself is attacked by their peers — you don't necessarily want to look like some dickhead who's wanting to go and study and be a good boy, so (particularly around 15 or 16) you tend to draw back from authority, draw back from being led by the nose to school, and hang out with your mates. The girls seem different; girls seem to be able to apply themselves as well as fit in, and, by doing both, they are not so attacked for academic achievement or towing the line.

The lads growing up in an environment where anything looked upon as towing the line is attacked get to 17, 18 or 19 and realise that their female contempories have actually got A-levels by that time: they have applied themselves, they have got options opened to them and they're probably going to move away in some way. But the boys didn't apply themselves at the right time, they hung out with their mates who are all in the same boat, with days lasting forever and spent watching daytime TV and hanging around the shopping centre. These boys seem to have a much shorter-term view of the future than girls. I don't blame them for that; I think it's a sad indictment of the education system, which I don't think is treating them very well. I know it has its own problems. This is also a reflection of an environment where most of the men you know don't work and may never have worked, and so the young men think why should they assume that they will ever work either?

There also seems to be a male ethic around work (even for those that haven't worked for donkeys' years) that there is something different for men, and, while it's alright for women to go and be chambermaids or do cleaning jobs because men see them as having other things in life that are important to them, to men work is something else, something special. Maybe it's to do with the tradition of being craftsmen and industrial workers (whereas women have their family, their friends and their home). If you went up to a lot of men and said, "Look, you can go and earn a bit more than your dole if you become a chambermaid", they wouldn't do it, partly because of the fear of being attacked by their peers for doing an unsuitable, un-cool job.

You mentioned mates, the way schools give up on young men, the lack of jobs. Which is cause, which is effect?

I think it's a complicated mixture and I would find it difficult to attribute it directly. I also think there is something intrinsically destructive in the nature of men, and, when you match that up against an economic social climate that is not favouring them, that destruction comes to the fore and exacerbates the situation. We don't look after ourselves well, and you can translate that in a number of different ways.

I don't think (and it's not meant to be in anyway an apportionment of blame) that the great moves that women have made in the last 20-30 years have helped men at all; if anything, I think the moves have backed men into a corner and made them at some levels quite resentful, a bit suspicious and also just generally feeling lost. Men can end up having a very poor image of themselves. Instead of helping ourselves and helping each other, we have a tendency to attack and destroy.

If we're talking 'innate tendency', we're talking about all men, all classes and all races!

Yes, I think so. It sounds an outrageous thing to say, but yes, I think there is an inherent destruction in men which is linked to aggression. This is probably really useful to us most of the time, but at the moment, in this phase of our history, it is not.

How does this differ from Charles Murray[1], who says young men are wild, and that women's role is to domesticate them and enable them to relate as human beings?

Well, I wouldn't go so far as to say that young men are all wild. By saying there is an innate destruction in them, it doesn't necessarily mean they're wild, because destruction can be a very quiet think. Suicide is a terribly angry act in a way, but it can also be a very quietly destructive act: it is not necessarily about outward aggression, it's about not showing your feelings, not asking for help, not allowing anyone else's pain or emotions to enter your space, but just shutting down and blocking off and compartmentalizing yourself. I actually think that kind of destructiveness is generally accepted, and that's more what I mean, rather than saying we're all screaming vandals, although that's another expression of it. There are some very, very quietly destructive boys who just aren't saying anything to anybody and are suffering, although they would probably not ever describe themselves as suffering.

Why would that be — because they don't experience it as suffering, or it wouldn't be something they would want to acknowledge?

It's something they wouldn't want to acknowledge; some may be able to express it in the right situation, but I'm not sure that a lot of them do. My personal belief is that an awful lot of young men (in fact, not just young men, but men generally) are so out of touch with their feelings and their emotions, that they can't actually describe what's going on for them and certainly can't link a lot of the feelings that they have with events that have happened to them.

I realise I'm making some massive generalisations. Some men can talk. Some men can talk to men, and not to women; some men can talk to women, and not to men; a lot of men don't talk to either. It just sounds so wanky, men not expressing their emotions, but how many times have we talked about this sort of thing? It's almost about men not expressing anything — not even just expressing it, but not addressing it, not acknowledging it, not investigating it, not even realising it's there. Anger is always above the surface — a violent act, a rage, fast driving, getting drunk, all those sorts of things. What's actually below the surface, causing that anger, is just never looked at, often because it's not even understood that it can be there. I think that obviously we encourage this ourselves, and that women may also encourage it, although they say the opposite. I think we live in a society that encourages a male silence.

When I asked you were we in a crisis, you said no, not really.

How do you gauge a crisis? Until something of tragic proportions happens, then we always seem to be just teetering on the brink of it, but it seems as though, of late, something's going to happen if something's not done about it fairly soon. An awful lot is getting acted out in depression, and you don't notice that — it's not as though there's going to be a riot, we don't even know who to blame. Part of my fear is that women will cop for quite a lot of the blame. I've said this recently and people went, "Tut, tut. That can't be right", but it's not meant as an accusation, just an observation. More men see their female counterparts accellerating away from them in all directions, and some think, "Hang on a minute, how come they've got it so good, and we haven't?".

As Minister for Men, given this evidence, what would you do about it?

It's a very hard question. I probably would want to look more to schools to help boys develop more broadly. Looking at ratios of boys to girls, the bigger the group of boys, the harder it is to get through to them. Breaking those groups down and possibly mixing the sexes (although that's arguable) and just trying to give time to people would assist. A lot of the time, girls are much more receptive and responsive — they're much nicer; people want to teach them. As you teach them, you get more back from them, they grow and they become more interested — for educators, it's a fulfilling experience. (Having said that, I think some teenage girls are becoming more 'masculine' and are already becoming harder to handle, and we are going to start seeing increasing problems).

There's a lot of support for girls, a lot of information, a lot of culture. There's a lot of socialisation for them; they are generally building up patterns of living which will take them through their lives, whereas, with boys, there doesn't seem to be those patterns, there doesn't seem to be the same socialising at all. Again, we are looking at a group of boys who will attack first. That seems to be the safest instinct, you know — if anyone shows a weakness, you attack it because it's much safer than support, and it's at that point the damage seems to start being done, the rot sets in.

For a teacher with boys, you are often fighting against peer pressure, you're fighting against a lot of misinformation that they are gathering in the playground; educators want to be with them less because it's harder work. For teenage boys, we may need to double the number of teachers through positive discrimination towards 11-14 year-old boys. Looking at the curriculum and things like class sizes and the ratio of boys to girls would be important.

Some 11-14 year-olds were interviewed in Belfast recently[2], and what came across was they said they didn't have a problem with big classes. What they had a problem with was when teachers couldn't control those classes.

If I were Minister for Men, and had a budget, I would pay teachers more. I would have more of them, and I think I would also look at who and why people are attracted into the teaching profession. I would want to attract some different personalities who are able to cope and understand young men. It's not meant as a criticism of teachers in any way. I know what it's like — you've got a big class and you're knackered and you've got a load of lippy 13 year-old boys — you just want to get out of there as quickly as possible and just contain them if possible, but, unfortunately, containment isn't proving to be good enough.

So what kind of characteristics do these people need, what sort of people are they?

I don't think there necessarily are strict criteria, but if we went to a lot of youth facilities, we'd find people working amongst groups there who know how to do it. They're not necessarily teachers, but they have been working with that age group and understand how to cope and how to communicate, how to break groups up and how to navigate their way through. You see, I don't think you can apply the same technique for teaching teenage girls to teaching teenage boys.

I think we need to start working now on 9 year-olds, basically. It would lay some important foundations for the future. If we don't solve it, there are going to be a lot of guys in 10 years' time who are going to be in their 30's who've still got fuck all, always had fuck all, who are getting older and even more bitter about it.

We need to create feasible employment for the late teens and early 20's (in a time, as well as a financial, sense), because I think that a lot of the behavioural patterns young men fall into when they are not working are quite depressive. You drink and smoke if you've got money, you watch a bit of tele (because there's nothing else to do) during the day, and those things are generally quite depressive and depressing. Part of the problem is that business of not wanting to be a member of any club who wants you as a member — once you call something a whatever 'scheme' or 'workshop', you can bet your bottom dollar that the guys you actually want there ain't gonna be there because they're put off right from the start by the fact that it's something that's designed for people like them.

Earlier, you said that young men see work as a special thing. Does that mean that attitudes should be changed, or do we respond to that need — do we start a mining industry?

It's a good point. I think the quickest result is, yes, create a mining industry. An industry that lets men do what a lot of men think of as men's work and earn a man's wage will keep some of them happy, but, at the same time, if you could change their attitudes, it would be far better for the future because you could work at erasing that mind-set. A lot of people talk about men having an increasing role in the family and home and so on and so forth, and I think that there are obviously men who welcome that and enjoy it — I've always said there are some incredibly maternal instincts among men that are very rarely allowed to come out. At the same time, there are also huge groups of men who do not respond to any of that. It couldn't be further from their perceptions of who they are, and it's almost like you have to be able to cater for both ways of thinking. To say that you can make it easier for men to be house-husbands, or whatever, is fine and great for a

199

portion of the population, but, for the rest, you've got to look for something else and maybe that is creating work for them. I often don't think men's needs are that great.

What would they be?

Well, they vary obviously from man to man, but I think there are some men that could be satisfied with a lot less then their female counterparts at the moment. I think, in women, you've opened up a can of worms — you've excited something within them where they want big things and big times. There are some hugely ambitious, hungry women around, and that's a wonderful thing. There's great potential there in terms of the country's creative and commercial future: there is no end of talent that is being nurtured amongst women by women. But I think there are a lot of men who don't have that same hunger, that size of ambition, at all, and who would actually be quite happy with a fairly straightforward, conventional, traditional existence.

Things are getting out of kilter — I mean, you'll find vast rafts of women in various professions at the moment who cannot find men. They've reached their 30's, they've got great jobs, they own their own flat, they own their car, etc., but can they find a man? They don't see their male equivalents. There are a lot of men who come along and say, "What I want is a housewife. I want a traditional role where I've got a job, I go out and bring back a bit of wedge, and my home and my family are looked after". We seem to have forgotten this in some ways, you know: we've been forced to forget that a lot of people are actually very comfortable with this.

So, as Minister for Men, you'd need to be flexible yourself and not assume that all men want the same thing. In terms of that mind-set you referred to, are there strategies that you could develop? Does it mean we offer therapy on the NHS?

When you asked that question, there were two things that went through my mind. I was thinking about NHS therapy, and wondered what sort of response would you get placing an advert

200

in the *Sun* tomorrow saying, anybody who wanted therapy, just turn up at your local Doctor and hand in your coupon. My immediate reaction would be you'd get a lot of 'sad men' who would trot up and do it, and most of the men who really needed help wouldn't go. Whereas, if you had a third world war tomorrow, you would get the men that really needed help signing up to go and fight — they'd want to see some blood-letting, they'd be charged with it. It's funny, on the one hand we're talking about therapy, but an instinct in me thinks actually what men want to do is go to fucking war. I'm not sure if a lot of that apathy and depression is about a complete lack of a vehicle for those emotions, although that does sound a bit bizarre.

While I'm sure you wouldn't want to advocate a third world war, are you saying that we have to package a response that will re-direct men's destructiveness? What might that be?

My first instinct always is that, whatever you do is going to be attacked, really for the sake of it, and it's like you almost have to do six different things simultaneously so that certain groups can attack and others respond, and you'll kind of cover everyone eventually if you think of the right permutation...

Do-it-yourself gladiators through the NHS! Some men need something, you see, like that to attack. There is never a moment when men are more together than when they're attacking something. For one of those six things, we need an 'enemy'. If we could invent a virtual reality enemy that can never actually be harmed, but that everyone believes in, you could muster up all that anger and passion and direct it there. But there is also a part of me that thinks, "What a terrible waste — if only you could suck that passion and anger off and do something else with it", but, as yet we've never been able to come up with what that something might be.

Did families provide this?

Yes. The increase in the divorce rate and the breakdown of the family model has removed the feeling that you have a family for life. The old-fashioned way of looking at families meant it was not just your duty, but your desire, to protect, nurture, feed and make it grow. Then it would blossom and look after you as well. If that no longer exists, have we taken away part of the drive that men traditionally had? It does seem as though men are forces of energy — some good, some bad — that needs to be focused and channelled, and, if it's not, it comes out sideways and causes all sorts of problems. Maybe the history of repression for women has given them a direction — we gave them the women's movement and it's like, to a certain extent, men are the enemy for them; there is the focus. Men as yet don't have an enemy and... there is a fear in my heart that one day women will become the enemy.

This would definitely be a pre-occupation for the Minister for Men, wouldn't it? It's how we locate those enemies that do not do anyone any harm, including the men themselves.

Yes. You said it there... the Minister for Men should spend a lot of money finding an enemy, a safe enemy, the 'Enemy Budget'!

REFERENCES

1. Murray, C. *The Emerging British Underclass.* London. London Institute of Economic Affairs (1991).
2. LLoyd, T. *Young Men's Health — A Youth Work Concern.* Belfast. The Health Promotion Agency for Northern Ireland (1996).

Righting the Wrongs and Putting Love before Profit

Neil Lyndon

Apart from a spell in the 1980's as political and media consultant to the Californian industrialist Dr Armand Hammer (when he wrote the best-selling book 'Hammer'), Neil Lyndon has been a full-time journalist in the national media since 1969. In 1992, his book, 'No More Sex War: The Failures of Feminism' was published, causing great controversy. 'Sexual Impolitics' (a collection of writings about gender issues) is due to be published in 1996, and Neil is currently writing a political thriller and preparing a study of the history of atheism.

The Left (which has been my political family home for 35 years) and its followers (among whom I have found most of my lifelong friends) have never been much good at admitting fault. Unless they have been dragged out of them in Show Trials, penitent confessions of error have never come speedily to the lips of those who believe they have discerned and share a comprehensively correct social analysis. The Left, speaking broadly, saw no wrong in the Russian Revolution before 1956 and was vicious in its treatment of those, such as Muggeridge, who did report evil there. It saw no harm in Maoism in the 60's (where are the Fanshens of yesteryear?) nor in the Khmer Rouge in the

70's. In America, in 1971, I knew many orthodox leftists who would say that there was no important political difference between Richard Nixon and Eugene McCarthy. In the early 80's in England, I was often in the homes of Labour Party members who would say that the Party should support the Provisional IRA.

Some of these stances were not just wrong, but evil; not merely mistaken, but mad. Those who took and espoused those opinions at the time will not repeat them now, or they will say that they were misled. Rarely will you hear them say they were wrong.

In our own age, the Left has been most comprehensively and fatally wrong in its analysis of the relative social positions of men and women. Led by the women's movement (if there ever was such a thing), the sexual politics of the Left since Kate Millett's book[1] was published in 1968 amounts to a comprehensive misprision and misrepresentation of a vital social and political issue. Wrong in its essential presumptions and fundamental tenets, the Left has also been poisonously wrong on most points of fact about the changes that have occurred for men and women since World War Two. The evidence about men gathered by WWM and reproduced at the front of this book makes one single point incontestable: if you put all that evidence together, it is logically impossible to say — as the Left has been saying for nearly 30 years — that ours is a patriarchal order of society.

If, as those statistics show, British men who have jobs work longer hours, for less pay, for more of their lives than their European counterparts, how can we say that ours is a society organised by men for the benefit of men? That is not what those men will say. If you ask them and listen to what they say, you will hear men who work say that they want to work fewer hours for more pay for less of their lives.

If men throughout Europe live seven years less than women, commit suicide in the ratio of 3:1 compared with women, are imprisoned in the ratio of 50:1 compared with women, receive less than half as much medical attention as women, get less favourable attention at school and, with or without educational qualifications, are less likely to get a job, how does anybody imagine that ours is a patriarchal order of society? Are those the characteristics of a society organised by men for the benefit of men? If so, we must think them very ineffective or foolish organisers, which, in its turn, must make it very puzzling to understand how people so stupid can ever have gotten themselves in charge or stay there.

Consider the position of a man who wants to be an active father to his children and tell us, if you can, how it is to be reconciled with the proposition that ours is a patriarchal society.

If he has no legal rights for those children so long as he is unmarried, and all rights of parenthood belong to the mother, how are you going to tell that man that his is the privileged status of the patriarch? If he has no legal right to time off work when his children are born, will you tell him that he is equal in parental standing with the mother who has that right? If he has no chance (and we know that he has no chance) of getting equal treatment with his wife over their children, their property and their money in a contested divorce, will you tell him that his are the advantages of a male in a society organised for the benefit of males?

If it is true, as Jeremy Andrew claimed in an article in The Sunday Times on Father's Day last year, that as many as 80,000 children a year are forcibly separated from their fathers by an insidious process of "family cleansing" sanctioned by the Courts, why does the Left go on insisting that all gender inequalities and disadvantages in our society are inflicted on women? Are you going to tell those men that the legalised abduction of their children is a personal advantage to them?

If it is true, as was shown by the MORI survey for the BBC Programme Here and Now, that 11% of men have been violently attacked by the woman they live with, and that 6% of women have been violently attacked by the man they live with, why does the feminist-led Left go on repeating the lie that women generally are in physical danger of attack from men? Why does anybody continue to believe what feminist criminologists have insisted upon for a quarter of a century, that domestic violence against women reflects the distribution of patriarchal privilege and power in the wider society? If, as the MORI survey and others have shown, it is true that men are eight times less likely than women to report an incident of domestic violence, why do we repeatedly hear that the figures for reported crimes of domestic violence show only 'the tip of the iceberg' of violence against women? According to available evidence, what those figures actually show is less than the tip of the iceberg of violence against men.

If, as WWM's evidence shows, it is true that women who have jobs work an average of 13.6 hours a week less than men who have jobs, why do we routinely assume that the reason why men fail to do an equal share of domestic work is because they are lazy and slobbish old patriarchs who deem it to be woman's work? Why do we not include in our thoughts on this subject the truth that men are given less time at home with their families?
I could go on. I have.

I have been asking many of these questions for the last few years and some of them for about 25 years. No persuasive answer has returned. Learned feminist scholars and their supporters have said that I must have a small penis; or that I must be impotent; or that I must have trouble getting a woman. Such are the refinements of argument in the gender debate. Of all the thousands of printed words of personal abuse directed at me, none has ever been given to answering these most essential questions. They all boil down to one question which, again, I have asked in every argument or debate about feminism for nearly 10 years:

If ours is a patriarchal society — which must mean that the interests of women are, at best, secondary to the interests of men — why is it impossible to name any inequalities for women in law, other than the prohibitions in some churches against women becoming priests and the rule that prevents a woman from inheriting a peerage?

It is no answer to say that societies before our own were self-evidently patriarchal: that's as relevant as saying that earlier ages took a standard rule of measurement from Henry VIII's foot; it has no bearing on our own times.

It is no answer to say that, women having been oppressed for centuries, it's about time men caught a dose of the same medicine. That's as intelligent and sympathetic as saying that young Germans today ought to be gassed to make up for the crimes of their grandparents.

The only answer that makes any sense to me is to say that the Left — we — were wrong. Our analysis was dunderheaded; our evidence was misconstrued; our prescriptions were worthless. We need to admit that we were, simply, mistaken.

We were wrong to believe that women had to fight a war of emancipation against male authority to achieve changes in their social, familial and sexual standing: that was all happening anyway, and feminism was nothing more than an ideological parasite upon those changes. We were wrong to say that men resisted change. The truth was that they — we, I and almost everybody I knew and know today — welcomed change, both for women and for men.

We were completely wrong to say that ours is a patriarchy. In doing so, we wronged men and their children. We wronged our age and we inhibited its promise.

What difference would it make if we could admit that error? Who would benefit by that confession?

The answer is that we all would benefit, not just men, but women and children as well. Families would benefit, and relations between men and women would benefit, if they were no longer encouraged to see each other as social and personal antagonists. These are the answers that I gave in my book, 'No More Sex War'[2]. They were intended to reinvigorate the sexual politics of the Left. They were absolutely ignored in all the published reviews of that book, but, in my mind, they remain the most radical, egalitarian and libertarian proposals to have emerged from discussions of gender issues in the last 25 years; so, in my temporary role as Minister for Men, I would like to repeat them here.

If we admit that we have been wrong and that men have been wronged, we might begin to recognise that the social interests of men and women are usually identical, and that, where they differ, they are harmonious. As a first step, we might start treating boys better. We might not suppose, as distinguished humanitarians such as Dr Rosalind Miles have said, that boys have a congenital disposition towards violence because they are closer to the animal state. We might believe that a boy's right to a good education is equal to a girl's; and we might forbid teachers to act as we know they have acted in the last 25 years — as if it was their social duty to give preferential treatment to girls.

If we can admit that we have been wrong in our general suppositions about men and their powers, we might begin to admit that men are genuinely unequal in family law and that the position of fathers in divorce is a major human rights issue. We might recognise that the elimination of fathers from their children's lives by legal process is a catastrophe for everybody — the children and the mothers, along with the fathers and the wider society.

If we admit the idea that men and women ought to be equal as parents, whereas at present it is men who are unequal, then we might adjust our family laws and practices to make men and women more equal at work. This means, along with other effects, that men would have equal rights with women to time off work to look after their children.

If both men and women are expected to do much less work when their babies are born and during their children's infancies, the professional disadvantages of women will disappear: they will evaporate. If both men and women are entitled to equal rights of leave from work, and all the concessions and encouragements a modern society can provide by way of tax-breaks, subsidies, subventions and honours, women would be less frantic in trying to resolve the demands of family and career, and men would be better fathers.

Young people who want to have children must be lavished with every form of encouragement we can provide in order that they may care for their children themselves. The State is a poor mother and a mean father. The State has no love to give, because love cannot be raised in taxes, nor dispensed by officials. Love is not the business of the State. It is the private work of individuals.

We could help young parents. Governments must apply some radical intelligence to their immense powers of social engineering to ease the pains of parents and to ease the present and future strains upon their own exchequers, imposed by parents who simply cannot raise their children and work full-time. Governments must extend the munificence of tax breaks to employers who give equal rights of maternity and paternity leave. They might, via subsidy and tax advantage, give active encouragement to employers and couples who work out job-sharing arrangements.

If, meanwhile, tax concessions and improved benefits were available to both men and women when they want to care for their own babies, we might begin to see some real change in the position of women at work, of men at home and of children presently in the care of others.

All these measures are, however, trifling tinklings with the problems we face — how to manage the labour market and how to care for our children. Trifling tinklings are likely to be the best we get, as governments fudge and mudge their way through the difficulties ahead. There is, nevertheless, a truly radical option available for consideration. There is one measure in the powers of government which might settle these deeply troubling problems and failures of care in one go. It is a fantasy — but the Minister for Men should be dreaming of an ideal state.

The most radical approach would be simply to impose a national minimum wage at double the present average earnings and, simultaneously, halve the hours of the working week. If the legal maximum number of hours an employer can demand from an employee were 20, rather than the 40, 48, 50 which are allowable today, our society would, instantly, be revolutionised in all its aspects, most particularly in child-care. If a couple could support a household and their children on two incomes derived from 20 hours' work each, they could sympathetically and efficiently divide the duties of child care. Meanwhile, the change in employment law would take care of our horrible problems of unemployment among the young and the redundancy of the elderly. If employers were prohibited by law from demanding more than half a week's labour from their employees, they would have to employ other people. The pool of unemployed among the young and the retired would be mopped up.

"What about our profits?", the corporate managers will be screaming. The answer is, chaps, that something has got to give; and it's your turn. The god of profit must be toppled from its plinth: the god of love deserves more collective worship, both in the home and in the finance department. I'm not saying that you can't make a profit; I'm just saying that you're going to have to make do and manage on a lot less of it. You'll have plenty of time to think about the ways to achieve this management while you are at home with the babies.

That's what ought to be next for men. It would be good for all of us.

REFERENCES

1. Millett, K. 'Sexual Politics', New York: Doubleday (1968).
2. Lyndon, N. 'No More Sex War: The Failures of Feminism', London: Sinclair-Stevenson, London (1992).

Why Do Men Want to be Victims?

Kerry Young

Kerry Young is an independent training and development consultant. Her background is in youth work, where for many years she was centrally involved in the development of work with girls and young women. Her current work seeks to examine the meaning, purpose and practice of 'equal opportunities' and 'anti-oppressive work' by exposing the moral principles underpinning the concepts and creating models for the development of effective structures and relationships. Kerry is particularly interested in relationships between women and men, and black and white colleagues.

For many years, I have publicly (and privately) acknowledged the negative and harmful effects of gender socialisation for men — a process which forces them into rigid and narrowly-defined roles limiting their range of experiences and de-humanising them as a consequence. The 1990's are no less pernicious, as the 'condition of men' at the start of this book demonstrates.

Statistics and current trends paint a picture of men as being more likely than women to 'under achieve' in the education system, be unemployed (particularly if young and black), suffer from ill-heath and be on the receiving end of violent crime (from other men). Men work longer hours than women (although this does not take account of women's domestic labour), die younger and are more inclined to suicide. At the same time, men's criminal activity continues to escalate, with instances of rape, indecent assault on females and gross indecency with children increasing dramatically over recent years.

In a way, this is not surprising. Gender socialisation encourages men to engage in risk-taking behaviour, to disregard their health and health needs and to respond aggressively, violently even, to (the slightest) provocation. Men are conditioned to seek self-identity through employment, the absence of which produces uncertainty, anxiety and stress. Men are also conditioned to be sexually compulsive and to associate sex with power, rather than with intimacy. Correspondingly, women's role is seen as not only 'looking after' men, but also as having a 'humanising' or 'socialising' effect on them.

In addition, racism and other forms of oppression exist to compound the experiences of black men, gay men, working-class men, Jewish men, differently-abled men, etc. Whilst individual men are clearly responsible for their own attitudes and behaviour, it is important to remember that men are part of a political and economic system and culture which structures and moulds all of our experiences, expectations and responses. The socialisation of individuals according to gender affects men as powerfully as it does women.

Men's current 'condition' reflects a quiet (and not so quiet) kind of desperation, and should be understood not only in the context of men's experience, but within the broader reality of the mass unemployment, poverty, ill-health, homelessness, recklessness and despondency which pervades contemporary British society. The weekly frenzy over the National Lottery is the most poignant illustration of the depth of hopelessness which sees 'winning' as the only escape from, or solution to, our predicament. The 'condition of men' is a part of this reality and is not simply, as some would have us believe, the result of feminism's efforts to create new possibilities for women.

Men are having a tough time — not only in material terms, but also emotionally and psychologically as they struggle to adjust to the new and changing demands of their circumstances. For example, they must deal with the material reality of unemployment, as well as come to terms with the emotional and psychological effects of what it means to be a man without the identity of a job. For, in this society at least, a man is defined by the nature of his production — a man is what he does (a miner, welder, electrician, plumber ...). The 'problem for men' is the recognition that age-old beliefs, attitudes, behaviour and identities are no longer applicable.

However, the current penchant for 'proving' the underdog status of men and promoting them as the 'victims of the 90's' is no solution. The conditioning of people into narrowly-defined roles is no more painful for one group than it is for another. The pain of men's gender socialisation is also the pain of women's gender socialisation. The effect for both is a range of (different) limitations which acts to restrict the nature and extent of women and men's experiences, shapes their expectations and aspirations, and, importantly, enforces their isolation and disconnection from themselves...and each other.

So, whilst accepting the material reality and validity of men's personal experiences, one is still forced to ask, "What is really the issue here?". The unfortunate truth is that, despite the progress made in equal opportunities for women, sexism is still alive and well in 1996. As a result, current debates about men take place within the framework of sexism. Within this, the tendency is to address the personal individual experiences of men, whilst failing to grasp the crux of the matter — the issue of patriarchy.

It is worth restating the elements of this oppression, given the current tendency to overlook its continued existence. Whilst gender socialisation has negative consequences for both women and men, existing social relations and institutions ensure that men are more powerful than women — economically, socially, politically. The effect of this patriarchy is the subordination and oppression of women (ie sexism). Feminism, in its struggle against women's oppression, is therefore not essentially a criticism of individual men, but rather a challenge to the institutionalised collective male power in society which ensures that women (as a group and as individuals) are systematically and consistently regarded as subordinate to men (as a group and as individuals). This is regardless of any individual man's particular circumstances, opinions or political commitments.

Sexism eases men's lives at every stage and in every sphere. As popular belief would have it ... if education is important, it is more important for a man; if unemployment is demoralising, it is more demoralising for a man; if domestic work is unfulfilling, it is more unfulfilling for a man; if success is important, it is more important for a man; if life is humiliating, it is more humiliating for a man.

Patriarchy not only determines the gender socialisation of both women and men, it also institutionalises a preference for males and 'masculine' values. For example, gender socialisation tells us not only that:

- men think/women feel
- men are strong/women are weak
- men are active/women are passive
- men are rational/women are emotional
- men are independent/women are dependent
- men are brave/women are frightened
- men are secure/women are vulnerable

but also that being able to think, being strong, active, rational, independent, brave and secure are positive 'human' qualities. The unspecified 'human being' is perceived in male terms, and the unspecified 'human' attributes are masculine. In some mystical and unwritten way, men become more worthy, more important, more respected than women. Men become the positive Self and women become the 'Other'. And, despite the attempts of some men to reclaim their 'feelings', the plain truth is that sensitivity, vulnerability, the ability to cry, or even the acknowledged need for closeness, are not actually qualities highly valued in/by society.

By contrast, men's apparent 'weaknesses' — insensitivity, incompetence in domestic matters, inadequacy as parents, compulsive sexual behaviour — are treated by society as relatively insignificant in relation to their (perceived) positive attributes of strength, clarity, power, reliability. Being good at housework or caring for others are not abilities highly regarded or rewarded by society — even if they ought to be. If women are indeed 'more human', then men are more powerful. And we know which, in society's terms, is considered to be of greater substance and consequence.

Cynicism could even suggest that society's increasing attention to men, as men, is simply another expression of the very same values which insist that men come first — their experiences, their needs, their opinions, their aspirations, their demands and now their anguish. It is this same reasoning and values which insinuate that, if things are bad for men, the very fabric of society is in shreds. The crisis of masculinity is the crisis of society itself.

The central issue is not therefore the personal experience of individual men (as important as that is), but rather the question of power — who has it, how they get it, what they do with it, and how they hang on to it. Whilst power has a personal dimension, interpersonal power relations are often little more than reflections of broader societal attitudes and behaviour. Therefore the issue of power is not only personal, but also political — ie the ways in which power relations are constructed and enforced in the institutions, structures, culture and values of society.

These power relations take many forms. At its sharpest, the fact that some men rape some women controls all women and implicates all men. This does not imply that all men are rapists, for they surely are not. It does, however, bring into sharp relief the dichotomy of gender relations. The single experience shared by all women (regardless of race, class, age, religion, disability, sexuality) is their vulnerability to male violence, and particularly to rape. For rape is a 'weapon of domination and repression' — a terror visited upon 6-month-old babies and 89-year-old pensioners. It is the form of control suitable for women because they are women. As Susan Brownmiller asserts[1]: "... rape is a part of a system of male intimidation that keeps all women in fear :... and in their place".

In this context, apportioning blame or attempting to identify men as 'victims' is, at the very least, misguided, and, at worst, a dangerous distraction from men's central task of creating a new masculinity appropriate for them in the present reality.

The question, "What do women want from men?" is often posed. But this is not the question. The question should be, "What do men want for, and from, themselves?". For, despite the now well-recognised negative effects of gender socialisation for men, men still cannot let go of the old patterns and stereotypes. It would appear that the privilege of being male in a patriarchal society is too much of an enticement. Unfortunately, we can only swim for shore once we have let go of the rotting debris to which we cling. The present 'crisis of masculinity' demands not sorrow, but celebration. For it represents a new beginning — an opportunity for men to finally break free from the rigidity and constraints which have for so long prescribed and structured their lives.

Indeed, it is only by grasping this opportunity that masculinity can be re-created in men's best interest whilst supporting the liberation of women, for you cannot have fixed roles and limitations for one group without the corresponding roles for the other group — you cannot have slaves without slave owners. Therefore the only true liberation lies in the elimination of the oppression, that is, the elimination of the institutional structures and systems which give privilege to some at the expense of others; the elimination of policies and practices which create systematic mistreatment, exploitation and abuse of one group for the benefit of another; the elimination of cultural attitudes and behaviour which regard one group as more worthy and another group as subordinate.

This means that men must give up sexism ... and come to terms with why that idea feels so scary — and why that reality seems so hard to achieve.

Men have to forget about 'what women want', and stop feeling sorry for themselves; stop trying to blame someone (women or feminism) for their predicament; or to prove that gender socialisation is just as painful, or even more painful, for men; or to show how misunderstood and badly treated men are — in general, stop trying to make themselves into victims.

Men need to:

— face the reality and accept responsibility for their own behaviour and the behaviour of other men (without explanation or reference to men's conditioning — this is a distraction)
— confront the worst feelings they have about men and being male (avoiding or denying this is not in their best interest — the only way forward for men is working through the shame, the guilt and the fear of being male)
— develop their understanding of sexism and learn how to challenge it (lack of awareness and understanding of the personal and political dimensions of sexism leaves men's 'liberation' in danger of becoming simply indulgence).

In the process, it will be essential to examine how enforced, institutionalised heterosexuality acts to define what 'real/proper men' are like and how they should behave. Equally, it will be necessary to understand how lesbian and gay oppression determines and controls relationships, not only between women and women/men and men, but also between women and men. There are many questions to be asked about the extent to which established stereotypes of 'male' not only fail to reflect the broad category of 'men', but are used to oppress certain groups of men (eg gay men, Jewish men, Asian men) who often do not conform to the aggression and the violence of the stereotype.

In the end, beating drums, hugging trees and romping in the woods — even workshops for getting in touch with their feelings — cannot sustain men though the long journey towards their own liberation. These pursuits are 'feel good' activities — they are short-term palliatives for those who feel lost, lonely or afraid. They offer no serious remedy for the private and public reality of men in a patriarchal society.

Indeed, as Audre Lorde comments[2]:

"the true focus of revolutionary change is never merely the oppressive situations which we seek to escape, but that piece of the oppressor which is planted deep within each of us and which knows only the oppressors' tactics, the oppressors' relationships".

Some men have misheard, misunderstand, or choose to misrepresent the feminist argument. Others want to make a virtue out of basic human qualities — kindness, compassion, helpfulness. And still it seems there are some who genuinely do not understand. The challenge, however, is not to 'humanise' men, for they are already fully human. The challenge — not only for men, but for all of us — is to become authentic human beings.

To achieve this, the sense of what is lost must be outweighed by the sense of what is to be gained. And what men have to gain is themselves. The dust is wiped from the mirror to reveal the brilliance of a true reflection. This is the exact opposite of abandoning one's own person. What is required here is not an escape from masculinity, but rather a rediscovery which enables men to recreate the people they have always been and to grasp, once again, their humanity. Such a task cannot be achieved by victims.

REFERENCES

1. Brownmiller, S. 'Against Our Will: Men, Women and Rape', London: Penguin (1976).
2. Lorde, A. 'Sister Outsider': The Crossing Press (1984).

Challenging Oppressions, Reconstructing Masculinities

Keith Pringle

Keith Pringle is Senior Lecturer in Applied Social Studies at the University of Sunderland. He practiced as a qualified social worker for ten years, mainly in the areas of child care and youth work. Since 1987, he has researched and written about men's sexual violence and also masculinity in general: his most recent book is 'Men, Masculinities and Social Welfare'. He is currently co-ordinating a Swedish-British comparative research project on fatherhood and writing a book on children and social welfare in Europe. He is active in re-creating masculinities and developing community responses to child sexual abuse.

The issue of men and masculinities has become the object of very considerable attention in recent years, both from the point of view of theoretical discourse and of practical action (and *Working With Men* has played an outstanding role in encouraging the latter). However, the vantage points of commentators, activists and practitioners focusing on the issue of masculinities vary massively — a fact clearly reflected in the range of contributors to this volume.

My own perspective is one which places more emphasis on the need to challenge oppressions generated within our society by certain forms of masculinity, than on seeking the well-being of men per se.

Having said that, I will attempt to demonstrate that challenging such oppressions may also be of benefit to many men for two reasons. First, because the oppressions being challenged often damage considerable numbers of men to varying extents, as well as many women and children. Secondly, because the reconstructions of masculinity which I seek may well, in some respects, offer many men more emotionally satisfying ways of living than they possess at present.

However, I would not wish readers to think that what I am suggesting is some nice, neat answer to the problems of gender relations for men and women. The solutions which I am advocating have their limitations, not least because the patterns of oppression associated with hegemonic or dominant forms of masculinity do benefit many, probably most, men in our society to an extent[1], and therefore the 'pay-off' to some men of reconstruction will be, at best, hard for them to grasp, and, at worst, non-existent.

Any selection of statistics about a social phenomenon is bound to give a particular shape to the stories that can be drawn from them about that phenomenon. The statistics which preface this book are no exception. One story that can be told from this data is that, in some aspects of existence, many men are suffering much dissatisfaction and pain: for instance, as reflected in the material relating to their health, life expectancy, suicide rates and their hopelessness due to unemployment.

I would not seek to discount such a story. However, I do wish to frame it within the context of two other extremely important and (to my mind) valid stories which are only partially reflected by the statistical evidence chosen to introduce this book.

The first of these two stories is the extent and range of the violences perpetrated by men and boys within our society. To gain what I would regard as an adequate appreciation of this massive social problem, one would need to address numerous sources of evidence which I have documented in detail elsewhere[2]. This evidence includes:

- community prevalence studies of woman abuse and child sexual abuse;

- a growing amount of relatively new data concerning the scale of sexual violence directed at particularly vulnerable groups within society, such as people with physical disabilities, people with learning disabilities, elders, and people who have suffered mental distress. Men and boys seem to preponderate as perpetrators in all these manifestations of sexual violence;

- increasing linkages being developed between patriarchal relations and the physical/emotional abuse of children;

- the extent and range of oppressions associated with dominant forms of masculinity to be found within virtually all types of organisation;

- the preponderance of men as perpetrators of not only physical, but also of sexual, violence against men and boys;

- the relationship between hegemonic manifestations of masculinity and the warfare which continues to ravage numerous areas of our planet;

- the relationship between forms of masculinity, capitalism and the associated exploitation of people and resources in this country and around the world.

I am not suggesting, simplistically, that dominant forms of masculinity can be held responsible for all the problems of the world. Nor am I ignoring the fact that women can perpetrate virtually all the forms of violence mentioned above, although their relative numbers in most cases are much smaller, and their violence has to be partly understood within the context of patriarchal relations. I am arguing that power relations associated with hegemonic masculinities are heavily implicated in many of the social, political and economic problems which confront western societies, and which are in many cases global as well.

The story set out above is one which we need to address urgently in asking the question, "What next for men?".

Moreover, there is a second story not fully told in the statistical data at the start of the book, and this story has to be addressed too. It is a story which recognises that, although many men are sorely disadvantaged (to different extents) within the structures of our society, on the whole, women tend to be disadvantaged to a far greater extent; and that many men also draw very considerable advantages from those structures (again to different degrees). Moreover, the structures are heavily shaped by the power relations mentioned above related to hegemonic forms of masculinity.

There is not space to detail this complex pattern of men's overall advantage here, but surveys are readily available in the literature[3]. Moreover, using this perspective, we can reframe three facts which this book's introductory statistical section mentions.

First of all, those statistics tell us that, in many respects, women's educational achievements are outstripping men's. What we then have to ask ourselves is why, despite this, should vertical and horizontal job segregation in favour of men still be so marked even in those professional occupations where women preponderate, such as the welfare services?[4]

Let us now reframe another statistic. We are told that there seems to be a trend towards fathers spending more time with their children, and that a considerable number of men demonstrate attitudes which reject traditional gender roles in terms of the breadwinner/homemaker dichotomy. Although I do not deny that both these assertions have validity in some situations[5], I would also echo the doubts expressed by many feminist commentators.[6] Involved fathers often tend to focus on parenting tasks which are more pleasurable, and men's attitude change towards domestic tasks does not, to a considerable extent, appear to be reflected in their actual practice. We also need to bear in mind that, apart from the material imbalances in domestic gender roles, there is also an emotional dimension where women often seem to carry an undue burden.[7]

My third and final factual reframe to illustrate the overall advantage enjoyed by men over women in our society relates to the finding that marriage, or cohabitation, with a female partner acts as a protection against ill-health for men. We surely need to place this in the context of another finding that, among married people, the rate of admission to hospital on psychiatric grounds is much higher for women than for men, whereas the reverse is true for people who are single, widowed or divorced.[8]

I think we should make no mistake in recognising that, along with other dynamics of power which we will address later, those of gender remain remarkably dominant within our society: to a very large extent, it is still 'a man's world' in terms of social advantage. This, too, needs to be urgently addressed in any answers to the question, "What next for men?".

To answer this question, we need to look beyond the evidence in the statistics provided for us. In addressing future policies and practices regarding men and masculinities, I would argue that the priority issues are:

- how do we counter the huge social problem of the violences and oppressions associated with dominant forms of masculinity;

- and how do we restructure society in such a way as to equalise, not just the life opportunities, but also the life experiences of women with those of men?

Relations of gender are not the only major power dynamics shaping structures of society and personal encounters. We need to imagine in any social situation an extremely complex and constantly-shifting interaction of dynamics around relations such as age, 'race', disability, sexuality, and class, together with gender. The picture drawn here, and indeed throughout this chapter, relies heavily on the analysis of masculinities developed by Bob Connell among others.[9]

That analysis can also be a starting point for thinking about creative and positive ways of reconstructing masculinities, in particular those dominant forms of masculinity which have figured so prominently in our earlier considerations of social structure. At the risk of grossly over-simplifying Connell's sophisticated approach, we can suggest that hegemonic masculinities (which are not envisaged as existing in any 'pure' form) are associated with the kinds of power relations we noted earlier (i.e. 'race', age, disability, class, sexuality).

Connell indicates that it is the very complexity in the social construction of masculinities which also offers the best hope of a transformatory gender politics, given the fissuring which such complexities imply — despite men's shared interest in patriarchy:

"Men continue to be detached from the defence of patriarchy by the contradictions and intersections of gender relations; new possibilities open up for reconfiguration and transformation of masculinities ... I think a fresh politics of masculinity will develop in new arenas: for instance, the politics of the curriculum, work around AIDS/HIV and anti-racist politics. I think it will require new forms, involving both men and women, centring on alliance work, rather than 'men's groups'. I think it will be far more internationalist than masculinity politics has been so far, contesting globalization-from-above as other democratic movements do. And, in some sense, it must be a politics beyond interests, a politics of pure possibility. Though that is, perhaps, another way of expressing the interest all people on this planet share in social justice, peace and balance with the natural world."

I now want to briefly describe an example of how practical ways forward may be explored in relation to "What next for men?". Drawing upon Connell and upon models of anti-oppressive practice[10], I have attempted elsewhere[11] to design a practical framework for a transformatory gender politics by men in one particular area of social existence — social welfare.

It is important to recognise that, in the world of social welfare, there are many examples of men who in some respects live their lives counter to those dominant forms of masculinity associated with control, oppression, hierarchical power and lack of emotional contact. Some of these men are workers, particularly those engaged in the more caring sectors of welfare. However, others are service users, such as primary informal carers for people who are older or disabled (often their spouses); men carers of partners/ friends suffering from AIDS; lone fathers; men supporting partners (of either gender) who are trying to deal with the trauma of childhood and/or adult sexual assault; men who are non-abusing parents supporting their children who have been sexually abused.

The experiences of such people may suggest not only the potential scope for all men in recreating their masculinities, but also some of the strategies by which this recreation can be achieved. For, in these cases, men have often found themselves confronted by other people's vulnerability, and this may have sometimes drawn out aspects of themselves which hitherto had been relatively unexplored — aspects less consonant with dominant forms of masculinity, including nurturance, emotional maturity, and sensitivity to the needs of other human beings.

It may well be that welfare agencies, and in particular male workers within those agencies, should more actively seek to positively support men who are placed in situations where they can act as informal care-givers to children or dependent adults. However, if this is not to be at the expense of other care-givers who are female, more resources are required, not simply a diversion of existing ones. This implies that anti-oppressive change is vital — not just at the level of individual workers, but also at agency, community and societal levels — so as to free up an increase of resources within a governmental context of retrenchment. This is, in fact, an example of a much wider issue, and, as we shall see later, transformatory gender politics in social welfare as a whole entail co-ordinated multi-level action.

Having said all this, it is important not to become over-simplistic or over-optimistic about the potential role for men in social welfare. After all, we saw earlier that some men, when confronted by the vulnerability of other human beings, do not react positively, but instead use such vulnerability for the purposes of abusing them. This happens both in families and in formal welfare settings. If men are to play a larger role as informal carers of children and dependent adults, this has to be done in ways that do not make those in need of care more open to abuse.

These considerations are even more crucial if we are to encourage men to act as professional carers in formal settings where the potential for abusing much larger numbers of dependent human beings usually exists. Elsewhere[12], I have suggested a range of strategies for reducing the risks of abuse posed by men who are employed in the welfare field. For the most part, these strategies involve such men adapting their methods of working to various extents, depending upon the specific situation of the service users with whom they are engaged; and I have developed particular criteria by which that situation can be assessed. However, in a very limited number of cases, I believe specific service users may be so vulnerable to abuse, as assessed by my proposed criteria, that the exclusion of men working with them should be considered. I recognise this last suggestion is a controversial one, and so I want to repeat again that I envisage it will only be applied in a relatively small number of cases. On the whole, I believe men can, and should, play an important role as formal carers in welfare services — as long as adequate steps are taken to protect the people for whom they are caring.

So, the positive roles already performed by some men as welfare workers and as informal carers remain grounds for encouragement to those of us seeking to promote reconstructions of gender relations within the field of social welfare. Further research is needed to examine the processes of masculinity transformation where men in welfare settings successfully fulfil such roles — and where they do not.

However, we can already make some suggestions about six central themes which should be addressed so as to challenge oppressive aspects of masculinity and promote more positive ones whenever men are working with men or boys in welfare settings:

- assisting men and boys to acknowledge their own capacity for acting oppressively;
- making explicit the links between men's oppressive acts and oppressive structures permeating society;
- countering societal attitudes which reinforce men's oppressions (myths about women, 'real men', violence, control, racism, heterosexism);
- recognising how peer group activities can reinforce men's tendency to oppress;
- devising strategies to avoid situations where oppressive behaviour is most likely;
- helping men look at their own masculinity and re-consider the forms of masculinity they want to develop in various aspects of their lives.

We need to emphasise that these themes are equally relevant to the men who are welfare workers themselves, both in terms of their initial training and their ongoing staff development.

Whether these themes are being addressed by men as workers and/or as users, one major problem is ever-present: the potential for collusion between men and thereby avoidance of the difficult issues about masculinity which have to be confronted by men. In all areas of men's practice, such collusion is an important barrier to progress. In some areas, for instance work with sex offenders and woman abusers, collusion is an extreme danger. Elsewhere[13], I have suggested a range of strategies to counter men's collusion which should be adopted in all work between men and boys, for instance video review and feedback; co-working with female colleagues; women consultation and supervision teams to monitor men's work; and effective involvement of women's groups in the management of men's projects.

Earlier in this chapter, I hinted that work by, and with, men needs to take place within a multi-level context. I now want to make that context explicit. A practical transformatory gender politics within the area of social welfare needs to be carried forward at a series of inter-acting levels by men, whether as welfare workers or as service users. This will involve:

- work with, and upon, one's own behaviour;
- individual work with men or boys;
- groupwork with men or boys;
- creating change at local, agency and community levels;
- change at societal levels.

Different issues need to be addressed at different levels. The overall project requires a multi-dimensional response by men. Depending upon his individual situation, each man will be in a position to address some issues better than others, and to work at some levels more than others. However, it is important that, as far as possible, men's networking with men and women should include activities which are occurring at different levels. For work at each level impacts on the others; co-ordination is therefore at a premium. Alliances by men as welfare workers with men who are service users are also likely to be crucial in this process.

To conclude, at the beginning of this chapter I emphasised that the primary objective of my approach to the future of men was to counter oppressions perpetrated by men and associated with hegemonic forms of masculinity. It is important to recognise that these oppressions are perpetrated against some men, as well as against women and children. However, the recreation by men of their masculinities in the manner suggested above may also benefit many men in other ways. The positive impact on men's own problems identified in the statistics at the start of the book, and earlier in this chapter, could well be immense: for instance, men's lack of attention to their health; their suicide rates; drug and alcohol abuse; unemployment and depressive responses to it. In saying this, however, I do not want to suggest that recreating masculinities is an easy option for men: I am not seeking to deny the central fact that positive masculine transformation still depends upon most men being prepared to surrender, individually and collectively, the many advantages which current patriarchal relations bestow upon them.

The proposals I have made are only viable if men can reconstruct their masculinities to be more emotionally open in the ways suggested here, and only if those structures of domination associated with hegemonic forms of masculinity can also be transformed in all spheres of life at the different levels identified above. This seems to be, and indeed is, a massive task. On the other hand, the opportunities available to work for change are ever-present. Let's get on with it.

REFERENCES

1. Connell, R.W. 'Masculinities', Cambridge: Polity (1995).
2. Pringle, K. "Child sexual abuse perpetrated by welfare personnel and the problem of men" in 'Critical Social Policy 36' (1992); "Gender issues in child sexual abuse committed by foster carers: a case study for the welfare services" in Ferguson, H., R. Gilligan and R. Torode (eds.) 'Surviving Childhood Adversity', Dublin: Social Studies Press (1993); 'Men, Masculinities and Social Welfare', London: UCL Press (1995).

3. For instance, Abbott, P. and Wallace, C. 'An Introduction to Sociology: Feminist Perspectives', London: Routledge (1990); Connell, R.W. 'Gender and Power: society, the person and sexual politics', Cambridge: Polity (1987) and ibid. (1995); Pringle, K. ibid. (1995); Segal, L. 'Slow Motion: Changing Masculinities, Changing Men', London: Virago (1990).

4. Grimwood, C. and Popplestone, R. 'Women, Management and Care', London: Macmillan (1993); Hearn, J. and Parkin, W. "Sex at Work": the power and the paradox of organisation sexuality', Brighton: Wheatsheaf (1987); Hugman, R. 'Power in the Caring Professions', London: Macmillan (1991); Pringle, K. ibid. (1995).

5. VanEvery, J. "De/reconstructing gender: women in antisexist living arrangements" in 'Women's Studies International Forum, vol.18, No.3' (1995).

6. For instance, Segal, L. ibid. (1990).

7. Duncombe, J. and Marsden, D. "Workaholics' and 'whingeing women': theorising intimacy and emotion work — the last frontier of gender inequality?" in 'The Sociological Review' (1995).

8. Barnes, M. and Maple, N.M. 'Women and Mental Health: challenging the stereotypes', Birmingham: Venture Press (1992).

9. Brod, H. and Kaufman, M. (eds.) 'Theorizing Masculinities', Thousand Oaks Ca.: Sage (1994); Connell, R.W. ibid. (1987) and (1995); Cornwall, A. and Lindisfarne, N. (eds.) 'Dislocating Masculinity: comparative ethnographies', London: Routledge (1994); Morgan, D. 'Discovering Men', London: Routledge (1992).

10. Ahmad, B. 'Black Perspectives in Social Work', Birmingham: Venture Press (1990); Dominelli, L. and McLeod, E. 'Feminist Social Work', London: Macmillan (1989); Thompson, N. 'Anti-discriminatory Practice', London, Macmillan (1993).

11. Pringle, K. ibid. (1995).

12. Pringle, K. ibid. (1995).

13. Pringle, K. ibid. (1995).

Fathering Beyond the Archetype
(An interview with Adrienne Burgess)

Adrienne Burgess was educated mainly in Australia before receiving a degree at Bristol University. Currently a research fellow at the Institute of Public Policy Research, she has been working as a journalist, specialising during the last 15 years on family relationships and structure. Her newspaper and magazine writing is extensive — Adrienne has provided features to British newspapers from The Guardian to The People, has written for leading broadsheets in the USA and Australia, and has been a contributor to Cosmopolitan since 1981 — and her work has been translated into more than a dozen languages. She has held research posts with senior lawyers (academic and practitioners), and, as Senior Researcher for Roach & Partners, developed television series for the BBC and Channel Four. Over the past 10 years, she has done much freelance work in industry, designing employee communication programmes using audio-visual techniques. Adrienne is co-author of 'Men and their Children' (IPPR, 1996) and the forthcoming 'Fatherhood Reclaimed: the making of the modern father.'

From the evidence you've seen, do you think there's a fatherhood crisis?

I think it is an unnecessary panic. There have always been men who have been unhappy. The pressures on men have always been

230

phenomenally high, particularly since the late 19th century with the pressure to go out and be the breadwinners. Before then, as far as I can see, they were multi-tasking (as women are now), but suddenly they had to be channelled into a workforce, which meant that they had to try to take their mind off being away from their families. Fatherhood was very important to them, and so they had to be convinced that it was alright not to see their children for most of the day; that they would still be loved; and that they still had a very important family role to play. When they went to the factory gates, they hated it; they used to be dreadfully bad employees, they used to chat to their friends and take Mondays off. They were offered two parenting roles — playmate and breadwinner — whereas before that they had been carers too.

So, if there is a crisis in fatherhood, it is not something that has just happened in the last 10 years because of unemployment: men have been asked to re-focus for the last 150 years as fathers have been de-skilled. I do wonder if the whole crisis thing is a bit of a backlash, a media creation, because of the fact that women are more visible now in the workplace. It's not that women never worked — working-class women were always employed — but there has been a steady increase in women's employment throughout this century: what's new is that women own their labour and therefore are visible.

Are you saying that women are now going through the same separation experience that men went through in the 1850's and 1860's?

Yes, except that most of them are not being separated from their children to any great extent. The vast majority of mothers in this country are part-time employed. Even among the full-timers, the average hours worked are 25 per week — compared with the average working father's 47 hours. The children are at school most of this time.

But there is a huge split in fatherhood — the public/private split. We don't know how fathers behave at home. We always thought that we knew about men's lives, but we didn't; all we knew was about men's public lives. It's only in the last 30 years that people have been carrying out family research. Fathers' private lives have been hidden from history, in exactly the same way as women's lives have been hidden from history because they only had private lives. We are still relating to men's lives in terms of the archetype. That's why, in a recent media study[1], you've got your monsters, heroes and villains — not because men are really like that, but because we still know very little about them.

Where do these archetypes come from?

It seems to me that archetypes are socially constructed, and the father archetype has really been hardened in the 20th century, for example, Freud's myth of Oedipus. We're trapped with these myths that don't necessarily express the essence of fatherhood, although we think they do. If we look at Henry Moore's sculpture of the father and child and his sculpture of the mother and child, the father and child seem to be wrestling and the mother and child are intimate. These are myths that have been constructed to tell men how to behave as fathers. There has been a lot of work on how these myths have impacted on masculinity, but they haven't looked to see how these myths have influenced fatherhood. In law still, the man who wins the custody battle may not be the man who wants to take time off to look after the children, but the man who is a good provider[2]. Women have often complained that men are not tough enough according to some ideal that everybody has been told fathers are like. They approve of a caring father on a personal level because they see what pleasure he brings, but at the same time they disapprove, as they view him as weak compared to the archetype. Charlie Lewis[3] fully believes that, in many homes, men in our fathers' generation were quite involved with the rearing of small children: he believes that, as we grew up, our fathers stopped being involved because no-one does childcare for children over the age of five in a kind of physical sense. Gradually the fathers pulled away, and the children pulled away too. Fathers are not needed to do things in the same amount after this time, so you get the impression that your father never did anything.

Nowadays, proportionally, mothers are doing a little less domestic work, and fathers are doing a lot more domestic work. Fathers are doing about 34% — as much domestic work as women are doing breadwinning. The whole idea that men are some kind of drones who are immobilised by the successes of women in the workplace seems to me to be out of the window. Some people reckon men aren't adaptable, but men seem to have been adapting as required.

When we ask how have women changed, it's said that women change because they are really good people who are brave and can tackle all that. In fact, women's lives have changed out of all recognition in the last 100 years, mainly because of the fecundity decline and the lengthening of their lives. It's not because the opportunities suddenly came in the 1960's and they took them: the fecundity decline did not happen with the Pill — it occurred 60 years earlier. When women were pregnant and breastfeeding all the time, the number of years they had at home after their youngest child had grown up and left was hardly any before they died. It was in the late 19th century that middle-class women started hardly having any children, and, by the 1920's, working women were in the same position.

Everybody says that the expectations of families are completely different now, that people used to only value their children in a functionalistic way as people who would support them in later life. This is complete rubbish: love has always come into it, and people have always valued their relationships with their children — the joys and the sadness. Even people who are starving still value their children for that. Nowadays, the whole purpose of the family has become about preparing our children emotionally. In this country, we don't worry about whether our children are going to survive anymore: we see the family as essentially about intimacy and teaching emotional maturity. We also know that we cannot prepare our children for the complexity of the world on our own. People try to buy services for their children from very early on; children are in training from a very early age.

If we have to buy in this education, what are parents for? We say what mothers and fathers are all about is love: it's about nurturing and understanding and children being able to express how they feel, and home being the place where they can let their hair down and get angry.

Children are being organised outside the home to do things, and coming home to let off steam. They call this 'dual socialisation'. Outside the home, children are using all kinds of socialising skills and negotiations; when they come home, they need to do different things. You have to have a balance.

Too long in daycare, or too long in the mother's care, and kids do not necessarily do very well, depending on the quality of care. Mothers are still able to provide intimacy and love and caring and nurturing the way they balance work at the moment, but fathers aren't able to do this. I am appalled at the hours they work. All of this is structural — laws to regulate the behaviour of the family have been coming through thick and fast for the last 200 years, from the Factory Acts to the Children's Act.

So many authors now refer to their disappointment in their parents, particularly with their fathers. If the function of the parents is now seen to be about love, intimacy and caring, are these expectations really more about our archetypes?

When they did childcare studies in the 1960's, mothers were talking about their own mothers in this very hostile and disappointed way. They were saying, "They were too busy; they never had time for me". Nowadays, you might think that was someone talking about their father being cold and never showing much emotion. In general, I think it's a split between the archetype and the reality. A lot of today's children are going to remember their fathers in the same way. The father is going to say, "I did so much when they were little". And you say, "Yes, but they don't remember that".

Maybe it is a crisis of imagery and the cultural pressure against men. We've had this idea about the mother relationship since Rousseau started saying that men and women have different roles and women are emotional and men are rational. And then psychoanalysis has emphasised thr mother and told the (breadwinner) father that all he had to be was a symbol! We are still anchored to this idea of the mother as the key to the relationship in all our thinking about parenthood. For example, we know hardly anything about men's fertility. Whilst women are seen as reproductive, men are seen as sexual performers. Their sexuality has been regulated by marriage, but the amount of control men have over fertility is zero. Even though there are very few women going around using men as mobile sperm banks, they could go sperm-napping if they wanted to very easily. Men cannot go egg-napping in the same way: they can't cheat women into getting pregnant. In fact, couples rarely discuss whether the woman should go off the Pill. So men start fatherhood from a very passive position.

I think men need to have control over their own fertility — they have to decide whether to become fathers. That doesn't mean giving them control over women's fertility — just their own. One interesting thing emerging about gay fatherhood is that gay men who become fathers have to think about it very consciously. They have to think, "What kind of father do I want to be? Do I want to be just a donor with some lady friend, or what?". They have to consider what kind of involvement they would want with the child after the birth. They have to think about it because they are not going to accidentally fall pregnant.

I also think that it should be mandatory to have good ante-natal involvement for fathers. Nobody in Britain even asks a father, when a pregnancy is confirmed, what his feelings are. We don't even know men's attitudes towards abortions. It is against the 1967 Abortion Act to counsel the father when a woman comes in for an abortion because of pledged confidentiality. It seems extraordinary to me that his views are not sought. This is nothing to do with controlling the abortion, but with how he feels, whether he'll go out and get someone else pregnant because of some unacknowledged loss.

We have this dissuasive attitude towards men all the way through. They are still allowed in the birth room, because hospitals are understaffed and the men can be useful, but there is a lot of distrust from some birth professionals. People still go on about how traumatised men are by birth, when actually hardly any are. A Royal College of Midwives survey[4] showed that only 8% of men had felt any pressure to go, and many of these still wanted to be there themselves anyway! Margaret O'Brien[5] recently asked 15-year-old boys and girls whether fathers should be present at the birth: 95% said yes, the girls commenting they should be there to help and support the woman, and the boys because it's the father's baby. So these young men wanted to centre themselves in the process. Both the Natural Childbirth Trust and the Royal College of Midwives say that, when men's courses on ante-natal care are held in the evenings and advertised properly, the take-up is phenomenal; the courses are booked up months before they open, which they never used to be.

What we have said to fathers is, "You can be a playmate and you can have an important role in child development (because Freud has said so). You don't have to be there all the time — in fact, it's better if you're not, because real fathers should be distant and uninvolved, and then they are able to make good judgements which can help direct their family in the right way". And yet new research is showing that fathers do not have a unique role in childcare — children develop their gender socialisation, their language, their emotions, irrespective of whether their father is there, irrespective of whom they are with. Children take from whomever is around them — men or women. That doesn't mean that fathers are irrelevant, it just means that fathers' relevance is exactly the same as mothers', depending on how much they put in, what they do, and what their intimate relationship with their child is like.

There is no free ride for fatherhood here, and that is extremely sad for men, because they have been told they've got it anyway and don't need to struggle for it: "You'll be the playmate, and they'll love you for it". It's certainly true that the playful father has been very good, but it is a double-edged sword. It has given fathers easy popularity with their young children — American fathers are more popular with their children than Swedish fathers, even though Swedish fathers do more care — because dads are fun, and everybody likes that. But the kids love you for being their playmate until they are about nine or 10, and then, if you are still pulling the funny faces and making them laugh, they hate you for it. And lots of fathers never progress beyond that.

If you ask men and women what they think a father is for, a lot of them say breadwinning. But if you ask fathers what they think is important about them, personally, being a father to their own children, they put breadwinning way down the list. Again, you've got this split. What we think is right for fathers to do, in their archetype's sense, is not the same as what we believe in the personal sense: we think the father should be present, emotionally available for his children, loving them, and the children knowing that he loves them.

I think men are also tremendously under strain from the point of view of the fact that they lose their children after divorce. Just as women are at risk after divorce if they haven't kept a stake in the workplace, because they can't earn sufficiently (some can never earn sufficiently, even if they have kept a stake in the workplace), so men have to keep a stake in the family, otherwise, after divorce, they lose their children. I think Families Need Fathers just waited for the Children Act: in their fantasies, all these kids were going to rush into court and say, "I want to live with my father". But they didn't. As the relationship between the parents deteriorates, alliances tend to be built between mothers and their children, so the father becomes the outsider, and, by the time the divorce actually happens, father and child have become more distant than they ever were before. If they were pretty distant to start with, then that puts the father in a very bad position: men who don't have a strong relationship with their children before divorce are not likely to have one afterwards. Edward Kruk[6] created a great deal of fuss by saying that the men who were most likely to lose touch with their children after divorce were the men who were most involved with them beforehand, but Charlie Lewis[7] has now replicated his research in Greece, where the opposite was shown — the fathers with the strongest connections before divorce had the strongest connection afterwards too.

If being a parent is about loving, intimacy and caring, these are the aspects which (given the realities of their work) men have been most separated from. What do we do about that?

We have to know that whatever we do will take time. What we are asking for is something so huge that no bits of parental or paternity leave (even though they are important) are going to solve it overnight. We are looking at a complete revolution in work and family life to enable fathers and mothers to have independent relationships with their children. One nurse said, "I think it's good that the mothers work at the weekend — it gives the fathers and children a chance". I think that's right because my innate respect of my own ability as a mother is such that, if I am around, I interfere and get in the way an awful lot; my partner does not find out what it is to be a father and develop his own relationship with our daughter.

Is this about opportunities to be responsible?

Exactly. Opportunities to make your own mistakes, your own decisions, not to have somebody say, "They don't like cheese on toast that way". I think of all the funny ideas I had about bringing up children and what I was, and wasn't, going to do. When I made mistakes as a parent, nobody put me down for making them — they said I was just learning. A father makes a mistake and too often the mother steps in instantly and he steps back. The way things are set up disables men from active, care-taking parenthood.

For some men, then, maybe being breadwinners is the best way they are going to be fathers.

Maybe. And breadwinning is an important part of being a parent — whether you are a father or a mother. Our expectations of our parents are changing. We know that, for instance, children whose fathers (or, for that matter, mothers) die, often do extremely well in later life, because the image of the parent is kept alive in a positive way. But a father — or mother — who just breadwins, who has very little time for the children, and who doesn't give the children the sense that they are known and loved for themselves, is not remembered positively.

We can only be disappointed by something if we've got something to compare it with.

You never used to hear adult children saying to their fathers, "You didn't give me closeness and love", but now they do. Most fathers today recognise its importance. I was interviewing this stiff-upper-lip dad and he said, "In our family, we never hugged anybody. Then you see other people's families, and you think that's rather a good way to be". He tried writing his son letters, and it turned out that quite a lot of the other boys at school were receiving these special letters from their fathers saying, "I love you really".

But is this reality, or is this again just the images people have of how they ought to be?

All we know is that the survival of the species depends on our attachment to, and giving to, our young, and that this seems to be arranged around family groups of different kinds. Babies seem to have that way of making fathers love them, just as they have that way of making mothers love them.

So, as Minister for Men, what would need doing?

I think we need to change the image of fatherhood. I would set up a resource centre to pump out information. I think people are very ignorant: I think they will often do better if they just knew about things. Changing images of fatherhood is absolutely crucial; I think that it does need consciousness-raising, it needs government campaigns, it needs unions thinking, and it's all tied in with job opportunities for men.

I think you need to inform advertising agencies of what the problem is. They have no idea. When you say, "Do a father", they present a playful father because that's what they think fathers do. When I asked a nappy company why they had an advertisement with a father failing to change a nappy, they said,

"Women like it". I often don't feel that these things are very well thought out; they're knee-jerk reactions. They don't do serious marketing testing. I think a lot of women would adore to see a man in a TV commercial lovingly and successfully looking after a baby. Companies offer benefits to employees like club membership, cars and healthcare, but they don't think about offering childcare support, or similar benefits, which can help retain male (and female) employees.

In Sweden, advertising campaigns make a huge difference. Parental leave take-up went up to 44% when they did two things: one was to say, "This is OK: real men do it", and the other was they extended the period over which it could be taken, so that men could take it beyond the first six months or year when many women were breastfeeding. I think you could manage it so that men did not have to leave the workforce completely, so they need not be worried about their jobs. I would feed storylines to the soaps: they currently show you a father hardly touching a baby, or, if he is looking after the child, he usually fails.

I would also work on the benefits system so that more part-time working is made possible. I would gather examples of good practice in businesses throughout the world: in Australia, there is an insurance company which has organised workers into teams to take account of the different stages of people's lives (each team will have a young worker, who might still be at university finishing off a Masters Degree and working shorter hours; then they'll have a couple of young people working all the hours God gives; and then a couple of people with parental responsibilities working fewer hours). I would develop a terrific system of childcare, so there could be drop-in childcare — a partnership between the state and individual parents, encouraging parents to spend time together with their children, but also to be in employment.

I would be looking for family-friendly policies. No-one sees childcare as men's responsibility, although, in fact, it is, because they can't work if somebody isn't looking after their children. Dupont asked their employees, "What do you want?", and lots of men whose wives were having children wanted to have bleepers so that they didn't have to worry about missing a birth because they could be contacted. The male employees also wanted parenting courses. The workplace seems to be a good environment in which to run fatherhood courses (at Dupont, they've had mentoring with older fathers), so I would put resources into that and generally develop father-friendly employment policies.

I would also put a lot of resources into men's infertility — not just fertility treatment, but also developing contraceptives for men so that more men have to make decisions about contraception (which a lot of men want to do). I would work with young men as well: you can get young men interested in fathering quite easily when you start them talking about their own fathers.

You're inviting men to participate, so are you assuming that, if you withdraw some of the social barriers, men will come forward?

Women will have to be educated too. That's very important because it's their area of power and control I am talking about. I think that a lot of them are just not aware of it; they have no idea that what they're doing is excluding men, because the definition of a good mother is one who copes alone. No wonder so many new mothers are depressed! It would help them enormously to let men in.

I would look at the position of unmarried fathers because I would want to treat non-married fathers in the same way as married fathers: at the moment, there is Parental Responsibility, which they can apply for to give them the kinds of rights they would have if they were married to the mother of the child, but only 2,000 of these are awarded every year, because so few people are aware of this facility. It would be very good to have some kind of ceremony around the registration of a child, where the father gets to state his interest. It would be ideal for married fathers too. I think, when you go to a wedding service, and it's all to do with the relationship between the couple, "and from this shall come children", this is very bad for men because it's suggesting that the relationship with the child is always through the mother. Men have to be able to have relationships with their children independent of the mother, and the statement needs to be made: "Whatever happens to my relationship with this woman, this is my child, to whom I am committed".

I would also do something about access. There is incontrovertible evidence that, the more fathers are involved with their children on every level, the more they pay child support (providing they've got the money to pay it), and so there's a direct link with access. The Child Support Act should be set in the context of valuing men for all the other things they can give their children in terms of the emotional support of the networks they provide through their own families, which are so important for their children, and which can be lost after divorce.

The whole family network of the father's side and all the caring and just being there matters, and so I would set up systems to facilitate that. I would have drop-in mediation and I would really tackle this question of co-parenting after divorce, not in a mandatory way, but to enable parents to do it. People after divorce are beginning to co-parent successfully in a way we could never imagine 20 years ago. They manage to get grown up and set aside how they feel and put the child first. I would try to give support services for when they hit other crisis points, like one of them getting a new partner. It would be quite an expensive programme, all this, but it would save us a lot. It's all part of prevention being better than cure.

REFERENCES

1. "Fathers in the Media: An analysis of newspaper coverage of fathers" in Moss, P. 'Father Figures — Fathers in the Families of the 1990s', London: HMSO (1995).
2. Collier, 'R. Masculinity, Law and the Family', London: Routledge (1995).
3. Personal conversation.
4. 'Men at Birth', London: Royal College of Midwives (1994).
5. O'Brien, M. "The Absense and Presence of Fathers", in Bjornberg, V. (Ed) 'Men's Family Relations', Goteborg: University of Goteburg Publications (1996).
6. Kruk, E. "Discontinuity between pre and post-divorce father-child relationships" Journal of Divorce & Remarriage Vol. 16 (3-4).
7. Personal communication.

Increasing Men's Involvement with their Children

Peter Moss

Peter Moss has worked as a researcher in the Thomas Coram Research Unit at the University of London's Institute of Education for over 20 years, and has had a particular interest in early childhood services and work/family issues. Since 1986, he has also been Co-ordinator of the European Commission Network on Childcare and Other Measures to Reconcile Employment and Family Responsibilities, where he has been involved in developing a programme of work on the theme of men as carers. Peter has three children.

The problem about writing about 'the problem' is considerable, whatever the subject, and 'the problem' of (or for) men is no different. There is the implication of a 'Golden Age' — that somehow everything was great until 'the problem' came along. Yet I do not remember my father having had a particularly satisfying life, denied access to university, suffering unemployment in the 1930's, six years of war in the 1940's, before he got into permanent, full-time office work — then worrying endlessly about money and spending much of his home life in front of the TV before dying prematurely of heart disease. Of course, I might be wrong — we never talked about it. But, looking back at this most barbaric of centuries, what cries out are the millions of young men who died (and continue to die in the Majority World) through war and other atrocities. Read Robert Graves, read Pat Barker, read any account of the First World War or the aftermath of the Great Depression, and it helps put today's 'problem' into some sort of historical perspective. For those of us who grew up after the Second World War, in what Eric Hobsbawn[1] calls the 'Golden Years' of the late 1940's to the 1970's, it is particularly hard to find that perspective and to realise that those few years — of high employment, rising living standards, relative security and so on — have been the exception, rather than the rule.

'The problem' is also usually a variety of problems. There may well be connections, but striving too hard to find some global explanation risks over-simplification and post hoc rationalisation. It also risks losing sight of what are general problems, experienced, though perhaps in different ways, by women and men. Last but not least, how you perceive the problem depends on who you are. As a middle-aged, middle-class, white, married, heterosexual father, I cannot avoid bringing all sorts of personal baggage to the issue. All I can add to this collection is one particular, and necessarily partial, perspective.

For the last 10 years, I have been coordinating an 'expert' group working for the European Commission on the issue of the 'reconciliation' of employment and family responsibilities, in particular the care and upbringing of children — the European Commission Network on Childcare and Other Measures to Reconcile Employment and Family Responsibilities of Women and Men. As this work has coincided with the latter part of my own fatherhood, the issue of 'reconciling' employment and family responsibilities has been central to both my working and personal life. Interestingly (though, as with most things European, virtually unknown about in the UK), the European Union and the Commission have placed considerable emphasis on the need for change in men's role, in particular, men taking a greater share of family responsibilities. In 1992, the Council of Ministers (ie all Member State Governments) adopted a Recommendation on Child Care, Article 6 of which recommends Member States to "promote and encourage, with due respect for the freedom of the individual, increased participation by men [in the care and upbringing of children], in order to achieve a more equal sharing of parental responsibilities between men and women". Over the last few years, the Network has paid particular attention to what this might mean in practice — how to promote and encourage increased participation.

However, before looking at 'what can be done', what is the problem that this 'doing' needs to address? In essence, it is the relationship between employment and family life and the management of that relationship, finding a balance between these two large and disparate areas of life that is satisfactory and satisfying to all concerned — men, women, children, employers, society. Ever a source of tension, the relationship is facing new stresses and strains.

If we look at employment, we find increasing polarisation and inequality — affecting women as much as men. There is the emergence of what Will Hutton[2] calls 'the 40/30/30 society', with 30% outside the labour market, 30% clinging precariously and insecurely to it, and only the final 40% enjoying relatively secure employment. Within this general picture, there are more specific age-related trends. Employment is more and more concentrated on the 'prime age' group, roughly from 25 to 50 — a period which increasingly coincides with parenthood, as men and women now enter parenthood on average in their late 20's. Prior to that age, employment has dropped as studying and youth unemployment have risen, and, after 50, there has been a rapid fall in male employment, due to a combination of redundancy and early retirement.

Employment is a source of growing insecurity — "Can I get a job? Will I keep it? What will become of me in 10 years time — or even next year?". For those with jobs, it is a dominating activity. British fathers work the longest hours in the EU, averaging 47 hours a week. It may even be, though we cannot be certain, that, for those with jobs, work demands are intensifying and becoming ever more obtrusive.

Many men will be feeling they have to invest more in their paid work to hang on to a job or make out in an increasingly competitive, 'flexible' world, in which new technology increasingly erodes boundaries between employment and the rest of life (I am writing this at home on Sunday afternoon because I have my own pc here and it is ever so easy to slip upstairs and work). Moreover, an increasing number of men have work where the drive to do ever more is not only, or at all, external, but is, instead, an internal urge to achieve.

Yet the value of this increasing investment in paid work has to be questioned. Not only are the employment and financial returns increasingly hard to predict, but it can limit, or damage, other parts of life of equal, or ultimately greater, importance. As employment increases among women, and particularly women with children, arguably there is an increasing need for men to invest more of themselves in their family lives — to assume more family responsibility, do more domestic work, give more time to children. The alternatives are either to disadvantage women's employment prospects (which happens widely today, when so many mothers take on poor quality part-time jobs to ensure they can continue to manage the relationship between employment and their family's life), or for parents (if well-off enough) to essentially contract out family responsibilities to paid servants, or for families to struggle, and often break, under the strain.

Family life is also changing. Like employment, it is increasingly unpredictable. While fathers are probably more involved with their children than in the past, more and more fathers are losing their children — what one Norwegian researcher has referred to as the 'paradox of closeness and distance':

"The new role of fathers is characterized by contrasting patterns. While some men actively involve themselves with their children, others distance themselves, voluntarily or not ... As mothers became financially less dependent, husbands were 'freed from' their responsibility as supporters. At the same time, they were also 'freed' to take on a greater share of the responsibility for their children. Through a process of selectivity, fathers who both live with their children and assume the new role of fathers will be among the most dedicated and committed. The new role of fathers is associated with changes among these men. The paradox of this process is that fathers are becoming more emotionally attached at the same time as an increasing proportion of fathers are becoming physically detached from their children ... Two partly counteracting tendencies in the relationship between children and fathers seem to be at work. First of all, forces at the individual level work in the direction of closing the gap. Secondly, structural forces work in the direction of widening the gap between children and men."[3]

Apart from reminding us of the danger of over-simplification when there are contrasting trends and increasing diversity, we see here one major problem facing many men — that they may lose out both ways, in employment and family life, left at 50 or 55 without rewarding employment or sustaining relationships.

There is, to be cliched, no simple answer. Partly because people differ in what they want and how far they are able to get what they want. Partly because economic trends seem, in some ways, at odds with individual and family needs, but at the same time unamenable to social needs. The Childcare Network, however, has sought to identify how it might be possible to encourage and promote more participation by men in the care and upbringing of children — on the basis that greater male investment in child-rearing, and a better balance in men's lives between employment and family responsibilities, will be good not only for men, but for children, their partners and the wider society. Indeed, a worrying feature of modern life is the growing 'feminization of childhood'.

The starting point has to be to help men, from an early stage, to reflect on what they want from their lives and on the importance of having a spread of investments — not only in paid work, not only in leisure interests, not only in public life, but also in family life and in relationships with partners and children. While there are many ways of supporting reflection, one condition must be that the issue of men comes onto the public agenda, in particular the issue of 'men as carers', using this as shorthand for the whole area of relationships and family life.

At present, this is not generally the case. Two years ago, the Network monitored newspapers for a month in seven EU countries, to see how they covered issues such as fathers, fatherhood and men as carers. The results were salutary:
"Such issues rarely make front page news unless they touch upon the exceptional and sensational, nor are they often examined in any great depth. Newspapers reflect, rather than lead, public opinion in relation to gender roles in employment and family life: leave arrangements and part-time work are predominantly discussed in relation to working mothers, while fathers attract attention in relation to custody and maintenance. Only in Denmark is there any substantial evidence of a different public discourse, which recognises and addresses men's role as carers, and, in this case, it is more likely again that newspapers are reflecting, rather than forming, public opinion."[4]

A large responsibility falls on leaders of public opinion, not least politicians and other powerful figures, to open up debate about men in their family and caring roles and the relationship between these roles and employment — while recognising that this is particularly difficult since so many 'movers and shakers' are men themselves who have probably devoted limited time to their family lives and may feel threatened by the whole issue.

It is also important to recognise that change comes in many ways, from many sources and through many relationships. Change in gender roles and relationships cannot be decreed from the top, nor can change be forced on men or women who do not want it. Having accepted these caveats, however, over the years, the Network has come to the view that there is a role for more formal interventions and that government, employers, trades unions and other formal organisations can play an important role as enablers of change. Social intervention involving these groups can contribute to cultural change (for example, helping to redefine 'childcare' as a men's issue, as much as a women's issue); provide support and increased opportunities for men and women who have decided they want change in their lives and relationships — or who are, at least, interested in exploring what change might mean; and influence the power balance in negotiation in the family, the workplace and other settings where change may take place.

In short, the Network believes that something can be done to support change. It is likely to be modest in effect, but still worthwhile. There is no excuse for doing nothing. There are plenty of good ideas for what should be done, and it is quite easy to produce a shopping list of measures to be taken (a call for ideas would quickly extend the shopping list still further). However, before preparing the shopping list, it is necessary to go one step back — to have a strategy for promoting change, based on some concept of how change takes place and how that process can best be supported. The Network has identified[5] a number of points which are relevant to developing a strategy:

- the strategy for promoting change should be based on detailed analysis of the context within which change is sought — whether it is a whole country, or a particular factory, or an individual nursery. Such analysis will define the context, the assets available to support change and the likely obstacles to change;
- a strategy to support change must recognise and take account of diversity — not only gender, but class, ethnicity and other important dimensions;
- a successful strategy must recognise the strong and negative feelings that can be aroused by change in this area, not least among many women — indeed, it is undesirable to consider men's role in the family in isolation from women's. It is important to provide means of recognising and responding to these feelings and concerns, including the provision of safe and secure places where men and women can explore change and its implications, both separately and together;
- a strategy for change might target certain 'golden opportunities' in life when men and women are more responsive to examining issues of equality, sharing, caring, role and identity. These 'golden opportunities' include major transition points in people's lives (for example, becoming a parent);

- an important element in any strategy for change is the provision of role models — individuals, families, workplaces, services and, indeed, countries — where more equal sharing has been achieved or is being seriously worked towards;
- another important element in a strategy is to identify appropriate and effective incentives to encourage change. These may take the form of specific policy devices (for example, extra payments to men who take parental leave): alternatively, they may take the form of showing men the personal benefits they may derive from taking more responsibility for the care and upbringing of children;
- last, but not least, it needs to be realised that the process of change may well take a long time, running into decades — in Sweden, for example, it has taken 20 years to reach the stage where nearly half of fathers take some parental leave. There needs to be sustained commitment and a long-term strategy, with regular monitoring and review.

Within the context of a developed strategy, there is a wide variety of measures that can be pursued, in many settings and at different levels, and with a balance between 'top-down' measures and working at grass roots through existing networks, institutions and relationships. Two examples of measures that the Network has looked at in considerable detail include parental leave (leave available equally to mothers and fathers to enable them to spend more time with young children)[6] and the potential role of nurseries (and other services for young children), not only as an important means of promoting cultural change in society, but as providers (at a more personal level) of safe and secure places where men and women can explore roles, relationships and identities, being available to parents at one of those 'golden opportunities' when men and women may be particularly open to reviewing their lives[7]. This potential role for nurseries has led the Network to recognise the importance of having more men working in nurseries and other services for young children[8], in turn emphasising that the issue of 'men as carers' goes well beyond men in their role as fathers to the whole nexus of actual and potential relationships between men and children.

As I have already emphasised, I am not at all certain whether real change in men's relationships to children, caring and family life is attainable, at least for a significant number. The increasing power of economic competition and business values, the commodification of labour and the devaluation of caring are causes for deep disquiet. Yet, nothing ventured, nothing gained. So what about it, Tony Blair? On Day One, announce as a priority that your new Government will be taking action to fulfil the UK's commitment under Article 6 of the Council Recommendation on Child Care, setting up a 'men as carers' initiative to support and encourage increased participation by men in the care and upbringing of children.

REFERENCES

1. Hobsbawn, E. 'The Age of Extremes: The Short Twentieth Century', London: Michael Joseph (1994).
2. Hutton, W. 'The State We're In', London: Jonathan Cape (1995).
3. Jensen, A-M. "Fathers and Children — the Paradox of Closeness and Distance", in report of a Conference 'Fathers in the Families of Tomorrow', Copenhagen: Danish Ministry of Social Affairs (1993).
4. Deven, F. 'Men, Media and Childcare', Brussels: European Commission Equal Opportunities Unit (1994).
5. EC Childcare Network 'Men as Carers: towards a Culture of Responsibility, Sharing and Reciprocity between Women and Men in the Care and Upbringing of Children', Brussels: European Commission Equal Opportunities Unit (1994).
6. EC Childcare Network 'Leave Arrangements for Workers with Children', Brussels: European Commission Equal Opportunities Unit (1994).
7. Ghedini, P., Chandler, T., Whalley, M. And Moss, P. 'Fathers, Nurseries and Childcare', Brussels: European Commission Equal Opportunities Unit (1995).
8. Jensen, J. 'Men as Workers in Childcare Services' Brussels, European Commission Equal Opportunities Unit (1995).

Reversing the Descent of Man

Geoff Dench

Geoff Dench is visiting Professor of Sociology at Middlesex University and a research fellow of the Institute of Community Studies. He has worked on development and research projects in a variety of non-European countries, and has written several books on race and ethnic relations, and more recently on gender.

On virtually every indicator that anyone might want to consider, men in Britain and various other western states seem to be performing very badly at the moment, both for themselves and for the communities in which they live. And all the signs are that the situation stands to get much worse. What I want to argue here, however, is that this is to some extent not an unusual situation. Men everywhere are inclined towards being social outsiders. Their usefulness to communities varies much more than women's, and depends greatly on the way in which social institutions define and reward their roles. Whereas most cultures seem to recognise this, in the West we have increasingly pretended that it is not the case. And we are now paying for our mistake.

It is not too late to face up to the problem. But we have such an accumulation of policy errors to deal with that we require a thorough re-orientation of public discourse before we can expect any specific measures to have much positive effect. The sort of shift that we need encompasses a moral reinstatement of at least some key elements of the sexual division of labour, probably grounded in stronger marriage institutions, and certainly linked with a conceptual unscrambling of the private realm of interpersonal relations, revolving around families, and the public realm concerned with the impersonal organisation of collective life.

I will start by discussing this broad cultural transformation before sketching out some policy directions which would become feasible under it. My general approach may seem wildly speculative to some people. But I do actually believe it to be consistent with the way that public opinion is currently moving. Many people are asking themselves whether some of the radical social experiments attempted in recent generations are viable in the long term, or should now be ditched. Our journey along the path I am signposting may already be underway.

The first step towards pulling men back from their plunge into unproductive and anti-social behaviour patterns lies in acknowledging that the social orientations of men and women can never be identical, that there is sexual difference. Refusal to accept this, and pursuit of interchangeability and strict equality, rather than seeking more appropriate goals of gender equity, are likely to increase, not to reduce, social differences between the sexes.

The key to this is that women in all societies are more responsive to each other's needs, and to the value of a social contract. In the last analysis, this is because they need society more. The long and arduous process of child-rearing makes women become interdependent and value co-operation with others, in a way which does not so readily apply to men, who can more easily get along by themselves and thus avoid commitments to others. Society is at heart female, and is built around shared motherhood.

In all 'traditional' cultures, there is a more or less explicit awareness of the centrality of motherhood and of the need to create similarly distinctive roles for men in order to give them a comparable stake in society. We all need to feel needed by others, if we are to learn to be responsive to them. Unless adult men are given clear roles and duties, their attachment to society is very tenuous.

The highlighting of male roles which results, and which corresponds broadly to what we call patriarchy, has two main aspects. Firstly, men are made socially responsible for the support of particular women and children, usually (but not necessarily) their sexual partners and own offspring. This makes men more like women, by giving them specific people to care about in the way that mothers have to care for their children. Secondly, they are given formal rights and duties, usually linked to a 'head of family' status, in the structure of political and economic institutions which organise access to the means of support. This increases their motivation and opportunity to carry out their family obligations.

As David Gilmore's cross-cultural study of men shows[1], in the small handful of cultures without patriarchy, men live a narcissistic Peter Pan existence, putting very little into the community and leaving most labour to women. Such societies have not developed beyond a rudimentary level, and cannot compete with more highly-organised and structured neighbours. This is why there are so few of them. They are not a suitable model for modern industrial nations to copy.

Copying them is, however, effectively what we have been striving to do in recent decades as attacks have mounted on sexual divisions of labour. Since the Enlightenment, the philosophical doctrines of individualism have come into repeated conflict with ideas about sexual differences. During this century, as the state has offered increasingly direct supports to women, libertarians (especially in Protestant countries) have portrayed male providing roles as a major source of evil.

Eleanor Rathbone, for example, persuaded Parliament in 1945 to by-pass husbands and pay family allowances to mothers, after conducting a long campaign against what she dubbed the 'Turk complex':

" . . . it is easy to see what satisfaction the institution of the dependent family gives to all sorts and conditions of men — to the tyrannous man what opportunities of tyranny, to the selfish of self-indulgence, to the generous of preening himself in the sunshine of his own generosity, to the chivalrous of feeling himself the protector of the weak. ... Thus when a proposal (for direct support of women) presents itself which is obnoxious to the hidden Turk in man, he stretches up his hand from his dwelling in the unconscious mind and the proposal disappears from the upper regions of consciousness."[2]

Rathbone herself was mainly concerned with improving the status of motherhood by defining it as a public role deserving direct state support. But her breach of the divide between private and public realms, and dismissal of male family motivations (but not of female) as rooted in an 'instinct of domination', contributed to a de-legitimising of distinctive male roles. It was a factor in the emergence of a new statist political economy in which segregated roles are deemed harmful to society, and where men who still aspire to them are regarded as morally deviant or pathetic throw-backs.

This process has become intensified since the 60's, when the emergence of the Pill, allowing much more reliable planning of families, encouraged women to start claiming equal participation in the formerly male-oriented public realm. This development has, I believe, been the clinching factor which decisively weakened the framework of family responsibilities which previously underpined men's motivation to take on socially useful labour. Some of this is revealed in Neil Lyndon's retrospective baring of soul:

"If we didn't have to have babies when we had regular sex, it followed that we didn't have to get married. And if we didn't have to support families, we didn't have to have jobs or careers: and if we didn't have to have careers, ... what might we not do? Or be? A tabula rasa of adult masculinity had been presented to us, upon which we might (we supposed) make our marks as we pleased."[3]

It is now time to discard this legacy. I argue elsewhere[4] that it has led to a collapse, not only in male participation in public realm activities, but in family work in the private realm too. Far from leading to a more equitable sharing of roles, it has piled ever greater burdens on women.

Policies of strict gender equality are no longer what most women want — if indeed they ever did. Many women, especially older women with experience of managing families, see some emphasising of men's economic roles as an essential basis for turning them into caring and productive members of the community. There is popular support building up for a reformulation of equal opportunities policies to allow for differential involvement of men and women in family life.

This might best be done by attaching greater importance among younger people to women's employment rights — as they do not have so long to establish themselves in work before wanting to give much of their time to running a family — while reserving priority among people aged thirty or over to men, who are often slower getting started anyway, but whom most women would, in fact, prefer to occupy the main breadwinning role during the arduous years of childrearing.

A formal shift of emphasis like this would signal to men that there are socially valued roles waiting for them, and offer reassurance and meaning in life to the growing numbers of them who seem to doubt it.

Heavy rates of unemployment are widely seen as related to the collapse of male morale and motivation. But it is a mistake to regard joblessness in itself as the cause of men's problems. Male unemployment is no novelty, and reached high levels as recently as the 30's without weakening male resolve and family commitment or readiness to retrain for new types of work. Arguably, it even sharpened these.

What is new is the loss of morale and sense of purpose among men, and this is a cultural, rather than an economic, change, arising out of the libertarian assault on sex roles. Men are bombarded with the message that modern women value the opportunity for self-realisation through work. So the chivalrous thing to do these days (as Eleanor Rathbone was warned, but chose to ignore) is not strive too hard to achieve and hold down a job, but to stand aside and let women go for it themselves. This is the root of contemporary male economic and educational failure, and the reason why, although there are increasing numbers of unemployed men, the total number of jobs remains the same.

It is not possible to do much about this so long as the problem is seen simply in terms of the amount of work available. Boosting employment in the current climate is likely to benefit women much more than men, as they are the ones presently more highly motivated (by existing or anticipated family duties) to take it seriously. We need measures which endorse the greater relative importance of work to men as their distinctive contribution to society.

One step which could be taken quite early on in a process of reasserting the value of male work, and which would help start to rescue the self-respect of unemployed men, is to change the nature of supports offered to men when they are out of work. All of the main political parties are developing schemes for limiting benefits to the unemployed and replacing them with training schemes and job-seekers allowances of various kinds. But these all still rely on the private sector actually to create new work, while, through taxation, its capacity to generate such jobs is reduced.

It would be more constructive, and no longer likely to incur union wrath, to replace benefits for able-bodied work-seekers with wages for socially useful work. In some circumstances, this might be 'family work' of bringing up children, as proposed by Michael Young and Chelly Halsey[5]. Nominally, this could be open to men or women, but, in practice, few men are likely to choose it or qualify for it. More significantly, in terms of getting the nation working again, it could be low-paid (or part-time) work in state enterprises.

This would initiate a valuable shift in the structure of public spending. Part of Britain's economic malaise derives from trying to incorporate too many personal services and supports, previously (and often better) carried out in the private realm, into the welfare state. This has burdened the welfare system far beyond its original remit, and has competed with the budgets available for stimulating industrial investment and modernisation. Focussing public monies into public works schemes could get resources circulating in ways which revived men's interest in working and supporting families at the same time as assisting industrial renewal.

Such a public employment system will only result in a re-harnessing of male energies if it offers real and useful work, and is concentrated in areas which do not require massive and sudden re-culturation of men. It must utilise currently wasted male labour, as well as helping to generate new jobs in the private sector — which, in the last analysis, is paying for it.

Many people will be shaking their heads at this point and chanting that, "Traditional male work is in decline". But this is not fundamentally true, and is a cultural-constrained perception, related to the attempt in the West to merge public and private domains, and to pay for caring work out of public funds. If we treat more personal services as private realm obligations (to be negotiated within families, or paid for by families), and then look for traditional 'work', there is plenty that still needs doing and could be paid for.

A new wave of public employment could be directed mainly towards renewal and maintenance of the infrastructure needed by a modern economy. For example, an efficient public transport and communications system, where public investment has been starved in recent decades, is a heavy consumer of traditional labour. Also, the conversion of industry and agriculture to ecologically-sound techniques and practices, along with measures to clean up the existing environment, are essential to the long-term economic health and growth of the nation, and something which a progressive government should undertake. Such a programme would use massive amounts of labour, some of it perhaps organised into mobile task forces, and mainly of the sort to which today's men are already oriented. The public expenditure entailed would be financed partly by the major reduction in direct payments of benefits to men; but there would also be direct and indirect gains from the associated slimming-down of welfare bureaucracies. People fit to work but unwilling to participate in public work schemes could be given the last-ditch defence of accommodation in hostels, where most of the labour would be provided by the residents themselves. In this situation, people's family networks would soon re-emerge as valuable and valued sources of (reciprocal) supports, and this itself would help to further boost the importance of male 'providing' and thereby the private realm incentives available to men.

A general rebuilding of conventional families would produce a number of powerful reinforcements for men's morale, as Patricia Morgan's recent work shows[6]. Restoration of tax incentives for marriage would reduce the perverse incentives to family breakdown and male abdication which are created by the present benefits structure, and steer caring work back into the private realm, where it helps to stimulate reasons for men to work. Single people, in particular single childless men, should be taxed at a much higher rate because they are less likely to be engaged in the reciprocal support activities of the moral economy which limit the collective liabilities of the welfare state.

The proposals outlined here may be dismissed out of hand by some people on the grounds that they would push women back into domestic labour. But I would argue strongly that they need not have this effect, and do, in fact, represent an updating of patriarchy which most women would already, at some level, agree with. It is, in any case, absurd to talk of pushing women back into kitchens, because the vast majority have never left, and still do by far the larger share of domestic work even where they do have partners. Domestic liberation of women is due more to technology than to help from men, which is largely mythical, and, insofar as it does exist, is positively, rather than inversely, related to a man's breadwinning status. Men reasonably successful at work and contributing to families through this are also more involved than others in domestic chores[7].

Male breadwinning is turning out not to be the enemy of modern women. Once they have children, most women would actually prefer a male partner to carry the main economic burden, and to perform themselves the main family management and caring role. That this is not more widely understood is largely due to the personal inclinations of most social researchers, who are at variance with the bulk of the population. Recent research that I have participated in myself suggests very strongly that, not only are most women in favour of an up-dated sexual division of labour, but support for it is growing steadily at the moment, especially among mothers.

Women, who when younger may feel that equal participation in the public realm is essential to their self-respect, change their minds as their own children grow up and they find themselves becoming the linchpin in a wider family system. They become concerned at their sons' lack of motivation, at the shortage of suitable partners for their daughters, at the polarisation among younger people (between civilised women and increasingly uncivilised men, who find it hard to live together and even harder to stay together) and at the distress caused to children and older people too by the general weakening of family networks.

There is a strong class dimension to the problem of modern men, as the demotivating effect of equal opportunities rhetoric does not affect all men equally. It is regressive in class terms. As the male provider role fades as a source of respect in wider society, men who can only realistically hope for low status work are the ones most likely to lose the will to seek jobs or retrain as old industries decline. Middle-class men, with more chance of interesting and prestigious jobs, have incentives to succeed which need less boosting by family obligations, so they are not held back in the same way.

I believe this is a powerful factor sharpening the polarisation of our society into rich and poor sectors. The division is increasingly between an elite of 'two-career' families who live in affluence, and an underclass of 'no-work' families — or rather non-families, as it is in this section of the population that households are breaking up, with men increasingly unemployed, living alone, dying of self-neglect and losing faith that there is a useful place for them. Women in this underclass suffer great stress and poverty too, but they keep going because they know that they have valuable roles as mothers.

Taxation policy could play a significant role here in averting broader social conflict, at the same time as re-motivating men. Dual-earner households enjoy a disproportionate share of jobs, incomes and also of valuable incentives. There is much in their lifestyle that is against the common good, as they have augmented everyone's cost of living by taking out huge mortgages which inflate the general level of house prices, and have helped to undermine family life by pressing for separate taxation of domestic partners. In spite of sometimes hiding behind leftish politics, they are the essence of two-nation Thatcherism. High combined taxation of working couples is needed to compensate for the social costs to the community generated by such households.

Eleanor Rathbone was undoubtedly right in assuming that many men draw great strength and satisfaction from the idea that they are playing an important role in supporting families. What makes her position, and the dismantling of sexual divisions of labour which draws on ideas like it, so wrong-headed, even prissy, is the idealistic judgement that this renders men unacceptable. In the last analysis, any society depends on this type of reward structure and motive.

Throughout history, communities have found that the most effective way to lock men into useful membership of society is to link their status and rewards in the wider group to their acceptance and performance of gender-defined family roles. When this connection is weakened — as, for example, after the French and Russian revolutions — then men's morale and behaviour deteriorates and families suffer. This is now being discovered again, and it will not be long before we will all be exhorting each other to accept men as they are and work with the grain, and to forget ideas about how it is patriarchal culture that makes them different from women. Then, once again, they will become more like women.

REFERENCES

1. Gilmore, D. 'Manhood in the Making': Yale University Press (1990).
2. Rathbone, E. 'The Disinherited Family': Edward Arnold (1924).
3. Lyndon, N. 'No More Sex War': Sinclair-Stevenson (1992).
4. Dench, G. 'Transforming Men': Transaction Publishers (1996).
5. Young, M. & Halsey, A.H. 'Family and Community Socialism': IPPR (1995).
6. Morgan, P. 'Farewell to the Family': IEA (1995).
7. Dench, G. ibid (1996).

Discarding the Traditional Notion of Gender

(An interview with Lynne Segal)

Lynne Segal is Professor of Gender Studies at Middlesex University. She has written extensively on feminism, sexuality and gender. Her books include 'Is the Future Female: Troubled Thoughts on Contemporary Feminism' (1987), 'Slow Motion: Changing Masculinities, Changing Men' (1990), 'Sex Exposed: Feminism and the Pornography Debate' (co-edited with Mary McIntosh, 1992) and 'Straight Sex: The Politics of Pleasure' (1994).

There has always been a crisis around masculinity: there is nothing new about men not feeling good enough about themselves. The problem is the things men do to try to establish their 'masculinity' are very often both anti-social and self-destructive. Looking at your statistics, I believe that there might be a particular time in boys' lives today that is especially self-destructive and destructive to others.

I don't think that there is anything new about men's suffering either — having to be the dominant sex arouses a lot of anxiety. Masculinity has always been associated with anxiety, while femininity has been associated with depression. Some of the symptoms men experience are associated with powerlessness, but, if you are supposed to be the powerful sex, there will always be the problem of whether you can live up to the fantasy or the ideology, which for most men, most of the time, isn't easy.

Obviously, those men who think women should be equal and believe in equality have fewer problems when their wives are out working and earning; it is those who think that it's all wrong who get most anxious. We cannot generalise about the effects of changing employment patterns on men, but certainly those men who are already having problems feeling secure in their masculinity (because their circumstances are at odds with what they think is right for men) are the ones who are most likely to fall back on traditional ideology about how relationships between men and women should be.

You are making a relationship between the social circumstances you find yourself in and levels of anxiety and self-esteem, and how men respond to these experiences — what is cause, and what is effect?

Another factor I would bring in is the problem with the notion of gender itself. It is dependent upon the idea that somehow men ought to be the more authoritative and dominant sex; although certain men are suffering, the men at the top of the social hierarchy are still secured. Men still head the leading religious, political and financial institutions. The image of a successful and powerful man is still in place, institutionally and culturally. In terms of Hollywood portrayals, he may need a gun these days to assert his power, but the image of masculinity is still very much in place. So for me, we can't really think of the 'problems of men' outside traditional concepts of gender, which are dependent on the fact that we have had hierarchical relationships between men and women as far back as we know. We know employers want women in jobs because they take less pay and work in poorer conditions and so on. So, the fact that gender relations are hierarchical is also part of the problem, and I think we need to keep hold of that, while not denying that boys and men suffer. There are particular reasons why certain significant groups of men are feeling most dislocated and most removed from the everyday satisfactions of life (which all people should be able to experience) — the feeling that their lives are meaningful and important and that they have a role in society.

Certainly, many men today are not able to feel that their lives are meaningful and important, and that they have a role in society, because of unemployment and other types of social disruption. While we have to aim to give all men a sense of having a significant, meaningful place in society, we have to acknowledge the importance of the shifts for women, whose growth in independence and confidence has had an enormous impact on men. This is also connected to rising divorce rates. Although we usually hear that we have to get rid of the high divorce rate to protect women, the reality is it's men who suffer more from divorce, even though women are likely to be economically disadvantaged by it.

You have so far detailed how you understand the problem. Suppose you're the Minister for Men; you're expected to do something about the data presented, so what would you do?

At one level it's straightforward: we need to have full employment. Unemployment is always going to have very bad effects, particularly on men (although it has bad effects on women too, who don't like being unemployed either. See Brown and Harris's work on depression[1]).

So there are all sorts of social reforms needed to make it more possible for men to feel that they are playing a meaningful part in society. I think it is important to be carrying forward a feminist message as well, particularly the message of feminism in the early seventies, of a new world for men and for women. In this new world, equality between men and women will be something that we would be expecting everybody to be aiming for, and, of course, that does mean that some of the traditional assumptions about masculinity, and the type of privileges men had simply as men, would go. For example, men's release from domestic duties would no longer apply. Some of the statistics show that men who are involved in caring and sharing in the home are the least likely to be those men who are depressed and are worried about masculinity. But, of course, that is partly economic, because the men who are most successful in balancing their family lives and working lives are the men who are in the best position to do this, and not the men in jobs working overtime. It's going to be the men who are more privileged in class and economic terms who are going to find it easier to adjust to the changes. Working-class men (if in work) are more likely to be doing masses of overtime to pay for mortgages; at the time they are most needed at home, they are going to be most absent. It's only in certain types of families (where the man and woman have dual careers) that there are real opportunities to share the domestic and emotional difficulties in the home, as well as the prestige or financial security that comes to them from work outside the home.

So, as Minister for Men, I would say it's crucial to see the importance of men being able to have a place both in the home, and in the workplace (just as it's important for women). The needs of men and women are always posed against each other, but the needs of each group are actually much the same. Another important area is a shorter working week — absolutely crucial, particularly for people with children. This Government is going in the opposite direction, treating paternity leave, for example, as only for 'wimps'. Paternity leave is, of course, crucial for men when they have young children. When they have more responsibilities at home, they should be able to feel that they can play some part there, as well as having some stake in the world of work.

So, full employment, shorter working hours (particularly for people with children), and parental leave — all these will remove the barriers and therefore provide some choice for both men and women. Are there more barriers to remove?

One of the other barriers to be removed is the remaining sexist and traditional gender thinking which blames women for men's problems. This is a real barrier to men feeling better about themselves. Working together with women is a much easier way for men to work out how to help create lives and worlds that are going to be better for them in the longer term, even if not immediately in the short term. I suppose, in the short term, traditional misogyny and sexism and blaming the wrong person for the problem might be a bit soothing, but it doesn't head you in the direction of finding a solution. Most of the changes in women's lives, while in general they have been good for women, have come about because employers have used the existing lower status of women for their own advantage. Women are being exploited in ways which affect men — which, again, has always been the case, nothing new about that. To deal with the problem, we have to begin seeing that, whatever differences there are between men and women, they're not so great that we don't have very similar overlapping goals. These include men and women wanting the best of all worlds, to be able to integrate their home lives with their working lives, to have a place in the community. To pose the interests of men against the interest of women prevents us from finding the creative way forward. Portillo's opposition to the Social Chapter and paternity leave is part of a direction which is going to exacerbate the problems which men face today, and so it is really important to adopt the traditional socialist feminist agenda of seeing men and women together trying to create new worlds. That does actually involve undermining much of traditional gender ideology, like our understandings and beliefs of sexuality and parenthood and so on.

Alongside trying to give everyone better lives in the workforce and create shorter hours so they can have more time at home or to do other things, for instance, playing political roles and engaging in cultural activity, it really is important to be re-thinking what the foundations of masculinity and femininity are, and to be questioning what I see as the traditional myths about the idea that masculinity and femininity should be defined in opposition to each other. We create ridiculous problems with such binary thinking, that not only links up with many men's coerciveness and violence, but also with homophobia and the way in which men police other men.

Another thing that is clear from your statistics is the continuing problem of men's violence. Of course, men are the main targets of violence. Men's need to police other men is absolutely enormous from very early on; no doubt it begins in the home and continues when a boy is at school. Those men who are seen as the more effeminate or gentle — perhaps just because they're slim, or look frail — are at a much higher risk of being beaten up, and all that has to be seen in terms of the hold of traditional gender patterns and of the idea that men have to prove their manhood by asserting some kind of toughness and virility, which is unfortunate, not only for women, but for men themselves.

It sounds like an education project is needed.

A very big education project. It has been attempted, particularly in Sweden, where they do have 'Ministers for Men's and Women's Affairs', or something similar, where they do try and promote basic equality measures, talk about their implications, and how you organise domestic lives in relation to how the workplace is organised. Once you connect home and workplace, look at where men and women actually are, and what their desires actually are, then you do have to start rethinking everything, because, unfortunately, all our institutions and all our ways of thinking are gendered. We see so much of the workplace as the man's place, despite the fact that women are in there; and we see so much of home and family life as the woman's world, despite the fact that that's where men live their lives too. We must continue re-thinking these things and not fall back on traditional solutions.

An ideological offensive is needed to counter much of the traditional meanings and imagery of gender. Men should get satisfaction from being breadwinners or having jobs, but not from the way in which that is made definitive of masculinity. We've got to become less attached to notions of masculinity and femininity themselves as fixed categories. Men have problems with masculinity because of the way in which gender ideology plays such a crucial role in our society, but that's something we need to look at and question. We need to be infinitely more flexible about ways in which both men and women pursue their lives and find work and happiness. I accept the Freudian definition of happiness as the capacity to love and to work — both men and women need to be able to love and to work, and those things aren't opposed to each other: love involves work, and work, ideally, would involve certain levels of love. Again, that's something which isn't usually thought about because gender ideology precisely sees work as the male thing, so it can't involve love and emotions. In fact, a big problem for unemployed men is that all the emotional support they were getting from talking about football, etc., with their mates at work no longer takes place, and so a lot of their important emotional needs are not being met once they're out of work.

So, re-thinking how we've 'gendered' all aspects of society is going to be crucial for this Minister for Men, though I also think it would have to be a Minister for Men and Women. I don't think one can ever separate the two — our lives are always interconnecting.

When you ask young men what do they like about being men, they usually say things like, ''I don't have periods. I don't have to have babies,'' so, for some, their identity in terms of masculinity is in relation to what they perceive as the rough end of being a woman.

That's right. That's why, in 'Slow Motion'[2], I keep arguing that it's so unclear what 'masculinity' is meant to be, except this denial of 'femininity'. The denial or repudiation of femininity is a terribly destructive and ironic thing for men: for much of what's supposed to affirm masculinity, and the more a man strives to affirm it, the more it can shade over into its opposite. So, for instance, male heroism usually begins to evolve into forms of suffering, or self-display, or other aspects which can also be seen as quintessentially feminine. There is actually no way of separating out these two things, and the more one tries to separate them out, the more one's likely to end up in a mess. There are not two contrasting ways of being in the world, and, ironically, the more one tries to polarize experience, the more one sees the connections. For instance, the funny thing about male body-building is that, the more you pump up your body with cortisone and so on to appear more manly, the more your testicles shrivel!

So are we talking about a publicity campaign?

What I'm talking about is something to undermine or disrupt the significance of gender in people's minds, and to help them see the similarities and ambiguities and contradictions in the desires of both men and women. It is hard to think of a campaign that says there is something wrong with our notion of gender, yet, in another sense, we are faced with the contradictions all the time. In fact, all forms of emotional literacy, like political literacy, must involve facing up to complexity.

It's hard to put a focus on it without emphasising it.

Yes, that's right. Some people see the solutions in terms of recognising androgyny, and saying, "Actually, everybody is equally masculine and feminine; men can play their part in the home and women can play their part in the workforce, and we need to have women at the head of everything, the same as men, sharing the world of politics and the world of the City". That's what seems to be the solution. But the problem here is that it still seems to leave the images of femininity and masculinity much as we found them. Our images of femininity, for instance, tend to be connected up with images of nurturing, caring, softness. But to be a woman, whether in the workplace or the home, also involves being tough, and rational. This is as true for successful mothering, as for successful career work. The images of masculinity are around rationality, independence and assertiveness. But much of what male heroes are meant to do involves obeying orders, a passive obedience to the authority of others. What I'm saying is that there is something fundamentally contradictory and silly about polarizing these images. That's why we cannot argue for androgyny, although this is probably what we want. There is something farcical about gender, and that's partly why men are always going to be anxious about their manhood.

It seems what you're saying is that we have to separate the attributes from the labels.

Yes, but I'm also saying that the attributes, for example 'toughness', only gain their meanings because they are linked to an activity or space already seen as 'manly', such as boxing. Otherwise, meanings just slide around. The attempt to tie masculinity/femininity to activity/passivity is a case in point. Whether we label behaviour as active or passive will depend upon how we define the context in which it occurs. As I argue in 'Straight Sex'[3], in intimate encounters we can be most 'active' in search of apparently 'passive' pleasures, and most 'passive' or 'dependent' when we 'actively' try to please another person.

Women are now entering into all areas of what have been seen traditionally as the pursuits and activities of men; women engage in sports, choose their sexual partners — all the things that men traditionally did. There is thus no new way of shoring up masculinity through excluding women, nor can we simply think of new ways of defining masculinity which don't involve excluding women from certain spaces.

So, there are certainly very real questions and problems for men today, and certainly many men are suffering, perhaps more so than in certain times in the past — although I think it's crucial to see that men have always suffered from the problems of trying to live up to the idea of masculinity. Everyone I know is currently reading Pat Barker's latest trilogy[4], which is all about the problem of masculinity during what should have been the most manly time of all, the First World War. Men went off to fight for their country, but, stuck down in the trenches, they developed hysteria en masse, so many suffering from what was then seen as the main female disease of the day: hysteria. The books are all about how the First World War totally undermined men's 'masculinity', even in an all-male environment.

So men's problems today have to be seen in terms of the agency and the spaces that everyone needs to claim in society, and, insofar as men are experiencing problems, the more directly they're tied up with images and ideals of masculinity, the further we are from finding a solution. This isn't to play down the real effects of change on men, but, alongside assessing the effects of change, we do have to re-think the categories of 'masculinity' and 'femininity' altogether: we have to loosen them up so that there is no way any longer we can think of men and women being in different social spaces, or think of what they do as being so very different. That's where categories of responsibility come in: that is what makes human life meaningful — and that's true for men and women equally, and really in ways which aren't so dissimilar. I think that sums up what I'm saying.

REFERENCES

1. Brown, G. and Harris, T. 'Social Origins of Depression'. London. Tavistock (1978).
2. Segal, L. 'Slow Motion: Changing Masculinities, Changing Men', London: Virago (1990).
3. Segal, L. 'Straight Sex: The Politics of Pleasure', London: Virago (1994).
4. Barker, P. 'Regeneration', 'The Eye in the Door', 'The Ghost Road', London: Penguin (1992-96).

EMERGING THEMES

At its most basic, the idea behind this book is, given the evidence offered, how do we understand what is currently occurring for men, and what can we do about it? The book aims to stimulate understanding and thoughts and ideas about policy and practical solutions. Our contributors represent a variety of perspectives, interests and positions: we have writers thought to be on the 'Left', the 'Right', 'radical' and 'reactionary', and operating within parliamentary, policy, media and personal contexts. Some contributors have chosen to talk about men in general, some about specific groups of men, and others about the context in which men go about their lives, and the impact men have on women, children and other men. A number of very clear themes emerge from a reading of the various articles, but a summary of these, or an overview of what contributors have said, would be inappropriate here, and — given the wide range of contributions — would also be overly-complex and lengthy. Instead, this final section highlights some of the themes in an attempt to structure the ways in which we can consider the different contributions.

Crisis or opportunity?

A number of contributors have stressed that, if there is a crisis for men, in many respects this is to be welcomed and taken as an opportunity for change to occur. Individual men feeling the impact of the changes in their lives can be encouraged to alter their attitudes and behaviours because this is more appealing than the internal and external strains which accompany continued resistance to our social evolution. Other contributors were not quite so upbeat about the changing circumstances: they were of the belief that masculinity has always been in crisis, or that the nature of masculinity is one of adapting to change and therefore always appearing to be in crisis. In fact, the idea of a crisis, as such, did not appeal to most of the writers, although there was a view that the media and policymakers usually 'needed' a crisis to generate interest and action.

Is there a sex war?

Most of the contributors believe that the needs of both men and women are best looked at in tandem. There is very little talk of 'sex wars', of men's and women's interests being in conflict, or, indeed, of women's gains being men's losses. Part of the reason for this seemed to be that most of our contributors have approached the evidence primarily from a gender perspective which stresses the differences between men and women, rather than a gender relations analysis that emphasises power imbalances between men and women. This isn't to say that our contributors have ignored sexism, but that an analysis involving men needs to be based on an understanding of both gender and sexism.

Following the same line of reasoning, a number of contributors identify the importance for both men and women of finding solutions to the problems described in 'The Evidence'. Most agree that men, women and children all have a lot to gain from understanding and solving the difficulties that confront men. Some stress a need for urgency, and others a view that the problems will not go away unless tackled head-on. All agree that we cannot turn back the clock, and that masculinity has to change (although there were differences in view of how far changes need to occur).

What circumstances have contributed to 'The Evidence'?

There is widespread agreement that external factors (particularly changing work patterns) have contributed substantially to the issues raised within the evidence at the beginning of this book. Women's higher expectations of men, and their own rapidly changing role and status, have also contributed to the situation — although how much this has been due to a feminist agenda, and how much has arisen from the needs of the economy (to reduce wages and, in turn, employ women), is debatable. Many of the writers have stressed men's apparent inability to adapt and deal with change, particularly their reduced status within the economy and within family and society.

Having said that external factors have forced us to address these issues, most believe there is now an opportunity for men to move away from their traditional positions, and also to take a more active social responsibility. Power, a number of contributors have suggested, is much more complex than most gender commentators acknowledge. While many reinforce a view that, at most institutional levels, power is still lodged tightly within (particular) men's hands, there have been some dramatic changes elsewhere, especially within personal relationships. Sexual and physical violence (and abuse) are still, of course, important issues within relationships between some men and women, but a number of the contributors implore us not to see this as a simplistic "men have power over women" issue, but to develop our understanding of individuals' changing relationships within a theoretical and ideological backdrop. Ehrenreich[1] makes a very useful distinction:

"I want to talk about the decline of patriarchy, and, I should explain right away, I do not mean the decline of sexism, of misogyny, or even male domination. I mean patriarchy in the original sense of the word, as the intimate power of men over women, a power which is historically exercised within the family by the male as breadwinner, property owner, or armed defender of women and children".

She argues that patriarchy is in decline, while other related issues have possibly increased, suggesting for instance that men now protect women less, but have taken on more of a predator role. Our contributors have tried to grapple with a complex picture of gender, sexism and masculinity, rather than a more simplistic allocation of blame or a 'victim' bun-fight.

Understanding is hard enough, let alone solutions!

When posed with the question, "What, as Minister for Men, would you do?", many of the contributors struggled to come up with answers. Some told us that understanding the problem was difficult enough in itself; others said they had not been asked to think about solutions before. Most, at some stage, were nevertheless excited and stimulated by the question. Bearing in mind that virtually all of the writers have made gender a central part of their work and personal lives, and therefore know what the gender business is about, the challenge of finding solutions has, we feel, highlighted the general lack of thinking that, as a society, we put into looking practically at the problem with (and for) men.

Incentives or coercion?

Interestingly, most of the contributors have emphasised proposals that would remove perceived barriers for men and enable them to become involved in activities and aspects of society — often those activities they have been relatively absent from. A number of contributors, for instance, have made suggestions that would 'invite' men to become involved in childcare, and policies that would 'enable' men to take more responsibility in this area.

This is relatively unusual in our social policy approach to men. The target groups for our social services, for instance, are usually women and children who are 'at risk' or 'victims', whereas the probation and prison services are seen as addressing men (as perpetrators and criminals). In current government social policies that address men specifically, coercion is more apparent than incentive — for example, the views that punishment must overshadow rehabilitation in the criminal justice field; that fathers must be made to take financial responsibilities for their children;

and that unemployed men must be made to take up 'training opportunities'.

The approach taken by our writers suggests a number of basic assumptions about men. It proposes that men have been excluded, kept out and hindered from involvement from areas such as childcare. Contributors have often given men 'the benefit of the doubt', and the invitation to participate has been seen as an important part of changing men: some, too, have proposed the view that, in order for men to treat others with understanding and respect, it is helpful if they can first understand and respect themselves. These would appear to be important starting-points for policy makers.

There are, of course, those men who will not respond to incentives. Connell[2] has suggested that a weakness in the gender analysis has been its reluctance to acknowledge the benefits and advantages that many men seek, and take, within gender relations as a primary incentive to maintaining those relations as they are. However, our contributors believe that change will involve a combination of 'carrots and sticks'. The fact that our present Government only seems to know about 'sticks' may account for contributors' obvious leaning towards 'carrot' incentives.

Minds over matter

Obviously, whether we give men the benefit of the doubt is very important, but do we really think men are able to change? Will they do it voluntarily, or will they have to be coerced? An understanding of incentives, benefits, motivations, and levels of coercion that will bring change (and not backlash) amongst men was viewed as important.

How much do we tackle the external factors that have impacted on the situation, and how much do we need to address the attitudes which are believed to be common amongst many men? While policies such as the creation of jobs, removal of barriers to fathering, and more pronounced careers and life education in schools were seen as very important developments, most contributors return to the central challenge of changing men's minds. While some have come up with imaginative publicity campaigns, new components within the school curriculum, therapy on the NHS, and counselling and advice for men at a variety of transition points in their lives, this issue of how much we are able to change men's minds is one that clearly needs further consideration and development.

Staying on this theme, at least two contributors emphasise the importance for all of us — men and women — in reflecting on our own attitudes, understandings and beliefs about each other. How much power do women actually have? How much do we all operate and work off a series of stereotypes of men, only taking in data and opinion that confirms what we believe already? Surveys, for instance, that suggest that women are involved in an unacceptable level of domestic violence towards men[3], don't fit neatly into the accepted views that many of us have about men and, indeed, women.

The counterview that seeks to make men the victims and reverse the stereotype of 'bad men' and 'good women' is also highlighted by at least one contributor as a distraction if we are to find solutions and move forward. A complex, informed and pragmatic approach is suggested as being essential to avoid the many ideological distractions and achieve progress.

The importance of work (and home)

Our writers have tended to focus particularly on employment, both in terms of the need to create jobs, but also to challenge men's over-attachment to work. The creation of jobs is seen as an important means of drawing men back into the economy: this does not mean a return to traditional men's roles, rather a need to provide an incentive for men to be offered the involvement, dignity and independence that work so often provides. In tandem with this is the need to challenge traditional views of men's relationship with work itself, the status and identity that so many men get from their work role, and the hole this leaves when work is taken away.

The parallel status of domestic work was also seen by many as needing to change. Views of 'women's work', fixed views of what men and women do, are in need of deconstruction. Contributors saw school (or early education) as the place where this questioning, reviewing and changing of attitudes should go on — although many recognised that schools were already burdened with an overambitious curriculum.

Men, emotions and change

Another aspect of the traditional male mindset that contributors addressed was that of men's emotions. Some have placed men's inability to express their feelings about the difficulties they face at the base of many of the health, education, and even the crime, statistics. Men would not, or could not, reflect on, discuss or express the way they feel, and therefore their problems were not acknowledged, nor, in turn, dealt with. This ostrich approach was seen as inhibiting men's ability to change and adapt.

Directly and by implication, some contributors have also suggested that many men lack skills, such as flexibility and adaptability, that are regarded as essential for the rapidly changing environment that most men find themselves in. Many talk in terms of 'role strain', where individuals have had difficulties adapting to the changes occurring around them and the mismatch between what society needs from them as men and the kind of men they want, or expect, to be.[4]

A number of different skills (such as the ability to express feelings, or to be flexible) were seen as essential if men were to learn and develop. Again, schools were often viewed as the appropriate propagation site, although some writers were more impatient (especially with adult men), demanding that men "just adapt and move on". Some acknowledgement of men's 'inner turmoil' by men themselves, as well as by women, institutions and government, was seen as essential for men's difficulties not to continue to be ignored, belittled or played down, although there was also concern that men might then be regarded as 'the new victims'.

Facing up to the problem

Indeed, there was a commonly-held view that we have to recognise that we have a problem before these issues can, or will be, addressed — and that, to date, that recognition has not occurred. Suggestions for achieving this included a governmental 'standing committee', publicity campaigns, and wider distribution of the type of information within our 'Evidence' section. While currently the media reports on anything that suggests a 'sex war' or 'men being redundant', a more genuine debate about the 'state of men' was thought to be an essential pre-requisite for useful policy development.

All men and groups of men

The importance of seeing the commonness between men's experience (even if this is the hegonomic image of the traditional man) was thought to be important, but also acknowledgement of clear differences between groups of men was considered essential. A number of sub-groups were mentioned within the text — young men, gay men, black men, older men, divorced and separated men, unemployed men, working-class men, etc., etc. The trends catalogued in 'The Evidence' obviously impact on different men in general and specific ways, both of which, our contributors have suggested, need to be addressed and acknowledged.

Getting the balance right

A number of similarities between men and women were highlighted. Writers have stressed the importance of finding a balance between work and family, for example. While men and women are travelling down opposite sides of the work/family highway (women spending increasingly more time at work, and men at home), they are both thought to be looking for a balance between the two. Other contributors have usefully questioned whether this is, in fact, one of those untested assumptions that policy is inadvertently built upon, and have suggested we can't ignore the power imbalances and the possible reluctance of both men and women to leave their 'traditional' roles.

Male transitions

The importance of transitions for men was a feature of several contributions and may, in part, be related to the difficulties that men appear to have in adapting to changing circumstances. For younger men, it may be the transition into school, followed by junior to secondary school; school to college; college to work, or a training scheme or unemployment; and always the transition of 'boy to man'. Bly[5] has, of course, highlighted the loss of adolescent transition points, particularly in Western cultures, and suggested that we need to reintroduce these to avoid the fall-out from this lack of process — for example, levels of adolescent criminality, violence and risk-taking. Health statistics suggest that these transition points continue to be a problem after adolescence, particularly when men are made redundant or retire — often critical times for men's physical and mental health. Some contributors have suggested that teaching flexibility and adaptability will ease these transitions; others that making men more aware of the impact of these transitions, and putting a series of 'safety nets' in place to catch those that find transitions difficult, should be important strategic policy aims.

Negotiating without violence

Violence tended to be an issue that was implicit in many of the contributions, and conflict resolution skills, to counter some of the 'defend before attacked' and 'get one over on them' attitudes that many men have, were seen as essential for both men's adaptability as well as others' safety. Schools were again seen as an important site for such skills to be learnt, although domestic violence and similar projects were also regarded as central to the development of these skills.

Role models for men

Surprisingly, role models and leadership were not a strong feature of many contributions, although, when they were mentioned, they were viewed as important. The morality of government ministers, the violent nature and lack of co-operation and care in our politics were highlighted as problematic and in need of dramatic change. There was a call for strong, decisive men who could be trusted, who acted with dignity, could be respectful of others and were able to tell the truth: such role models were seen as essential for men, and for society as a whole. There was concern that many of these values had all but disappeared, and that many men currently in leadership modelled a 'screw you' approach to others — a level of competitiveness that reflected the hegonomic man at his very worst.

This will take time

A recurrent theme was that we are not talking about an overnight change. Men and women are gradually adapting to the current circumstances, regardless of thought-through policy interventions. However, the value of decisive intervention would be the possible avoidance of the pain, confusion, divorce, ill-health, even death, that 'The Evidence' currently reflects. While intervention was very important, we would need a number of short and long term strategies to address, and deal with, the wide-ranging issues facing men at this present time.

The 23 contributors have, of course, said so much more than the various points highlighted in this final section. Our own view of the contributions is that they all (irrespective of perspectives) say something very important about the ways we understand men and the policy choices that follow from these understandings. This is less a perceived liberal stance of agreeing with everyone, rather a more accurate perception that the current societal changes, the different perspectives we use to understand these changes, and the impact and response these changes have had on individuals and groups of men, are complex and full of untidiness. We currently lack certainty; we lack statements of generality; and we lack clear, straightforward policies that will impact on the problems which 'The Evidence' highlights.

While tidiness will be as elusive as ever, the contributors will hopefully have challenged, extended and developed your own thoughts, as well as contributed to our collective clarity about what, indeed, is next for men.

REFERENCES

1. Ehrenreich, B. "The Decline of Patriarchy" in Berger, M., Wallis, B. and Watson, S. 'Constructing Masculinity', London: Routledge (1995).
2. Connell, R.W. 'Masculinities', Cambridge: Polity Press (1995).
3. See "Men as Victims of Domestic Violence" in 'Working With Men 1995.1', London.
4. Kilmartin, C.T. 'The Masculine Self', New York: Macmillan (1994).
5. Bly, R. 'Iron John: A Book about Men', Mass.: Addison-Wesley (1990).

ABOUT THE EDITORS

Trefor Lloyd has been involved in developing work with men for over 14 years. He co-founded The B Team in 1985 to produce useful resources and publications for those developing work with men, and Working With Men to provide training and consultancy and a subscription journal to such professionals. He has written and spoken in Britain and abroad on issues affecting men, especially developing practice of work with men. Trefor's publications include 'Work With Boys' (1985), 'Working With Men Who Batter their Partners' (with John Lees, 1993), and 'Young Men's Health — A Youthwork Concern' (1996). He has also written articles for a wide range of publications, from *Cosmopolitan* to professional journals such as *Healthlines*. Trefor is currently writing a book on working with boys and a health professionals' guide to men's health (both for publication later this year), and a research report on young men and responsibility.

Tristan Wood has been co-editor of the journal *Working With Men* since its inception in 1990, and prior to that co-edited *For Men*, also with Trefor Lloyd. A founder member of an agency in Lambeth which works with men to erradicate domestic violence, Tristan is employed full-time as the Special Needs and Supported Housing Director of Threshold Tennant Trust, a housing association operating throughout West and South-West London and North Surrey. Author of 'Drive It! The Complete Book of Formula 2 Motor Racing' (1984), Tristan has also contributed to 'Squatting — The Real Story' (1980) and the Labour Housing Group's 'Right to a Home' (1984) and edited another LHG publication, 'Guidelines for Tenant Involvement' (1989). He is also a regular contributor to the Club Taurino of London's *La Divisa* magazine.

ABOUT THE PUBLISHERS

Working With Men is a not-for-profit organisation that supports the development of work with men through resources, publications, training, consultancy and advice. Outputs include a quarterly journal for professional workers; a number of high-quality games, packs, posters and booklets, all to assist professionals to develop their work with men; and also a number of consultancies and projects for organisations such as the Health Education Authority, Youth Action Northern Ireland, the Royal College of Nursing and the Gulbenkian Foundation. We can be contacted at 320 Commercial Way, London SE15 1QN (tel./fax 0171 732 9409).